Web Words That Work:

Writing Online Copy That Sells

MICHAEL MILLER

800 East 96th Street,
Indianapolis, Indiana 46240 USA

ISBN-13: 978-0-7897-5059-4

ISBN-10: 0-7897-5059-7

Library of Congress Cataloging-in-Publication Data is on file.

Printed in the United States of America

First Printing: December 2012

Trademarks

All terms mentioned in this book that are known to be trademarks or service marks have been appropriately capitalized. Que Publishing cannot attest to the accuracy of this information. Use of a term in this book should not be regarded as affecting the validity of any trademark or service mark.

Warning and Disclaimer

Every effort has been made to make this book as complete and as accurate as possible, but no warranty or fitness is implied. The information provided is on an "as is" basis. The author and the publisher shall have neither liability nor responsibility to any person or entity with respect to any loss or damages arising from the information contained in this book.

Bulk Sales

Que Publishing offers excellent discounts on this book when ordered in quantity for bulk purchases or special sales. For more information, please contact

> U.S. Corporate and Government Sales
> 1-800-382-3419
> corpsales@pearsontechgroup.com

For sales outside the United States, please contact

> International Sales
> international@pearsoned.com

Editor in Chief
Greg Wiegand

Executive Editor
Rick Kughen

Development Editor
Rick Kughen

Managing Editor
Sandra Schroeder

Project Editor
Mandie Frank

Copy Editor
Barbara Hacha

Indexer
Erika Millen

Proofreader
Jovana Shirley

Technical Editor
Karen Weinstein

Publishing Coordinators
Cindy Teeters
Romny French

Designer
Anne Jones

Compositor
Jake McFarland

CONTENTS AT A GLANCE

Contents

TABLE OF CONTENTS

II   WRITING FOR DIFFERENT VEHICLES

16 Writing Online Ads   179

17 Writing Online Press Releases   191

III   GETTING IT DONE

21   Determining the Right Delivery Formats   231

22   Dealing with Web Page Design   241

23 Working with Technical and Design Staff   249

24 The Final Word: Think Like the Reader   259

IV APPENDIXES

Appendix 200 Web Words That Work   265

Index   269

About the Author

Michael Miller is a successful and prolific author with a reputation for practical advice, technical accuracy, and an unerring empathy for the needs of his readers. He is known for his casual, easy-to-read writing style and his practical, real-world advice—as well as his ability to explain a wide variety of complex topics to an everyday audience.

Mr. Miller has written more than 100 best-selling nonfiction books over the past two decades. His books include *The Ultimate Web Marketing Guide, B2B Digital Marketing, YouTube for Business, The Complete Idiot's Guide to Search Engine Optimization, Online Marketing Heroes, Teach Yourself Business Plans in 24 Hours, 80/20 Guide to Effective Presentations, Webster's New World Vocabulary of Success,* and *Management Secrets of the Good, the Bad, and the Ugly.* He has also written hundreds of articles for various websites and served as a consultant on the design of many others.

You can email Mr. Miller directly at webwords@molehillgroup.com. His website is located at www.molehillgroup.com.

Dedication

*To all the writers who have inspired and continue to inspire me: the list is too
numerous to detail.*

Acknowledgments

Thanks to the usual suspects at Que Publishing, including but not limited to
Greg Wiegand, Rick Kughen, Barbara Hacha, Mandie Frank, and technical editor
Karen Weinstein.

We Want to Hear from You!

As the reader of this book, *you* are our most important critic and commentator. We value your opinion and want to know what we're doing right, what we could do better, what areas you'd like to see us publish in, and any other words of wisdom you're willing to pass our way.

We welcome your comments. You can email or write to let us know what you did or didn't like about this book—as well as what we can do to make our books better.

Please note that we cannot help you with technical problems related to the topic of this book.

When you write, please be sure to include this book's title and author as well as your name and email address. We will carefully review your comments and share them with the author and editors who worked on the book.

Email: feedback@quepublishing.com

Mail: Que Publishing
            ATTN: Reader Feedback
            800 East 96th Street
            Indianapolis, IN 46240 USA

Reader Services

Visit our website and register this book at quepublishing.com/register for convenient access to any updates, downloads, or errata that might be available for this book.

Introduction

This is a book about writing. Online writing, to be precise.

How is online writing different from regular writing? It's a matter of how and where readers are reading your words and what their expectations are. There's no denying that reading something on a computer screen is different from reading it in a newspaper or magazine. You have to use a different approach, employ different techniques, even choose different words. What works well in one medium doesn't necessarily work well in another.

Online, you not only have to deal with a different presentation, but also different vehicles of communication. Although they're all displayed on computer screens, a web page is much different from a blog post, which is different from a Facebook update, which is different from an email or online press release. Again, what works well for one type of missive doesn't work nearly as well for the others.

So you can't just take what you might write for a print piece and import it verbatim into an online vehicle. Oh, the words will translate, but they won't be as effective. Both your content and your writing style have to be adapted to the chosen online medium.

But you probably know that, or at least sense it. That's why you're reading this book, after all. You want to know the rules of online writing so you can more effectively communicate with your online readers.

As much as I'd like to comply, I'll be honest with you: there really aren't any rules. (Damn!) That is, I can't tell you absolutely positively every time that you should do A, B, and C. It doesn't work that way; every situation is different. But then, you probably knew that, too.

There are, however, some overall guidelines you probably want to follow, approaches that have been proven to generate better results, and that's what I address in this book. I've done my share of online writing of various sorts, and I know what works and what doesn't. So if I can't offer you hard and fast directives, I can make a few suggestions you might find useful.

As you'll discover, this online writing thing can be tricky. Sometimes it's a matter of making a subtle shift in tone; other times it requires a wholesale rethinking of your content and approach. The goal, however, is to adapt your writing to be as effective as possible for an online audience. All you have to do is keep your target audience in mind—what I call *thinking like the reader*—and you'll know exactly what to do.

Who This Book Is For

When it comes to online writing, it certainly helps if you have some prior writing experience. It's a lot easier to adapt an existing writing style than it is to start from scratch—even though there might be a lot of adapting to do. Knowing how challenging it can be to change the way you work, I'll try to guide you through the process as best as possible.

I also know that a lot of people being asked to write copy for web pages and blog posts and social media updates are not professional copywriters. A lot of you don't even have much in the way of prior writing experience, at least beyond what you did for your English classes in high school or college. If this is the boat you're in, don't despair; it's a fairly large boat of reluctant volunteers drafted into service. The good news is, you haven't learned any old or bad habits, so you can dive right in (off that figurative boat, presumably) and start writing online text the right way. I'm not saying it's going to be easy, but it might not be as difficult as you fear.

How This Book Is Organized

About this book—what's it about, exactly? Well, as the title implies, it's about learning to write for an online audience, using a variety of Internet-based communication vehicles. I'll guide you through some general guidelines that apply for all types of online writing, and then get specific about how to write copy for various types of online publications. There's a lot of useful information here, so be ready for that.

Knowing that organization is important (I mention that in the book, by the way), I've structured the content of this book into three main parts, as follows:

- **Part I, "Online Copywriting 101,"** walks you through the basics of writing online copy. This is the place to start if you're new to copywriting in general, but also presents the guidelines an established copywriter needs to learn to be successful in writing online. You'll learn what's really different about online copy, some essential grammar and punctuation stuff, how to convey complex content, and the value of keeping your copy short and simple. You'll also learn how to organize your content, fire up your readers, find your writing voice, incorporate visuals and web links into your writing, and—this last bit is very important—optimize your copy for web search. Yeah, this is a crash course in online copywriting; you need to read this part.

- **Part II, "Writing for Different Vehicles,"** gets into the nuts and bolts of different types of online writing, each of which has unique requirements. You'll learn how to write web pages, online articles, blog posts, Facebook and Twitter updates, email promotions and newsletters, online ads, online press releases, help files and FAQs, and web page interfaces. You'll even learn how to adapt your copy for display on mobile devices—which is becoming increasingly important as more and more people access the Web via their iPhones and other smartphones.

- **Part III, "Getting It Done,"** wraps things up by offering some advice about the practical side of the online writing business. I'll help you determine the right delivery formats for your work, deal with the ins and outs of HTML and web page design, and work with the rest of the team assigned to create a website.

When all that is done, I offer a short appendix titled "200 Web Words That Work"—that is, a list of powerful words that will make any online copy more effective. (I felt I had to, given the title of this book.)

Taken together, these 24 chapters (plus appendix) will help you become a more effective writer of online copy. I tend to think that the book reads better in sequential order, but if you prefer to dip in and out, I won't get upset. As a writer yourself, you know best what works for you.

Conventions Used in This Book

As I stated up front, this is a book about writing. I hope that the writing within this book stands on its own, and that you can easily enough learn what it is you need to learn. If you can't figure something out, then I haven't done my job well.

Know, however, that I've employed some tricks of the trade to better present different types of information on these pages. These tricks—what we call *margin notes*—are well suited for print, which means you might not want (or even be able) to employ them online. Still, I thought I'd present them to you here, so you'll know what to expect.

 Note

A *note* is designed to provide information that is generally useful or interesting but not specifically essential for what you're doing at the moment.

 Tip

A *tip* is a piece of advice that might help you do a particular task more effectively or efficiently.

 Caution

A *caution* tells you to beware of a potentially troublesome situation. In some cases, ignoring a caution could cause your readers significant problems—so pay attention to them!

I've also added one or more *sidebars* to most chapters. These sidebars expand on a given issue that doesn't necessarily warrant additional coverage in the main text. Sometimes they represent more opinion than fact, which is another reason they're separated out. Read 'em if you like, or skip over 'em; it's up to you.

Let Me Know What You Think

As a writer, I always love to hear from readers—especially if those readers are other writers. (I'll qualify that; please don't email me about typos or grammatical mistakes. I'll just blame the copyeditor and proofreader.)

Anyway, if you want to contact me, feel free to email me at webwords@ molehillgroup.com. I can't promise that I'll *answer* every message, but I do promise that I'll *read* each one.

And if you want to learn more about me and any new books I'm writing, check out my Molehill Group website at www.molehillgroup.com. Who knows, you might find some other books there that you would like to read. Lord knows, I've written enough.

Enough preliminaries. You want to learn more about online writing, and I want to tell you about it. So settle back in your easy chair, adjust the lights, and get ready to turn the page. I think you'll like what you find there.

1

What's Different About Writing Online Copy?

You have some writing that needs to be done. Maybe it's copy for a page on your website, maybe it's an email bulletin, or maybe it's some posts for Facebook or Twitter. In any case, there's a big white hole where those words should be; somebody's got to fill that hole, and that somebody is you.

I'll be upfront with you. Writing copy for online use is a bit different from any other type of writing you've done. Oh, there are similarities; you use words and sentences and paragraphs and such, and grammar and punctuation still have a place. But what you write and the way you write it has to be tailored to the audience and the medium—both of which, when you're talking the Internet, are unique.

Examining the Different Types of Online Writing

Before the Internet, everybody read books, magazines, newspapers, and letters. Writing, then, was for physical media; our words got printed on paper and distributed the old-fashioned way.

The Internet has brought us more places to put our words. If you get paid for writing, that's a good thing—even if some of the newer outlets are supplanting traditional ones. So although there might be fewer opportunities for magazine writers and newspaper reporters, there are a lot more web pages and blogs and such that need our word-crafting services.

It might not seem like it, given the decay of traditional print publishing, but there's actually more writing going on these days than there used to be. It's just that the writing is a little different.

When it comes to the Internet, then, what kind of writing is needed? Given that most online media are inherently text-based, there are a lot of different vehicles for your copy. Here are just a few:

- **Web pages:** This is the big one. All websites need at least a little copy; most need a lot. All the pages on all those sites need descriptive text, and the more often a site is updated (many update frequently), the more new copy is needed.

 Note

Learn more about writing web copy in Chapter 11, "Writing Web Pages."

- **Online articles:** Whether you're talking about dedicated news sites or regular sites with a given topic focus, there are just as many (if not more) articles online than in print these days. Sometimes they're the same articles—print articles ported to the Web. Other times, they're articles written specifically for web consumption. In any case, there are lots of opportunities to write articles for online readers. Lots.

 Note

Learn more about writing for news sites and blogs in Chapter 12, "Writing Online Articles."

- **Blogs:** A blog is a type of website where one or more writers contribute articles of varying lengths. Most blog posts are text-based, even if they're only a few sentences. Other blogs encourage longer-form posts; still others eschew text for a photo-based approach. The thing that makes blog writing appealing, however, is the frequency. Most blogs have new posts on a daily basis, which means there's a never-ending need for new material. Lots of writing, of both a personal and a commercial nature, is going on in the blogosphere.

> ✉ *Note*
>
> Learn more about writing for blogs in Chapter 13, "Writing Blog Posts."

- **Social media:** Ah, the expanding world of social media—which, for most folks, means Facebook and Twitter. You're probably used to tweets and status updates that detail the poster's personal activities and moods, but there are also a lot of semipromotional posts from companies small and large. All those commercial tweets and posts have to be written by someone, even if they're only 140 characters long; in fact, the space constraints make social media writing a unique challenge. Can you get your message across in such a short space?

> ✉ *Note*
>
> Learn more about writing tweets and status updates in Chapter 14, "Writing Social Media Updates."

- **Email:** Email might be a dying medium (it's being replaced by social media among the younger generation), but it's still pretty big—and it's a long way from its digital grave. Most companies use email for promotional purposes, in the form of notices, newsletters, veiled advertisements, you name it. In this regard, email writing is a lot like traditional direct response writing; the copy must engage the customer and include a strong call to action.

> ✉ *Note*
>
> Learn more about email copy in Chapter 15, "Writing Email Newsletters and Promotions."

- **Online ads:** Speaking of writing, advertising does exist online—although it's much different from traditional print advertising. Online ads are typically shorter and more direct than most print ads; in fact, the largest category of online ads are so-called pay-per-click ads that contain a scant four lines of text—one of which is the link-to URL. No fancy copy here, not even in the larger banner ads; it's short and sweet with not a wasted word.

> **Note**
>
> Learn more about writing web advertising copy in Chapter 16, "Writing Online Ads."

- **Online press releases:** The world of public relations has migrated to the Internet and evolved accordingly. Traditional press releases were targeted at other media, in the hopes of getting a review or a mention in a newspaper or magazine article. Online press releases are targeted as much at consumers as at other online media (such as bloggers), and as such require a more customer-oriented writing approach.

> **Note**
>
> Learn more about online PR in Chapter 17, "Writing Online Press Releases."

Those are just some of the places where the traditional Internet needs copy. Most of what's online can also be read on any number of devices—computers, tablets, or mobile phones—and each type of device comes with its own challenges for copywriters. Writing copy for a traditional web page is one thing; writing for the mobile version of that page (or for that site's iPad app) is often something different. On the plus side, that's more paying work for starving copywriters. On the downside, that's more damned work for overloaded copywriters. Take it as you like.

Why Online Writing Is Like Any Other Type of Writing

If you're an experienced writer, you're probably wondering what's so freakin' special about writing for websites, blogs, and such. Words is words, after all; when you're talking about good writing, the medium shouldn't matter.

There's a certain amount of truth in those sentiments. The basic elements of good writing *do* carry across media; if you know how to write for magazines or newspapers, you should be able to ply your trade online as well.

It comes down to the value of solid writing skills. All online writing, much as all traditional writing, is built on a base of sound punctuation, grammar, sentence construction, style, and the like. If you already know how to write, you can adapt your writing for the unique needs of the various online media. If you don't know how to write, even casually, you face an uphill battle—online or off.

Successful online writing, then, starts with all that stuff you learned in English class and goes on from there. You choose the right words, arrange those words into sentences, and arrange those sentences into paragraphs to tell the story you want to tell. Your command of language and sentence structure and the like determine how and how well you tell that story. You can take the long route there or a shorter route; that's your personal style. But getting from point A to point B is still the goal, and you use the same tools to do that online as you do in print.

What I'm saying is that writing for online media shares the basics with any other type of writing. If you can write a solid print ad or newspaper article, or even a decent term paper or memo, you can write online copy, too. Of course, there are differences—all media have unique writing requirements—but you have the basic skills you need to get started.

The Unique Challenges of Online Writing

All that said, online copy is noticeably different from traditional print copy. That's due in part to how we read online copy, where we read it, and on what types of devices. Let's face it: reading an article on a harshly lit computer monitor or tablet screen is a lot different from reading that same article in a gently creased newspaper from the soft glow of a nearby table lamp.

When it comes to evaluating why and how online writing differs from writing for a book or magazine, you have to take into consideration things like readers' attention spans, their expectations, the need for content to be "searchable," and, of course, the different types of devices on which words are read.

Reader Attention Spans

Let's start with the attention span thing. Most folks would agree that our collective attention spans have been decreasing for decades. It's evident in all types of media, not just the written ones.

Take movies, for example. In the 1930s, the average shot length (ASL) in a feature film was in the 8- to 11-second range. Fast forward to today, when ASL is between

4.3 to 4.9 seconds. Try forcing younger viewers to watch a film from the golden age of movies, and they simply can't sit through it; they don't have the attention span to tolerate the considerably longer shot length of those older films.

You see the same thing with television commercials. Decades after the 30-second spot became standard, we're seeing the advent of shorter TV ads, in the 15-second range. Today's viewers are too antsy to sit through a 30-second spot, especially when they can press the fast forward button on their DVRs and move on to the next thing almost immediately.

 Note

What is causing today's diminishing attention spans? Experts have identified any number of causes, from the larger amount of content and media available and the quick cutting of modern television shows (especially music videos in the original MTV age) to the faster-paced and highly programmed lives of today's youth. Some even blame the attention span problem on texting and social media—although I tend to see both as responses to, not causes of, diminishing attention spans.

Why, then, should Internet users be any different when it comes to attention span? Well, they're not; in fact, online readers are even less likely to completely read something long and involved than are today's print readers.

Given this attention span issue, if you expect the average online reader to repeatedly press the Page Down key or click the Next Page button on a long web page or blog post, you're woefully mistaken. The typical online reader reads only the digital equivalent of what's above the fold; at best, you have the reader's attention for a single screen, nothing more. And, if you want your content read and not ignored, you'll have to adjust your writing accordingly.

 Note

How do you deal with short online attention spans? Learn more in Chapter 4, "Keeping It Short and Simple."

Instant Gratification

The short attention span thing becomes even more of an issue when you consider that the online generation is used to instant gratification. Think about it: Virtually every piece of information in the entire world is no more than a Google search away. If you want directions to a given location, a dinner recipe, biographical information about a historical figure, or whatever, it won't take you more than a few seconds to find whatever you need. You want it; it's yours—*now*.

This also goes for all forms of entertainment. Today's younger generation isn't used to waiting for anything; everything they want or need to view or read is available on demand. Forget scheduling your TV viewing a week in advance to catch a given show or movie; just go online or use your cable's on-demand feature to watch whatever it is now, at your convenience. It's all about gratification of the instant type, and that's what people expect.

The operative phrase for online users, then, is "no waiting." If the information isn't put in front of them *this instant*, they won't wait for it. If you can't give it to them, they'll find it faster someplace else. There's no patience for the payoff; you have to give them what they want now, right up front, without them having to dig for it. No waiting and no work—that's what the web reader wants.

They're Not Readers, Really

Here's something else interesting. When it comes to online readers, they don't view themselves as readers. Instead, they're users or visitors or whatever descriptor is trendy this week. Reading is something you do with a book; it's not something you do on a web page.

It's sad, but true: most people don't want to be forced to read anything online; all they want is that one particular piece of information they're seeking. Online readers (I'll call them that, even if they don't) don't have the time or the patience to "read" a web page. They want information now, no reading involved.

This means that any reading that gets done online is purely a means to an end. People don't read web pages for pleasure; they don't linger over the words and savor the sentence structure. Reading is a task that people have to do to get to the information they need, and the less they have to do of it, the better. Try to force online users to read, and you'll lose them; there's another site, not too far away, that will provide the pertinent information in a more direct fashion.

Screen Issues

Online reading is constrained by the container. That is, the screen size and shape that people use to read online content dramatically affects the reading experience—and, to some degree, the content itself.

Let's face it: reading online is not the same cozy experience as reading a traditional print product. With a book or magazine or newspaper (or even a comic book or catalog), the reader can slip on his reading jacket, curl up in his favorite chair with a snifter of brandy, light up his pipe, and look forward to an evening of enjoyable entertainment. Even if the experience is more like pajamas in bed with a cup of hot tea, or ensconced under a shady tree with a can of beer, it still leaves the reader comfortably in control of what's read, and how fast.

Reading online is different. Instead of sitting in a comfy chair or relaxing in bed, you're sitting at your desk. (Okay, if you have a notebook or tablet, you might still be in your comfy chair.) Instead of holding the familiar heft of a book or newspaper in your hands, you have a computer keyboard or tablet. Instead of looking at printed words on paper, you're looking at a small, flat, eerily glowing screen. It's not really that comforting.

And that screen is *small*, compared to printed media, which means that either the letters onscreen are also smaller than print or that you see less of a page at a glance. The latter is probably more common because most computer monitors are wider than they are tall. You can't usually read an entire page without scrolling, which—because most people prefer not to scroll—means that you either have to adapt your content to the smaller, horizontal screen or risk readers getting half the message and then clicking away.

 Note

A reading surface that is oriented horizontally—wider than tall, such as a computer monitor—is in *landscape* mode. A reading surface that is oriented vertically—taller than it is wide, like a book—is in *portrait* mode. We're more used to reading in portrait mode.

It gets even more complicated when you throw mobile devices into the mix. More and more Internet users are accessing the Web via smartphones and tablets, and the screens on these devices are even smaller and harder to read. Tablets aren't bad (although you have the issue of whether people are reading in landscape or portrait mode), but trying to read most web pages and other content on a tiny smartphone screen can be extremely frustrating.

Somehow or another, you have to take these different reading screens into account when you're creating your online content. It's a bit more challenging than trying to keep your newspaper lead above the fold.

 Note

Learn more about writing for smaller screen sizes in Chapter 20, "Writing for Mobile Devices."

Interactivity

Then there's the issue of interactivity, on which the Web is woven. Web readers expect websites and blogs to include all manner of media, not just text. You need to think in terms of text, plus pictures, plus video, plus whatever. And some of that whatever should be outside content hosted elsewhere.

The chief form of web interactivity is the lowly link to another web page. Online users like to click, so the more you can link your content to other relevant content, the better. Unless, of course, you include too many links or link to sites with poor or irrelevant content or content that's too good and upstages yours. It's complicated.

You might even want to embed content hosted elsewhere. For example, you can easily embed YouTube videos in a web page or blog post, if that's what you want to do. It's one more catchy element on the page—but also one more thing to draw attention away from your core content or maybe it enhances your core content. Like I said, it's complicated.

In any case, you don't have these types of interactivity issues when you're writing a book or magazine article. You do have them when writing for just about any online medium—and that's what makes it challenging.

 Note

Learn more about incorporating interactivity in Chapter 9, "Utilizing Links and Outside Content."

Search Engine Considerations

There's one more thing that's different about creating online media: you're not writing just for humans. Online, your web page or blog post is just as likely to be read by a machine (actually, a software program) than it is to be read by a living, breathing, humanoid life form.

It all has to do with online search and how people will find your content online. On the Web, most content gets found when people search for it. That means how high a given web page or blog post or whatever ranks on a search results page determines how many people will visit that page; the higher the page is in the search results, the more visitors that page will get.

It's important, then, to engineer your online content so that it ranks highly with Google, Bing, and the other major search engines. And that's done by construct-ing the container so that the spider software that crawls the Web for those search engines easily finds a given page or post and by writing the content in a way that best matches the most relevant searches that people conduct.

This task is complicated by the simple fact that search indexing is all automated. There aren't any real human beings at Google who look at pages on the Web and decide which should rank high on a given search results page. No, Google and the other search engines trust algorithms more than they do human judgment, and thus have designed computer software that attempts to analyze web content and match it to consumer queries. This software looks for various elements on a web page to try to determine what that page is really about, so that it can match the page to relevant queries.

To ensure high search ranking, you must write your copy (and design other elements of the page) in a way that appeals to the search engines' software. This is called search engine optimization (SEO). In an ideal world, writing unique and informative copy is the best way to optimize a website for search, but there are tricks that transcend pure content. As such, you need to be aware of the search issue when you're writing web copy and slant your writing in ways that court the search engines—while still appealing to real live human beings.

It's not always easy pleasing two masters, especially when one isn't human, but it's what you need to do to write effective online copy. Ignore the search engines and you might have the best-written content on the Web—that nobody knows about.

✉ Note

Learn more about writing for search engines in Chapter 10, "Optimizing Your Copy for Web Search."

What If You're Not a Writer?

I said upfront that if you have decent writing skills and experience writing for traditional media, you should be able to make the jump to online writing. But what if you're not an experienced writer? What if you've been appointed to do your company's social updates or blog postings, or even create new web pages, and you've never written anything more involved than a book report or interoffice memo?

Well, life for you is going to get real interesting, real fast. I won't sugarcoat it; without the proper training or experience, writing for online media is going to be challenging. Heck, *any* writing is challenging. It's unfortunate that some powers that be assume that if it's for the Web, anybody can do it. That's not really the case;

you still need a solid foundation of grammar, punctuation, and style to make your point, no matter what the medium.

You can, however, learn what you need to know to write what you need to write. There are rules you can follow and guidelines that can guide you. A lot of the unique aspects of online writing that are sure to vex experienced writers might seem second nature to someone who hasn't had to follow the old rules all along.

Learning to write is a little easier if you take advantage of various resources available to you. Obviously, this book is one of those resources. But I'd also recommend getting yourself copies of

- *The Elements of Style* (William Strunk, Jr. and E.B. White, Longman, 1918, revised 1999)
- *On Writing Well* (William Zinsser, Harper Perennial, 1966, revised 2006)
- *Writing Tools: 50 Essential Strategies for Every Writer* (Roy Peter Clark, Little, Brown and Company, 2006)

And if you plan to do any fiction writing, see *On Writing* (Stephen King, Scribner, 2000, revised 2010)

These are all helpful and, in some cases, inspirational books of value to any aspiring or practicing writer.

You can also, of course, seek out writing classes at your local community college. In addition, there are plenty of online writing classes of value. In other words, there are lots of resources available to you.

So tackling your first online writing project might be stressful, but might also be easier than you think. You just have to put yourself in the place of whomever you're writing for and give them what they expect. That doesn't sound so difficult, does it?

DO YOU NEED TO BE A WRITER TO WRITE ONLINE?

Even though I'm now known as a book author, I actually started my writing career as a marketing copywriter. Way back in 1987, I was hired into what was then called Que Corporation (the same company that's publishing this book!) to write copy for catalogs and the back covers of books. In fact, one of the first books I wrote the back cover for was Que's groundbreaking, million-copy selling *Using 1-2-3, Special Edition*. (If you don't know what 1-2-3 is, you're just not as old as me.) Boy, did that little bit of copy get a lot of scrutiny throughout the company!

My point is that, given my background, I obviously have a bias toward trained writers—for all writing tasks. Look, when you need some woodworking done, you hire a carpenter. When you need wordworking, you should hire a wordsmith. Seems simple to me.

However, I know that it isn't always that simple—especially online. Many, many companies need a lot of online copy written, and they farm it out to whomever's available at the time. That might be a trained copywriter, but it often isn't. So if you're one of those noncopywriters drafted into writing a blog post or tweet or whatever, you're not alone; there are lots of people just like you, thrown into the grammatical deep end.

The good news is, you can learn how to write. Hell, every writer learned how to write at some point or another; that's how we become writers. Don't panic: it'll come.

By the way, even though I just called myself an "author," I prefer the term "writer." Author sounds too damned pretentious. I think Mickey Spillane got it right when he said, "I'm not an author, I'm a writer, that's all I am." I write, so I'm a writer. I happen to write books, so that technically makes me an author, but my skill is in writing. That's all I am, and that's good enough for me.

2

Punctuation, Grammar, and Other Rules to Live By

Before we get into online-specific writing advice, it's probably prudent to examine some basic writing guidelines. You know, the kind of stuff you learned back in high school English class. (Yeah, I know, I hated that class, too—but it obviously did me some good!)

So if your writing is a little rusty, or if you haven't written professionally before, this is the chapter for you. Settle in and learn yourself how to write real good!

Why Punctuation and Grammar Matter—Even Online

Online, as in the real world, you want to convey a professional appearance. You want people to take you (and your website or blog or company) seriously, and you can't do that if your copy is rife with errors. Even a few simple misspellings or improper word usages can cause readers to click away to other, more reliable, sites; these kinds of mistakes will cost you your credibility and cause readers to dismiss all the content on your site.

To attract the largest number of visitors, your site must contain unique, useful, and authoritative information. If there are punctuation or grammatical errors, readers will question the accuracy of the content itself. If there are errors in the grammar, the thinking goes, are there also errors in the content? If the writer can't be bothered to double-check grammar and punctuation, maybe that writer doesn't check the accuracy of the other information. Errors inspire doubt, and doubt causes visitors to distrust your site's content.

The errors don't have to be big ones, either. Consider basic punctuation mistakes, such as the use of "it's" instead of "its," or simple misspellings. Some readers won't notice or even know there's something wrong, but a lot of readers will. Even tiny errors will distract certain readers from focusing on the content itself, and you don't want or need that distraction. You want readers to focus on what you're writing about, not how you misused that apostrophe.

Good writing, then, reinforces the credibility of your site. Mistake-laden writing, on the other hand, undermines that credibility. If you want your site to be taken seriously and to be trusted, you have to be precise in everything you do—especially and including your punctuation and grammar.

This speaks to the value of knowing how to write and to write well. Fortunately, it isn't that difficult; all you have to do is follow a few simple rules.

Practicing Proper Punctuation

Punctuation has an important place in your writing. Put simply, it's the use of a set of common marks and symbols to separate sentences and elements within sentences. Without proper punctuation, things tend to run together in a way that causes confusion. Proper punctuation, then, helps make your writing clearer.

With that in mind, let's look at the basic punctuation marks and how to use them.

Periods

The most used punctuation mark is the period, such as the one you see at the end of this sentence. And that's the most common usage; periods are used to end sentences. Well, most sentences, anyway; you use other marks in sentences that question or exclaim. Periods work with declarative and imperative sentences, which should be the type of sentence most used in your writing.

Note

Although some might have been taught different in typing class, you should leave only a single space after a period to separate sentences. In the days when typewriters ruled, two spaces were common, but in today's desktop publishing environment, one space is all that's needed.

Question Marks

When you ask a question in your text, you indicate that question by using a question mark (?) at the end of the sentence. Example:

Is this the right course of action for your business?

Question marks are used only for direct questions. If you're asking an indirect question (more pondering than inquisitive), use a period instead of a question mark. Example:

I wonder if it will rain tomorrow.

Exclamation Marks

You use an exclamation mark (!) when your text needs special emphasis or enthusiasm—literally, to exclaim something. Example:

There's a big crash on the highway!

As you can see, the exclamation mark conveys the excitement in the passage.

You can also use an exclamation mark to express urgency or surprise or to emphasize an important command. Example:

Act now!

▶ *Caution*

Don't overuse exclamation marks, especially when you're writing profession-ally. Too many exclamation marks diminish their value and call into ques-tion the sincerity of your text. (And never, *never* use multiple exclamation marks; that's just amateurish!!!)

Commas

Commas (,) have several uses. Let's walk through them all.

The first use of commas is to separate items in a series. Put a comma after each item except the last, like this:

He needed to purchase pens, pencils, and paper for school.

▶ *Caution*

Do not insert a comma after the final item in a list, unless the comma is serving another function—such as separating one clause from another. This sometimes is necessary if the list itself is a separate clause that could be removed from the sentence, as in this example: **He needed to purchase some supplies, such as pens, pencils, and paper, for school**.

You use a comma only if you have three or more items in a row. If you have only two items, put the word "and" between them and forgo the commas. Example:

He needed to purchase pens and pencils for school.

SERIAL COMMAS

There is an ongoing debate about the use of what is called the *serial comma*. (Serial commas are also called Oxford commas or Harvard commas, depend-ing on your school affiliation.) A serial comma is the comma after the last item before the word "and;" in the following example, the comma comes after the word "blue:"

I like the colors red, yellow, blue, and green.

Without the serial comma, you write the same list as follows, without the comma after the word "blue:"

> I like the colors red, yellow, blue and green.

I prefer using the serial comma, because it better delineates the items in the list. In this example, without the serial comma you might imagine a color called "blue and green." With the serial comma, it's very clear that blue and green are separate colors.

Although the serial comma is common in American English, especially in nonjournalistic writing, and recommended by the *Chicago Manual of Style*, not everyone agrees. Journalists who follow the *AP Stylebook*, for example, are encouraged not to use the serial comma, and it's also less common in British English.

You can go either way; there's no definitive rule. But I tend to think that writing is clearer with the serial comma than without it, which is why I recommend adding that final comma before the "and."

You also use commas to set off nonessential phrases and clauses—things that could be omitted and still keep the sentence intact. Example:

> Mr. Jones, the most recent employee hired, hails from Des Moines.

In this example, the key point is that Jones comes from Des Moines. The fact that he's the newest hire is interesting but not key.

 Note

A clause is a single thought within a sentence. Simple sentences contain a single clause; more complex or compound sentences contain two or more clauses.

Along the same lines, you use commas to set off any expression that interrupts a sentence. Here's an example:

> The weather report, of course, was incorrect.

The "of course" is the expression that serves as a bit of a road bump and thus is set off by commas.

Similarly, you use a comma after introductory elements—like the word "similarly" at the start of this sentence. Here's another example:

> In conclusion, I urge you to vote for me.

In addition, you use commas before the words "and," "but," "or," "nor," "for," "so," and "yet," when those words are used to join two independent clauses in a single sentence. Example:

He liked the taste of fresh bananas, but he hated banana cream pie.

✉ Tip

Sometimes you can use a semicolon to join two independent clauses, but without the "and" or "but" words.

Finally, you use commas when writing dates and locations. For dates (in American English format), put a comma after the date and before the year, like this:

February 14, 2014

In addresses, put a comma between the city and state, as follows:

San Diego, CA

You should also use a comma before any honorariums in a person's name, such as:

Scott Randolph, PhD

Apostrophes

Apostrophes (') have two uses: to indicate contractions and possessives.

Let's start with contractions—like I just did with the word "let's," which is a contraction of two words: "let us." Other common contractions include "can't" ("cannot"), "it's" ("it is"), and "you're" ("you are").

For possessives, when it's a singular noun doing the possessing, add an apostrophe and an "s" after the word, like this:

It was the nun's fault.

🔍 Tip

If the addition of the "s" after the apostrophe makes for an awkward pronunciation—typically when the single noun ends in an "s"—you should add only the apostrophe. For example, you should write **the bus' route**, *not* **the bus's route**.

When it's a plural noun doing the possessing (such as a group of nuns), add an apostrophe after the "s," and nothing else, like this:

It was the nuns' fault.

If the plural noun does not end with an "s", add an "s" after the apostrophe, as in

The men's team won the match.

It's *not* **mens team**; you have to add the apostrophe.

 Caution

> You do *not* use an apostrophe when writing possessive pronouns—words such as "ours," "hers," "his," and "its."

APOSTROPHE ERRORS

The apostrophe might be the most misused punctuation mark, period. Some people insist on adding apostrophes where they don't belong, perhaps in the mistaken impression that every word that ends in an "s" needs an apostrophe. That is obviously not the case.

Here are some of the more common apostrophe mistakes you're likely to encounter:

- Apostrophes in dates, such as when someone is writing about the **1960's**. There's no apostrophe needed here; it should be written **1960s**. (You can, however, drop the "19" and write about the **'60s**, using an apostrophe to indicate the contraction—in this case, the apostrophe indicates omitted numbers.)

- Similarly, many people mistakenly put apostrophes in plurals, especially those that typically require the addition of an "e" in the plural, such as **We have lots of potato's**. No, you have lots of **potatoes**. It's the same with non-"e" plurals, such as the execrable **No semi's allowed**; nope, it should be **No semis allowed**. Apostrophes are not needed to indicate plurals. Period.

- Another common mistake involves the words "its" and "it's." I can't tell you how many times I've seen people write sentences such as **It's brain was on hold**. That's clearly incorrect; in this instance the word "it" is not possessive, and "it's" is not a contraction. Obviously, this is confusing to many people, probably because "its" is a possessive pronoun; even though it is possessive, you don't use an apostrophe. The word "it's," on the other hand, is a contraction for the words "it is." In fact, that's the *only* time you use the word "it's"—when it's short for "it is." If you can't expand it, it's not a contraction and shouldn't be used.

- Then there's the "your" and "you're" confusion, which isn't necessarily an apostrophe problem, although apostrophes are involved. If you're writing the contraction of the phrase "you are," you use **you're**. If, on the other hand, you're indicating a possessive (that is, it's *your* thing), you use the word **your**. Keep your contractions separate from your possessives and you'll be fine.

- Along the same lines is the use of "there," "their," and "they're." In order, **there** refers to a place; **their** is possessive for a group of people's things; and **they're** is a contraction of the phrase "they are." Don't get them mixed up; there's a lot of confusion there.

I could go into a lot more of these apostrophe errors, but I don't have the time or space to do so. Just remember to use apostrophes for contractions and possessives only. Any other time, resist the urge to apostrophize.

Semicolons

A semicolon (;) is used in a single sentence to separate two or more independent clauses that are not joined by "but," "and," or similar words. Think of it as joining two sentences into one with the semicolon as the glue. Example:

Don't just dive in; read the instructions.

You can also use semicolons between items in a series if any of those items contain commas. The point here is to use the semicolon to avoid confusion. For example, take a list where nouns are accompanied by descriptors, as follows:

The new employees are Bill, Marketing Assistant; Jenny, Copywriter; and Rudolfo, Production Assistant.

If this list were written with commas instead of semicolons, it would be extremely confusing: **Bill, Marketing Assistant, Jenny, Copywriter, and Rudolfo, Production Assistant.** That sounds like you have six new employees, not three. (It would be even more confusing if you didn't use the serial comma.) So use semicolons to make things more clear.

Colons

Colons (:) are used to point to something following. That something can be a list, a statement, a quotation, or you name it. Example:

Remember this: colons are important.

Note that the word following the colon is *not* capitalized if it begins a list or makes a statement. The following word *is* capitalized if it begins a quotation or a direct question, or if it introduces two or more sentences. I know, it's a little confusing.

Dashes

You use a dash (—) to indicate a break in your thinking. There are two types of dashes: the longer and more common *em dash* and the slightly shorter and less common *en dash* (-). For our purposes, I'll assume you're using an em dash.

 Note

The en dash, which is half the length of the em dash, is typically used to indicate a range of values, such as **1–3 years** or **January–June**.

In many instances, the phrase you set off with dashes is an interjection, as in this example:

We were following the instructions—such as they were—when things got all screwy.

Other times, the dashed-off phrase is explanatory, as in this example:

The three main offices—New York, Chicago, and Miami—were targeted for major layoffs.

The problem with using dashes when writing online is that there is no "dash" character on the computer keyboard. The quick and easy solution is to type two hyphens (--), which kind of sort of looks like a dash. The more elegant solution is to use the HTML code `&mdash`, which inserts a real, honest-to-goodness em dash into the text.

Tip

> In American English, it is standard to *not* include spaces on either side of
> a dash—to "close" the dash, in other words. In other parts of the world,
> however, it's common to "open" the dash with spaces between it and sur-
> rounding words.

Quotation Marks

Quotation marks ("") are used to set off quotations, with one at the beginning and
the other at the end, like this:

"The dog is part of the problem," Mark said.

You can also use quotation marks to set off defining words, titles, and other
sources. For example, here's the way you use quotation marks with the title of a
song:

Jimmy Webb's most-played work is "MacArthur Park."

▶ *Caution*

> You don't use quotation marks for all types of titles. For example, song
> titles typically have quotation marks, but album titles are typically itali-
> cized instead. Book and movie titles are also italicized.

By the way, when you're doing the quotation mark thing, put all ending periods
and commas *inside* the quotes. Colons and semicolons, on the other hand, should
go *outside* the quotes.

The placement of exclamation and question marks, vis a vis the quotation marks,
vary depending on the meaning of the sentence. That is, the ending quotation
mark should be right next to the text being quoted (or the title text). Note the following example, which places a question mark outside the quotation marks:

Did the band play "MacArthur Park"?

Parentheses

The final punctuation mark I cover here is the parenthesis. (That's the singular;
when you have two of them, which you most often do, they're parentheses.) As
you might have noticed from the previous sentence, you use parentheses to set

off material that does not fit within the normal flow of the surrounding content. Think of parenthetical material as an aside, something that can be removed without affecting the rest of your writing.

You can insert parenthetical content as whole sentences, or within a sentence, like this:

> It was a wonderful evening (not too cool, not too hot), which made the dinner that much more enjoyable.

Getting Grammatically Correct

We just spent a lot of time on simple punctuation. The whole issue of grammar is more complex and takes a lot more time and effort to get right.

First off, just what is grammar? In a nutshell, grammar is the structure of language, defining the way words fit together in sentences. Not surprisingly, there are grammatical rules for how your words should fit together—lots of rules, like the following:

- Make sure your subject and verb agree with each other. If it's a singular subject, use the singular form of the verb, not the plural form. Don't say **The dogs is barking**, say **The dogs are barking.** Plural nouns *are*, a singular noun *is*.

- Keep the same tense throughout a sentence. Don't switch back and forth from past tense to present tense. For example, **I was cautious, but think it is okay** isn't okay because **was** is past tense and **think** is present; the tenses don't agree. You need to rewrite this one as **I am cautious, but think it is okay.**

- Never end a sentence with a preposition. Instead of writing **She's someone I can't cope with**, write **She's someone with whom I can't cope.** Or instead of writing **Where are you at?**, drop the preposition and just write **Where are you?**

📩 *Note*

The preposition thing is one of those rules honored more in the breach than the observance. When following this rule causes the sentence to sound stilted, it's okay to break the rule and use a more natural construction.

- Don't split your infinitives. The most famous example is *Star Trek's* **To boldly go where no man has gone before.** It should more properly be written **To go boldly where no man has gone before**. (Although this one is like the preposition rule, it's often broken to make the sentence sound more natural.)

- Always write complete sentences. Well, almost always.

Now, you might not know precisely what some of these rules actually mean. I'm with you; I can't tell a participle from a predicate, let alone conjugate irregular verbs.

However, a lot of writing instruction focuses exclusively on grammatical rules. The thinking is that if you learn all the rules, you'll learn how to write well.

 Note

Even if you do follow the grammatical rules, know that every rule is meant to be broken, as circumstances demand. So there.

I beg to differ. I think you can learn to write well without knowing every single grammatical rule. I also think that even if you learn all the rules, your writing can still be stiff and uninviting.

When it comes to grammar, I really don't pay much attention to all those supposed rules. Instead, I follow one golden rule—your writing must be easily understood. That's it. Make your writing so that others easily understand what you're saying, and you'll be successful.

Here's how I make my writing understandable—by making it speakable. That is, I pattern my writing after the spoken word. If a sentence when spoken sounds right, has good flow, and is clear to the ear, then it's a good sentence. Forget all the prepositions and clauses and such; focus on what sounds right, and you're most of the way there.

 Tip

Lloyd Short, one of the first editors I worked with when I was a beginning copywriter, gave me one invaluable piece of advice. He said it didn't matter whether a sentence was technically correct; if a reader stumbled over it, it was wrong. His point was that writing needs to be clear and direct, without drawing attention to itself. The goal is for the reader to easily understand the information being presented, and nothing should detract from that goal.

So I won't go into all the pieces and parts of English grammar and tell you what you should or shouldn't do in every possible instance. Instead, I urge you to write as clearly and succinctly as possible and to read your work aloud. If it sounds good when spoken, if you don't stumble over any given word or phrase, if it's clear what it is you're talking about, then it's good writing.

✉ Note

It would take a book to detail all the various grammatical rules you're supposed to follow. In fact, there have been many books written about just that. If you want a good grammatical guide, I recommend the venerable *The Elements of Style,* by William Strunk Jr. and E.B. White. Written way back in 1918 (the current fourth edition was published in 1999), "Strunk and White" (as it's often called) is a short and inexpensive book that contains everything you need to know about proper grammatical usage. Keep a copy nearby for reference, if you need it.

DIAGRAMMING SENTENCES

One way to learn grammatical rules is to diagram your sentences. That is, you identify all the component parts of a sentence—nouns, verbs, adverbs, and the like—and put together a diagram of those parts. This supposedly helps you learn the different pieces and parts and how they should be used together.

I must confess, I hate sentence diagramming. When it came up back in high school, I did my best to avoid it. Not that I couldn't do it, because I could, I just found it extremely boring and mostly useless; who, after all, really cared about the difference between a participle and a predicate? And here's the thing: even though I avoided sentence diagramming like the plague, I still learned how to write, and to write pretty damned well, or so I've been told. In other words, not diagramming sentences didn't hinder my writing one iota.

On the contrary, I learned how to write by reading. I loved to read, still do, and tried to figure out why I liked what I liked. Why was Hemingway's writing so effective and Faulkner less so? (At least in my opinion...) By figuring out what made my favorite writers tick, I learned by emulating those writing styles. After I had that figured out, everything else was easy.

But it didn't come from the mechanical diagramming of sentences, of making sure this article of speech always followed this other grammatical cog. Sentence diagramming is soulless; learning from other writers has a lot more heart and soul.

Capitalizing Correctly

Given my caveat about learning grammar organically, there are still a few grammatical issues worth your attention. One of these is capitalization, which gives some writers the heebie jeebies, especially those more used to texting or tweeting than writing complete paragraphs. That's okay; capitalization rules are relatively simple.

 Note

> Don't confuse the state of anxiety known as the heebie jeebies with the 2005 film, *Heebie Jeebies*. (Note the title case for the film title.)

Capitalization Styles

There are three common styles of capitalization:

- Sentence style, where the first word of the sentence is capitalized but no other words are: **The song remains the same.**
- Title style (sometimes called headline style or initial caps), where the major words are capitalized (but the minor ones aren't): **The Song Remains the Same.**
- All uppercase (sometimes called all caps), where every letter is a capital letter: **THE SONG REMAINS THE SAME.**

For most body text, use sentence style. For titles within text, use title style. For headings and titles on a web page or other document, you can use any of the three styles, depending on what you want to employ. Just make sure you employ a consistent capitalization across your entire site or document; consistency is paramount.

▶ *Caution*

> Avoid the use of all lowercase (**the song remains the same**) in formal pages and documents. What might be okay in casual communication comes off as amateurish in more commercial uses.

First Words and Proper Nouns

Whatever style you choose (save for the recommended-against all lowercase), the first word of every sentence should be capitalized. This becomes problematic only when the first word is a proper noun that itself is not capitalized or is capitalized in a distinctive fashion. I'm talking brand names here, such as iPhone and eBay.

If you're faced with this situation, the recommended course of action is to rewrite the sentence to avoid starting with the brand name. (Yes, discretion is the better part of valor.) Because you can't always do this, however, the second-best approach is to make that initial lowercase letter uppercase, like this:

EBay's profits exceeded expectations.

Although this approach is perfectly proper, it seems awkward to me (as well as potentially offensive to the company's trademark attorneys). It might be less awkward (and increasingly more common) to use the brand name as is:

eBay's profits exceeded expectations.

This is why you might want to rewrite the sentence to sidestep the situation, like this:

The profits of eBay exceeded expectations.

(To be honest, that sounds awkward, too—which is why I really hate these inter-capped brand names!)

Beyond the first word in each sentence, you should also capitalize all proper nouns. That means names—of people, places, and things. Also, if you're doing how-to writing, capitalize the names of all buttons and switches and other important parts, such as:

Press the Esc button to close the Print dialog box.

Using Active Voice

Here's another grammatical rule that is worth following. When writing, try to use the active voice whenever possible. Avoid writing in the passive voice.

What, exactly, are active and passive voice? They're different ways of approaching the same content. With active voice, you have a direct subject-verb construction; something does this, or someone did that. With passive voice, the action occurs offscreen, as it were; this *was done* by someone. It's a matter of doing (active voice) versus having been done (passive voice).

So why, then, is active voice better than passive voice? For the simple reason that active voice is more...well, *active*. It's more direct, and it pulls the reader into the sentence.

Take, for example, this sentence written in passive voice:

The cabinet was built by Johnson & Sons.

Nothing is really wrong with that; it states a fact, and it's easily understood. But rearrange the sentence to put it in the active voice, and it looks like this:

Johnson & Sons built the cabinet.

The result is a shorter, more direct, and more powerful sentence. That is why you should structure your sentences in active voice whenever possible.

How do you change passive voice to active voice? Simple—remove the "was" or "were" and move the subject (the person or thing doing the action) to the front of the sentence. For example, if you're presented with the following passive sentence:

It was determined by the committee to review the contract.

Start by removing the "was." Then move the subject ("the committee") to the front. Smooth it out and you get the following more active sentence:

The committee determined to review the contract.

A simple, yet effective, fix.

Dealing with Gender Issues

Given that we're living in a post-sexist society (in theory, anyway), I need to address the use of gender in your writing. Trust me, it'll come up.

Typically, you run into gender-related issues when you're talking about a hypothetical someone doing something. You often see something like the following:

When the customer reaches the checkout phase, he clicks the Buy button.

And here's the problem. How do you know this customer is a he? The answer, of course, is that you don't. So why did you call that customer "he?" Are you some kind of sexist pig or what?

Of course, you're not a sexist pig, so you could reword the sentence to reference a female customer instead:

When the customer reaches the checkout phase, she clicks the Buy button.

Fine. But the same question remains: how do you know the customer is a female? Will you alienate male readers by introducing the feminine?

You could try to appease both sides by going with the "he or she" approach, like this:

When the customer reaches the checkout phase,
he or she clicks the Buy button.

Unfortunately, this approach is a bit awkward and really doesn't please male or female readers. You're trying to split the difference, and it just doesn't work.

Some less experienced writers might try to use the generic "they" approach, like this:

When the customer reaches the checkout phase, they click the Buy button.

That's a fool's errand, however, because you're now mixing singular and plural subjects in the same sentence; the customer (singular) is not a they (plural). Don't do this.

You could, I suppose, rephrase the sentence to be all plural, like this:

When customers reach the checkout phase, they click the Buy button.

That works, sort of, although it kind of sounds as if you have a large group of customers all working together to buy a single thing. This type of plural reconstruction can also get tiring if you do too much of it over the course of a piece.

You can also try rewording the original sentence so gender doesn't enter into it. For example, you might reword it as follows:

At the checkout phase, the customer clicks the Buy button.

"The customer" in this example could be of either gender.

All that said, sometimes the best approach is the simplest. Go ahead and use a gender-specific pronoun (he or she), but vary the gender references throughout the page or document. If you start with a "he" reference, make the next one a "she" reference." Change it up and you end up pleasing everyone over time.

Tip

A notable exception to this gender solution is when a piece or page is targeted specifically at a single gender. For example, if you're writing an article for new mothers, you gain nothing by using the pronoun "he" because most mothers tend to be "shes." When in doubt, go with what your audience expects.

Proofreading Before You Publish

Given how important punctuation and grammar are to your writing, it pays to have a second set of eyes before you publish. That's right, I'm talking about having your work edited and proofread—by real human beings.

I know that Microsoft Word and other software programs have built-in spell checkers, but a spell checker checks only spelling. A spell checker will not tell you that you should have used "their" instead of "they're" because they are both valid spellings. You can use the wrong word but spell it correctly, and that satisfies the spell checker.

I also know that Microsoft Word and other applications include rudimentary grammar-checking functionality. Word will try to tell you if something is grammatically incorrect. Really. It'll try. But this sort of machine-based grammar checking isn't terribly accurate; it'll flag some things that are perfectly correct and miss lots of things that aren't.

Note

Back in the early 1990s, the publishing company I worked for acquired the company that developed the RightWriter freestanding grammar-checking software. (This was before grammar checking got incorporated directly into word processing programs.) I can tell you from intimate experience that there's no way a software program can parse and analyze every possible grammatical permutation; a computer program simply can't grasp the underlying meaning behind words on a page. It takes a human editor to do that.

In short, there's no substitution for human-based proofreading and editing. That's why I recommend having a human being take a pass at your copy to look for misspellings, incorrect punctuation, poor grammar, and the like. And that person, by the way, shouldn't be you. That is, you need someone different from the writer looking at what was written. Another set of eyes is essential; if you made the mistake in the first place, you probably won't catch it on later review. You need someone else—an editor or proofreader, or both—to look over your copy before it goes live online. It's a safety net that pays countless dividends.

Tip

If you don't have a proofreader available to you, you can try proofreading your own work, although you're likely to miss your own mistakes. Otherwise, there are many online editing and proofreading services available; rates often aren't too high for shorter pieces.

I think that every piece of copy that goes online needs to be proofread. It doesn't matter if it's a four-line text ad, a 140-character tweet, a long blog post, or a multipage website; you don't want errors to creep into your work. Every word you put online matters. A single misspelled word or misplaced comma can cause endless embarrassment for you and your company. This is why everything you post online needs to be error free, period.

Take the time to do it right in the first place, and then have someone else give it a final look over. It's worth it.

3

Conveying Confusing Content, Clearly

One of the key things you need to do when writing for online media—for any media, actually—is tell the readers what they need to know in an understandable fashion. Dump the fancy language and jargon; the reader has to understand what you're talking about—which, with some topics, is a challenge.

It's important, then, to learn how to make complicated things simple. This involves your content (simplifying the complex) and your writing style; both need to be as user friendly as possible. With online content, writing over the heads of your readers is not the way to go.

Who Are You Talking To?

Before you write a single word, you have to be very, very clear about who your audience is. That's because you need to write differently for different people.

This is particularly true when you're talking about conveying complex or specialized information. If you're talking to someone well versed in the given topic, you can assume they know the basics and write at a more advanced level. But if they're newcomers to the field, you can't assume they know anything at all. You especially can't assume they know as much as you do about the topic; thus, you have to do a lot more explaining (in plain English, please) about what the topic is and how it works.

It goes the other way, too. If you're writing for a knowledgeable audience, you can insult them by pitching your content too low. If you cover ground that your readers already know, you run the risk of boring them and sending them to other sites that are more level appropriate.

It's key, then, to be very, very clear about who is going to be reading the content you write. Figure out who the audience is, how much they know, and why they're reading it, and then give them what they want at the level and in the style they want. Don't pitch too high or too low; make it just right.

And What Are You Talking About?

It also helps if you know exactly what it is you're writing about. Your content must be clear not just to you but also to your readers. That starts with you having a distinct understanding of the topic; if you're not that knowledgeable about a topic, it will be difficult for you to write with the necessary authority.

Before you write a single word, you need to have in mind the key message(s) you want to convey. Your message can't be fuzzy or confusing; it has to be simple and easily grasped by the reader. And there can't be too many messages, or what's really important will get lost in the mix.

For this reason, I like to do a little outlining before I start writing the main text. Even if it's just writing down the main concepts as a series of bullet points, looking at the bare bones of the thing before you start adding text will help you focus your thoughts on what's most important. Start with these key elements and then embellish them; build your story around the essential bullets.

Translating Complex Topics to Plain English

Topicwise, online content can be—and is—all over the board. Some websites specialize in pop topics, others in technical ones. Whatever the topic, however, you need to be able to convey it in a manner that casual readers can understand. That often means taking complex content and presenting it in a simple fashion or taking an "insider" topic and making it accessible to outsiders.

It's really a matter of translation.

That is, you need to translate those complex terms and topics into plain English—words and concepts that your target audience can understand. Assume that you and your insider pals are talking a foreign language, because you are, at least to the general public. Take those fancy terms and buzzwords that you throw around like dime-store Frisbees and express them in everyday language. Translate, if you will, your jargon into English.

How do you simplify complex content? The key is to know your audience. You have to get outside your own head and recognize what your readers do and don't know—and what they need and want to know.

To do this, you essentially have to forget everything you know. Forget all the jargon and industry speak. Forget the inside information and technical details. Forget the inside stuff you find fascinating, and forget what your boss or colleagues think is important.

Instead, ask yourself how much you'd know if you were coming to this topic completely fresh. Think of yourself as an absolute newbie, without years of experience and exposure. Just what would a newbie really know about this topic?

The answer is, of course, not much. Depending on the topic, there might be some knowledge gleaned from the popular press, but the more inside the topic is, the more likely it is that a newbie wouldn't know much at all.

That's where you start—at the very beginning. Assume your reader doesn't know anything and build from there.

This means that you should gently introduce core information, using language that an outsider will understand. You'll need to avoid jargon and industry-specific terms; you'll also want to keep your sentences short and sweet and use words that just about everybody knows.

GETTING OUTSIDE

Look, I know how it is. When you're familiar with a given topic, it's tempting to assume that everyone else knows as much as you do. That's seldom the case, but it's how a lot of bad copy gets written. I'm talking about copy that starts midway into the story, leaving newcomers scratching their heads as to what's going on. Copy that's dense with industry terminology and jargon that no one outside the industry can comprehend. Copy that doesn't bother to explain arcane or confusing points. Copy that you and your friends and coworkers understand, but nobody else does.

This type of "inside" content is often incomprehensible to anyone just outside of your immediate crowd, and thus a fairly ineffective way to communicate with anyone visiting your website or blog. You can't assume that everyone just visiting your site or blog knows the same things you do or cares about the same things you do—or as much. Get too "inside" in your writing and you will turn off everyone outside your immediate group.

This is why you need to get away from your daily echo chamber and go outside the company or industry, where your readers and customers are. Hear things the way the uninitiated hear them, see things the way outsiders do. Leave the inside to become an outsider—at least while you're writing.

By the way, insiders often refer to those outside the industry as "civilians." That's as good a description as any; unless you're specifically writing for industry insiders, explain things in a fashion that civilians can understand.

Limiting the Detail

Then there's the matter of just how much your reader wants to know or needs to know. It's fairly common to assume that everyone will be as interested in your topic as you are, and thus will want to learn all the gritty details and inside scoop you find fascinating. Trust me; nobody but you is interested in that stuff. I'm sure you can go on and on about the history of this or the implications of that, but it's just so much yada yada to the masses. Keep your trivia and minutiae to yourself or at least wait until you're sure you have a more receptive audience. When you're writing for newbies, keep the amount of information to a reasonably digestible level.

That is, give the readers exactly what they need to know—not one word more. Don't embellish the information; don't get all insidey. Keep it short and sweet and to the point. You'll have plenty of opportunities later to provide more details, if that's necessary and what the reader wants. For now, start at the beginning and go only so far as is absolutely necessary.

How much information is enough? Again, put yourself in the shoes of a newbie reader. At what point do his initial questions get answered, and when do his eyes start glazing over? Get the key information out there before the reader starts getting bored. If anything, leave the reader wanting more, rather than wanting to click away.

Caution

The danger of boring online readers is that they click away from your site or blog—and never return.

The bottom line is that you can't write for yourself, or even for your coworkers (unless you're writing a company newsletter, that is). You have to write for people who don't know as much as you do and make the topic understandable and interesting to them. That means using popular language, not insider jargon, and explaining things in terms that the average person can understand.

Conveying Benefits, Not Features

Making complex information simple and meaningful also means writing not about the topic itself, but about how the average reader might relate to the topic. A reader might not be terribly interested in the details of how an artist created a new sculpture, but she might be interested in how that piece of art beautifies the public square where it's installed. It's not the piece itself that's interesting; it's how the reader interacts with it.

What I'm talking about is conveying benefits instead of features. Most people couldn't give a flying fig about the features and specifications of a product, but they are extremely interested in how they might benefit from those features. It's a matter of what you (or your topic) can do for the reader; everybody's interested in how things affect them personally.

Let's say you're writing about a new automobile. You could go into extreme detail about the car's engine and the transmission system and even its audio system. In doing so, you could probably spout all manner of specifications and use all sorts of industry buzzwords; you're probably also tempted to use the newly coined labels your marketing staff came up with for these new features.

Using a real-world example, one auto manufacturer talks about its 5.7-liter DOHC 32-valve V8 engine with Dual Independent Variable Valve Timing, its 6-speed ECT-i transmission, and its Entune audio system with JBL Synthesis. Without some sort of Toyota-to-English dictionary at hand, the average car buyer would have no idea what most of these items actually are. Would you, for example, know that ECT-i stands for Electronically Controlled automatic Transmission with Intelligence—or, for that matter, what that means? Of course not.

What you need to do in your copy is take this sort of technical nonsense and make it both understandable and meaningful to the reader. Instead of simply conveying the engine's specs, talk about how it gives the car the power to comfortably pass even on steep grades. The engine specs are the features; the passing power is the benefit. Instead of blathering about that ECT-i transmission, tell the reader how the transmission is smart enough to choose just the right gears to maximize the car's fuel consumption, and thus save you money on gasoline bills. Instead of throwing around trademarked names like Entune and JBL Synthesis, say that the audio system sounds great with any type of music from any device, including satellite radio and your iPod or iPhone.

Benefits, not features. It's a reader-focused approach that also helps to make technical information clearer and more meaningful.

Using Examples

Another good way to explain complex topics is to use examples. Show readers, by detailing a specific case, how this one complex thing is just like this other simpler thing that they're more familiar with.

You use examples in your writing to bring complex topics down to earth. Illustrate the concept by providing a concrete example that the reader will be familiar and comfortable with. It's illustrating the general with a specific.

For example, consider the challenge of explaining how to put together a household budget. When it comes to talking about inflow and outflow, two topics that some find hard to grasp, you could say, "For example, your paycheck is income, money coming into your bank account. The money you spend on groceries is outflow, money flowing out of your bank account."

See what I just did there? I used an example to illustrate the concept of using examples in your writing. Kind of meta, I know, but you get the point.

Writing Step-by-Step Instructions

The ability to simplify complex concepts is particularly important when you're trying to show readers how to do something. With how-to information, you have to lead readers step-by-step through a set of detailed instructions. By breaking a topic or process into its component steps, you simplify a complex procedure.

It's easier for readers to comprehend what's going on when you walk them through it one step at a time. Instead of forcing them to grasp an entire concept all at once, they become comfortable with it gradually as they move from step to step. And they actually learn how to do something in the process.

Writing step-by-step instructions also helps you to better understand all that's involved with a given process. When you take apart a process, as it were, it forces you to think about and better appreciate each step in the process. It's a good learning experience for writers as well as readers.

To write step-by-step instructions, you have to start at the beginning and finish at the end. This sounds painfully obvious, but you'd be surprised how many instructions start somewhere in the middle and stop before the thing is completely done.

So you'll need to think through a given process, and what you need to do, one step at a time. Start where your readers will be starting with their level of expertise. That means you can assume some basic understanding and preparation from a more experienced audience, but also means you'll need to start at the very beginning when you're dealing with less-experienced readers.

Take the example of showing someone how to high dive into a swimming pool. You might start the instructions by explaining how to position your feet on the diving board, but for some readers you've already skipped ahead too much. You might need to detail what type of swimming pool is best for diving, how high the board should be, or maybe even tell them that the pool should be filled with water and that they should have a spotter or lifeguard nearby. You then lead the reader up the steps of the ladder to the end of the diving board, and proceed from there.

The best way to convey step-by-step information is literally in steps—numbered steps, that is. Although you can write how-to content in paragraph form, it's a lot easier for the reader to grasp when the individual steps are broken out, like this:

1. As you enter the store, grab a shopping cart.

2. Push your cart to the produce aisle.

3. Find the banana section.

4. Choose a bunch of bananas that have a strong yellow color—not too green and not yet brown.

5. Place your bananas into your cart.

6. Push your cart to the store's checkout.

7. Pay the cashier for your bananas.

Notice how the instructions are clear and easy to follow. You know exactly what to do at each step; there's nothing left to guesswork.

 Tip

Make sure that you cover only one operation in each step. Avoid combining multiple operations into a single step, which can be confusing to readers.

Now, you might need to edit these instructions for different levels of reader. Using our current example, if someone is totally unfamiliar with grocery stores, you might need to explain in step 2 just what the produce aisle is and looks like; he might not even be familiar with the word "produce." Or, if someone is an experienced shopper, you might be able to skip step 1, assuming she knows to grab a cart when entering the store. It's a simple matter of fine-tuning for your target audience.

▶ *Caution*

Do not nest steps within steps. If there's a subprocess involved, either include it as a single step within the numbered list, or refer readers to another set of instructions for that subprocess.

Avoiding Jargon and Industry Speak

Now we come to one of the most important ways to simplify complex topics. It's a matter of using accessible language, by avoiding topic-specific jargon, acronyms, and such—what I like to call "industry speak."

As noted previously, it's easy (actually, lazy) to think that your readers are as well versed as you in a given topic. Maybe they are—in which case, use as much industry speak as you like. But in most instances, your readers are coming from a different place and won't know all the jargon and buzzwords that you and your pals toss around with abandon.

I like to think of it as being inclusive instead of exclusive in your writing. When your copy contains too much industry jargon and doublespeak, you exclude those who aren't already part of the club. Far better to be inclusive and invite outsiders into your club; that's how you attract new readers, new visitors, and new customers.

Consider this list of buzzwords gleaned from an online security website: botnet, clickjacking, cloud security, defense-in-depth, and typosquatting. Now, if you're big into online security, you probably know what all these mean. If you're not, you don't. So it won't do you any good to write about defense-in-depth if your audience doesn't know it has to do with employing a series of security countermeasures to protect an organization's information assets.

(Whoops! I just used another buzzword—"information assets" to explain the first buzzword!)

In any case, don't use terminology that your reader doesn't know or understand. Yeah, it's convenient shorthand for those in the know, but it's meaningless blather to everybody else. When it doubt, use a plain English explanation instead.

Then you have the issue of acronyms—words formed from the initial letters of other words. For example, BYOD (continuing our online security example) stands

for Bring Your Own Device; AHG is an Ad Hoc Group; and WEEE is Waste
Electrical and Electronic Equipment.

 Note

> Given the tendency of long terms to be condensed into short acronyms, we
> have the common acronym TLA—which stands for "Three Letter Acronym."

The problem with acronyms is the same as with other jargon—unless you're an
insider in that industry or environment, you won't know what they mean. In fact,
some acronyms have different meanings for different industries; ACE, for example,
can stand for American Council on Exercise, American Council on Education,
Adobe Certified Expert, Advanced Composition Explorer, Adult Continuing
Education, and a few dozen other things. Write ACE in your copy, and it will mean
different things for different readers.

The best way to use acronyms is *not* to use them, period. If you think you must
use a specific acronym, spell it out on first usage, like this: **He was a veteran of air
combat engagement (ACE)**. But better if you can avoid the acronyms, especially
when you're writing for a general audience.

 Note

> About the only times acronyms are acceptable are when you're writing
> for an "insider" audience, and when you're tweeting on Twitter. (With a
> 140-character limit, you need to conserve space whenever you can!)

That said, if you are writing for a knowledgeable audience, and they're likely all
familiar with a given acronym or buzzword, then go ahead and use it; you might
look kind of dumb or unknowledgeable if you don't. Along the same lines, if a
given acronym is more commonly used than the original phrase, then the acronym is probably okay. (For example, does anyone remember that DVD stands for
Digital Video Disc? We all know the acronym, not the original phrase.)

▶ *Caution*

> Along the same lines, you should avoid trendy terms that might date your
> content. For example, the word "mancave" is trés trendy today, but in five
> years will seem as outdated as the word "metrosexual" does now.

Writing in a Conversational Style

Finally, how you say something is as important as what you say. That means you need to carefully choose the writing style you use and match that style to the type and level of reader.

For a general audience, that probably means writing in a conversational style. Not too formal, not too stiff, not too technical; make your writing feel genuine and natural, just like you're having a conversation with someone in real life.

I'll talk more about writing style later in this book, but for now know that if your writing sounds overly technical or too inside, it's going to turn off the reader. Force yourself to write in a conversational style, and you'll find it easier to use the right words and include the right information. Using the right style for your audience will keep their interest, and everything else will fall into place.

 Note

Learn more about writing styles in Chapter 7, "Finding Your Voice."

4

Keeping It Short and Simple

One of the key things about writing online copy, of any type, is that the shorter it is, the better. People today have fairly short attention spans, and it's even more so online; we're talking a generation that's grown used to short text messages in lieu of more considered longer-form communications, such as letters or even emails. To readers today, anything longer than a pamphlet qualifies as a novel; anything longer than 140-characters is too long to scroll through. There's little tolerance for lengthy discussions, let alone learned digressions. Everything has to be seen at a glance, not read and contemplated over time.

You see what I just did there? I wrote a very long paragraph with very long sentences and very long words. The sort of thing you shouldn't do when writing for the Web.

Instead, you need to learn how to write more concisely. Keep it short and simple. Short paragraphs. Short sentences. Short words.

How do you do this? Read on and I'll tell you.

Why Shorter Is Better

Back in Chapter 1, "What's Different About Writing Online Copy?," we talked about how the nature of online reading necessitated shorter copy than you might find in traditional print media. It helps to fully understand the *why* behind the issue before we get into the *how* to deal with it.

Computer Monitors Aren't Made of Paper

There are some obvious physical limitations to reading online content. Reading a web page or email isn't like reading a book or magazine; a computer screen doesn't fit comfortably in your hands, nor does it reflect and absorb light like paper does. Instead, you're dealing with a flat screen, typically sitting on your desk, that emits light from behind the words. The comfort level simply isn't there for extended reading sessions.

Indeed, it's the backlighting thing that bothers many people who try to do serious reading on their computer or tablet screens. Many folks complain of eyestrain when reading on computer or tablet screens, and I can understand that. The longer you sit at a computer monitor reading, the more tiring it becomes.

 Note

The reading fatigue issue is why most dedicated ebook readers forgo the typical backlit LCD screen in favor of something called Electrophoretic Ink (E Ink), which mimics the light reflectivity of ink on paper.

Resolution Is Poor

You also have to consider the resolution of computer screens, which are noticeably inferior to ink on paper. Resolution measures the number of dots (pixels) that make up onscreen text and images—the higher the resolution, the sharper the picture.

A typical 15.4" notebook computer screen has a resolution of 1440 pixels wide by 900 pixels high. That's a pixel density of 110 pixels per inch (PPI). Apple's third-generation iPad tablet is better for reading, with a pixel density of 264 PPI. A fourth-generation iPhone is even better at 326 PPI. (All of which tells me that the larger the screen, the less resolution we're dealing with.)

Compare these resolutions with that of a printed book or magazine. Now, ink on paper doesn't translate exactly into screen pixels (the more appropriate measurement for print is dots per inch, or DPI), but you can compare the two. Newspapers, for example, are typically printed at 1270 DPI; most books are printed at 2400 DPI. (Image-intensive coffee table books are printed at even higher resolution.) Assuming a dot is similar to a pixel, put a 2400 DPI book side by side with a 110 PPI computer screen; there's significant difference in resolution and clarity.

So printed text and images are sharper than what digital media can offer. And that's one of the contributing factors to online reading fatigue.

Screen Sizes Are Small

In addition, many computer screens are smaller than book or magazine pages, especially when you consider the landscape versus portrait orientation. Take a typical 15" notebook screen; it's only about 8" high. Compare that to a typical hardcover book, which is about 9" high, or *Time* magazine, which is about 10.5" high. (Newspapers are even taller...) In short, large-format books have to be shrunk or reformatted to fit on a typical computer screen—or you have to do a bit of scrolling to see the whole page.

 Note

Display screens, whether for computers or television sets, are measured diagonally, from one bottom corner to the opposite top corner. Thus a 14" diagonal display measures just that (14 inches) from the lower-left corner of the screen to the top-right corner. We cannot easily ascertain the height or width of a given display from this diagonal measurement, because we also have to account for the screen's aspect ratio—the width versus the height. Widescreen monitors have a different ratio (typically 16:9) than standard screens do (which typically have a 4:3 ratio). It's all rather complicated.

The situation isn't much better on tablets, especially the smaller ones. The Amazon Kindle Fire, for example, is billed as having a 7" diagonal screen, which translates into a screen height of only 6". The larger Apple iPad is better, with a 7.75" high screen, but that's still better suited for reading paperbacks than it is for reading magazines or newspapers.

The situation gets really bad when you're talking about reading on a smartphone—which a lot of people do, whether that's web pages or books or tweets or whatever. The typical smartphone screen is less than 3" high, which isn't big enough to read anything of any length. Pretty much everything you read on your phone has to be scrolled—a lot. And that's inconvenient.

Attention Spans Are Short

So the physical screens used for reading online are small and not as detailed as traditional paper media. That's only part of the problem.

As a society, our collective attention span has gotten shorter over the years. It probably started with the widespread embrace of television in the 1950s, got worse with the advent of MTV in the 1980s, and shrunk considerably more during the personal computer revolution. (Phone texting also contributed to the issue, of course.)

In any case, people today don't have the patience for anything long, whether that's shots in a movie or words in a message. We want whatever it is we want to be short and sweet. We don't have time for long conversations, or for reading in general. Decry that as you will, but it's the way it is.

What this means is that you can't expect online readers to actually read anything. People are more likely to "graze" your text than they are to read every single word. And they won't put in the effort to scroll through a long web page or blog post; they have to see it all in a single glance.

That's not to say that some people don't read some things that are longer. Business professionals might read industry white pages; savvy shoppers might read detailed spec sheets. But in general, people don't have the attention spans to read anything long at all online.

Got that?

It's What We Expect

When you're writing for an online medium today, you're not inventing the wheel. There have been lots of writers before you, and they've established the way online writing looks and feels—which is short and sweet. Just look around the Web; most web pages are textually concise and don't require a lot of scrolling. It's what readers have come to expect.

So go ahead and write overly long web page copy. It won't be what visitors expect to see, and they won't like it. There's no point trying to break the mold; you have to do things the way everybody else does. It's a matter of meeting reader expectations.

And what happens if you do write overly long online copy? In the best case, people will just stop reading midway. In the worst case, they click away to another site that presents similar information in a more concise fashion.

In other words, long writing will drive online visitors away. So keep it short. Very short.

Keeping It Chunky

How do you deal with all these issues? It's simple—you have to present your information as concisely as possible.

This is, perhaps, the key difference between online writing and writing for traditional print media. Every aspect of what is read online must be short and quickly scanned; you don't have the luxury of creating dense and flowing prose.

Where print enables, even encourages, the writing of lengthy, involved passages, the Internet does not. Effective online writing recognizes the challenges arising from people with short attention spans reading on small screens and adjusts accordingly. People don't have the attention span to read long passages online, so you give them shorter passages. Small, low-resolution screens make reading lengthy passes difficult, so you make your text shorter and better fit to backlit screens. It's a simple matter of adjusting your writing to the medium.

You do this in a number of ways. You have to organize your content into more but shorter sections, keep down the sentence length, and even simplify the language you use. When you're online, shorter is better—however you accomplish it.

That doesn't mean delivering less information. Despite the attention span and screen size issues, many people still want and need a certain amount of information. What this means, then, is that you need to write and format that information in a way that is easily scanned on small, low resolution screens by people with short attention spans. Piece of cake!

I find that a good way to approach this is to think of your content not as something that's read in detail, but as something that's glanced at or scanned. That is, you want to present only as much information as a reader can absorb in a single glance. In most instances, that's a screen's worth of information, certainly no more, sometimes less.

That doesn't mean that you're limited to only a screen's worth of text. If you have a longer message (and you might for a given web page or blog post), spread it across multiple screens. Don't expect readers to scroll down a long page; instead, have them click to view another full screen. (It's true; web readers would rather click than scroll. I'm not sure why.)

This approach also dictates paragraphs that can be scanned in a single glance and sentences that don't roll on and on for multiple lines. Again, it's all about making your content scannable so that it can be absorbed in a glance.

What you end up with, then, is content that's been *chunkified*—broken up into short, easily digested chunks. Chunks of information is what you want—chunky text, you might say.

✉ *Note*

Yes, "chunkified" is a made up word. It's my book, so I get to do that. (It
is quite descriptive, though, don't you think?)

The goal, then, is to chunkify your text—break it into easily browsed chunks. You
can do this via a variety of methods, all of which involve making things shorter.

WRITING FOR THE SCREEN

One of the keys of writing for online consumption is working within the constraints of the display screen. Ideally, you want your content to fit within a
single screen, without readers having to scroll down to read more. The problem is, every screen is different.

Think about it. Let's say you tailor your content to fit on a 22" diagonal
desktop computer monitor, which actually can hold a lot of text. Well, that
formatting wouldn't work nearly as well on a 14" diagonal notebook screen,
or a 10" diagonal tablet display. (And don't get me going on formatting for
those extremely small smartscreen displays.)

There are other factors involved, as well. The font used onscreen, in terms
of both type and size, makes a big difference, as does the width of the page
or the lines of text on the page. A web page formatted with 12-point Times
Roman type is going to hold a lot less content than one formatted with
10-point Verdana—and you might not know in advance how your content is
going to be formatted.

So the challenge is to write to fill a single screen, but different screens are
different sizes, and you probably don't even know what size font you're writing for. Like I said, it's a challenge.

If you're writing for a website, you might be able to work with your site
designers to get a better feel for how much content will fit on a given page.
(Learn more in Chapter 22, "Dealing with Web Page Design.") If you don't
have this luxury, you'll have to play it by ear and trust your own experience.
You might also want to experiment a bit, if you can. Be willing to trim a little
here or add some filler there to create a better fit for the "typical" screen. It's
all a matter of fine-tuning—which is part and parcel of the writing process.

Writing Shorter Sections

Let's start with the macro and move down to the micro. That means starting with
the overall sections within your writing.

If you're used to writing papers for educational or professional use, you're also used to organizing your work into sections, with level one heads, level two heads, and such, kind of like a big outline. That's good because your content online should also follow this sort of sectioning.

What's different about sections online is that they should be shorter. In professional and educational papers, a given section might run a full page or more; online, a section should probably be only a few paragraphs in length. In fact, it's okay to have a section with just a single paragraph.

As previously noted, the goal is to chunkify your text to make it easily scanned. Employing lots of shorter sections (with the corresponding more frequent headings) does just that.

What's the right length for a section of text—that is, how many paragraphs should you have between headings? There is no hard-and-fast rule, but I'd say about three or four paragraphs, even fewer if the paragraphs themselves are long. People jump from section to section, often reading just the section headings, so give them a lot of headings to read.

You can shorten your sections a number of ways. First is to delete extraneous text from longer sections, although that might deprive readers of valuable content. A better approach is to insert descriptive headers every two or three paragraphs as the content dictates. This results in the headings creating a kind of running commentary on the underlying text; an impatient reader could read just the headings to get the gist of what you're trying to impart.

 Note

Learn more about organizing your content into sections in Chapter 5, "Organizing Your Content."

Writing Shorter Paragraphs

When it comes to chunkifying your text, nothing works better than writing shorter paragraphs. Online, you just don't want a paragraph to stretch from the top of the screen to the bottom; you want to be able to gently graze from one short paragraph to the next.

Let's also be honest: shorter paragraphs are effective in most types of writing. An overly long paragraph looks dense on the page and might discourage readers from tackling the whole thing. A shorter paragraph is more inviting and promises a quicker payoff. Readers are more likely to read a paragraph where the end is in sight than one that trails off somewhere down the page.

You can use several techniques to write shorter paragraphs. One is simply self-control; limit yourself, while writing, to no more than two or three sentences per paragraph. Another approach is to take longer existing paragraphs and chop them into two (or three or four). If you go the latter route, a little rewriting might be in order, to make sure that each new paragraph has appropriate first and last sentences, and that they flow well from one to the next.

> ✉ *Note*
>
> Short paragraphs are a staple of what some call "practical writing." This includes most journalistic writing, where the goal is not the writing itself, but rather conveying the facts of a story. In its own way, most online writing is practical writing; the facts are what's important, not the words you choose.

Take, for example, this single long paragraph:

> **We employ several stealth techniques when monitoring Darknet sites. First, we disperse our software agents through multiple secure servers located around the globe. In addition, software agents are programmed to mimic naturalistic human behavior, not the automated behavior typical of search spiders, thus concealing their presence. This non-intrusive process leaves little to no signature behind, so that monitoring can continue without detection or interruption. The data retrieved by our search engines are forwarded to the company's human cyber intelligence analysts. These professionals can then enter the targeted site or channel manually if more information is required or filter through the retrieved data and forward their analysis to the company's clients.**

Pretty dense, isn't it? You get better readability when you break this single long paragraph into multiple shorter ones, each of which are more easily scanned by the reader. The end result looks like this:

> **We employ several stealth techniques when monitoring Darknet sites.**
>
> **First, we disperse our software agents through multiple secure servers located around the globe.**
>
> **In addition, software agents are programmed to mimic naturalistic human behavior, not the automated behavior typical of search spiders, thus concealing their presence. This non-intrusive process leaves little to no signature behind, so that monitoring can continue without detection or interruption.**

> The data retrieved by our search engines are forwarded to the company's human cyber intelligence analysts. These professionals can then enter the targeted site or channel manually if more information is required or filter through the retrieved data and forward their analysis to the company's clients.

Still not ideal (I'd shorten some of those sentences—as I'll discuss next), but it's a lot more readable than the original single paragraph.

Writing Shorter Sentences

Okay, so you need to write paragraphs that are only a few sentences long. You also need to keep those few sentences relatively short.

The Internet is no place for picturesque prose. It's a just the facts, ma'am, medium, with no tolerance for wasted words.

That means you need to pare your sentences down to the bare essentials. Don't use a lot of rhetorical flourishes; do the subject-verb thing with a minimum of adjectives and adverbs. Use only what you need to get the point across.

Shorter sentences have the added benefit of being more powerful. A sentence is certainly more understandable when the reader doesn't have to negotiate a maze of commas and clauses. Shorter sentences are more direct; getting to the point more quickly helps the reader digest and ultimately remember the message better than with longer, more involved sentences.

The easiest way to write shorter sentences is to discipline yourself to do so. Beyond that, you can pare down longer sentences by removing unnecessary verbiage and by rewriting sentences with multiple clauses into multiple sentences. Don't try to say two things in a single sentence; use two sentences instead. (Not like I just did in that sentence, by the way.)

Here's an example of a long compound sentence, taken from the previous paragraph example:

> This non-intrusive process leaves little to no signature behind, so that monitoring can continue without detection or interruption.

You make it more readable by breaking it in two, like this:

> This non-intrusive process leaves little to no signature behind. Monitoring can then continue without detection or interruption.

Reads better, don't you think?

What's the right length for a sentence? There's no minimum; in conversational writing, a sentence can consist of a single word. (Really.) In terms of maximum length, keep it to no more than 10 or 12 words, if you can. Focus on the main idea and excise anything that doesn't contribute to that.

 Tip

Another way to reduce sentence length is to avoid lazy phrases and jargon. For example, instead of saying **at the present time**, say **now**. Instead of **in the majority of instances**, say **mostly**. You get the point; don't use three or more words where one will do.

Writing Shorter Words

We've now arrived at the micro level of writing—the words you use.

Look, I'm a fan of fancy words. I love 'em; the more inventive, the better. I even wrote a book about improving your vocabulary, filled with lots of ten-dollar words.

 Note

My book of ten-dollar words (maybe they were only five-dollar words back then) was *Webster's New World Vocabulary of Success*, published by Webster's New World in the waning days of the past century (1998, to be precise). I don't think it's still in print, but you can probably snag a used copy from Amazon if you're so inclined.

Most readers, however, do not share my love of language, nor do they have as large a vocabulary. Not that you should talk down to your readers, but you do need to write in a fashion they understand.

That means using language that your readers are familiar and comfortable with. Your web page or Facebook status update is not the place to educate the unwashed or show off your knowledge of synonyms. All you need to do is get your point across; use words that do that most efficiently.

That means using shorter words, more common words, and less-technical words. Don't break out the thesaurus; use words that your readers are likely to know.

And if you're a frustrated linguist—tough. This isn't about you; it's about the people reading your words and the content you're providing. Don't make it any more difficult than it has to be for your readers to get the information they want and need. If that means feeding it to them with a very small spoon, so be it.

Besides, I like small words as well as large words. When it comes to language, size really doesn't matter, does it?

5

Organizing Your Content

The Internet is no place for disorganized content. You might have been able to get away with a little organizational confusion in your last term paper, and I'm sure your personal letters swing and swerve all over the place, thoughtwise, but people just don't have time for that online. Online readers want to get to the main point as fast as possible, and if your content's roadmap is anything but a straight line from point A to point B, you'll lose them—literally.

It's important, then, to organize your content so that it's easily understandable and so that time-starved readers can quickly get to the good stuff. This involves not only determining what goes where in your copy, but also employing headings, lists, and other devices to make your content as clear as possible.

Putting the Most Important Stuff First

It might seem somewhat obvious, but the better organized a piece of text, the easier it is for readers to find exactly the information they're looking for. Readers don't want (and shouldn't need) to work hard to find what's important; the structure of the text should lead them directly to the main points or to subsidiary information of interest.

In many cases, this can be as simple as making sure you put the most important information first. Don't make readers wade through paragraphs (or pages) of less-important or less-interesting stuff to find the underlying nugget in your text; put that key point front and center so that it can't be missed.

It's not like fiction writing, where you drag the reader through dozens of chapters of plot before you reach the thrilling climax. With informational writing (sometimes called practical writing), there might be a story to tell, but you don't withhold the key information for the sake of the storytelling. In journalistic terms, you don't bury the lead; you reveal the main point in the very first paragraph, if not in the initial sentence.

The comparison to journalistic writing is apt. What you're doing online is conveying information—and the best way to convey information is to put it out there for all to see. Newspapers work in terms of headlines and section headings, and a lot of online writing works the same way. You put the important stuff first for all readers to see (even if they're just grazers), then provide additional details later for anyone still interested.

In journalism, this is called the *inverted pyramid*. As shown in Figure 5.1, you put the most newsworthy information first, at the base (now the top) of the inverted pyramid. You follow that with important details, then end the story with other general and background information. If someone reads only the first paragraph, she gets the most important information. If she continues reading a bit, she'll gather some more details; if she reads all the way to the end, she'll also get some interesting background info. A diligent reader is rewarded with the whole story, top to bottom; less-interested readers still get the important facts.

 Note

In newspaper writing, the top level of the inverted pyramid contains the who, what, when, where, why, and how of the story.

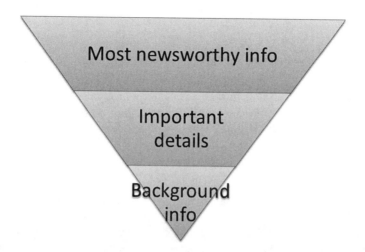

Figure 5.1   *The inverted pyramid of newspaper writing.*

When we're talking online writing, the inverted pyramid makes a lot of sense. Tell the reader exactly what he wants to know in the very first paragraph, and then fill in additional details through the rest of the page, post, or press release. Don't make readers sludge through an entire web page or blog post to find what they're most interested in. Give it to them upfront, and *then* tell the rest of the story and provide additional details.

For example, consider a blog post that reviews a local restaurant. You could write the post chronologically, starting with how easy it was to make reservations, how you were promptly seated, how you liked the appetizer, how you didn't like the main course, and so forth. In this scenario, your conclusion—how much you did or didn't like the restaurant—would be the capper to your story, appearing at the end of the post.

The problem, of course, is that more people want to know your conclusion rather than how you arrived at it. If someone wants to know only whether the restaurant is worth going to, you're making that person wait until the very end of your post to discover that essential information.

The better approach is to start your post with your conclusion—that you had a pleasant experience, were a little disappointed in the main course, but would probably return in the future. *Then* you can go through the chronology of events, from appetizer to dessert, supplying the details that informed your conclusion.

This inverted pyramid approach gives all readers the key takeaway right at the start. For readers who want only the conclusion, they get it quickly and can move on to something else. Readers who want all the details can get them if they keep on reading. It's a content structure with proven effectiveness.

Tip

The inverted pyramid structure also helps you repurpose content for different online media. For example, you might skim off the top-most layer of essential information for a short social media post, dive down into the middle layer of details for a longer blog post, and go all the way to the bottom tip of background info for a full-fledged news story.

OUTLINING HELPS

When it comes to writing longer online copy—for web pages, certainly, but also online articles and some blog posts—it helps to employ those outlining skills you were supposed to have learned back in your school days. You know, break the content into level one, level two, and level three headings, with body text underneath each heading.

Doing this sort of outlining helps you see at a glance what's your most important content. You can then reorganize the outline to put the most important stuff first. (Actually, you want to shift things around so that you put the *conclusion* first, right?)

This type of reorganization by outlining is fairly easy if you're doing your writing in Microsoft Word. Just click into Outline mode and you can drag and drop any given section into a different position and easily reassign outline levels. I recommend doing this with your headings *before* you start writing the body paragraphs, but you can rethink and rearrange your outline at any stage of the process. It certainly makes it easier to put your most important content first.

Breaking Your Copy into Multiple Pages

Yes, the Internet loves short content. But what do you do when you have a topic that demands more in-depth treatment? Not every story can be told online in a paragraph or two.

Long-form content does exist on the Web. Maybe it's an article, or maybe it's a blog post, maybe it's just a web page with a lot of information. Whatever the content, you need to find a way to present longer amounts of text so that it fits within the Internet's short-form prism.

The lazy approach is to put all the text on a single page. That's certainly easy enough to do, but it forces readers to keep scrolling down the page to read more. And online readers positively *hate* scrolling through long web pages.

The better approach is to slice and dice your copy so that it can be placed on multiple sequential web pages. That is, divide the copy into sections that each fit on a single screen. Readers click the Next button to advance to the next screen to read more of the article, which seems like a bit of work but is preferable to endless scrolling through a lengthy page. Because readers are seeing only one screen at a time, the content is more scannable than it would be on a single page (where you see only a small slice of the article per scroll).

The takeaway is that you should avoid scrolling and instead employ multiple screens when you have lengthy content. As with all things web related, break it up into multiple chunks for easier digestion.

Using Headings

It's important to announce the details of your text before throwing your readers into the deep end. It's kind of like the approach you see on local newscasts: tell them what's coming up before they start reading the story.

On the Web, that translates into dividing your content into short sections (as previously discussed) and then "announcing" each section with its own heading. Use the heading to describe what's in the following text.

 Note

Learn more about chunkifying your content in Chapter 4, "Keeping It Short and Simple."

Time-starved or less-interested readers can get the gist of your content just by reading the headings. More-interested readers can read all the text between the headings, too.

Figure 5.2 shows a web page that makes effective use of headers to organize its information. As you can see, you get all the key information just from the headers; the text itself provides the details.

If your text is really long, you can employ multiple levels of headings. That is, you break your text into major and minor sections, then assign level-one headings to the major sections and level-two headings to the minor ones. You can even get down into level-three and level-four headings, but let's be honest: no online copy should be that long or involved.

We go places on the Internet that you can't.

The Dark Web is a haven for criminal activity. It's where you'll find all manner of illegal transactions, from software piracy to ID and financial theft. It's where the bad guys hang out online.

Traditional intelligence methods can't always infiltrate this underground web—and even when they can, it can take *years* to set everything up. When you need information now, turn to Procysive's **CIPACS** online monitoring system. Our unique cyber intelligence technologies find websites and chat channels that you never knew existed, gaining access in a virtually undetectable fashion. Our software agents work 24/7 to monitor, detect, and infiltrate virtually every corner of the Internet, seeking out potential criminal activity—and reporting that activity back to you.

Protect your assets online.

Procysive's deep web monitoring scans the entire web so you'll know what people are saying about your company online—the good and the bad. We find unwanted instances of your brand, content, products, and intellectual property, and even track what's being said about you online. We ferret out threats before they become active—and protect your company, your intellectual property, and your people 24/7.

Stealth technology evades detection.

Procysive's deep web monitoring is done with a light touch. We hide our presence by dispersing our software agents through multiple secure servers located around the globe. Our non-intrusive process leaves little to no signature behind; our agents act like human beings, not typical search spiders. The bad guys never know we're there—or that they're being watched.

It's more than just a technology—it's an invaluable service.

Unlike companies offering technology-only solutions, Procysive also employs a staff of trained cyber intelligence analysts. These experts interact with the raw data compiled by our software agents to filter and identify the most significant and immediate threats for our client base. The combination of deep web monitoring and active human analysis provides the ultimate in online security for both intellectual and physical assets

Figure 5.2   *Web page copy with effective use of section headings.*

 Tip

> For most web pages and news articles, I recommend sticking to level-one headings. If you need to go the level-two route, that's a sure sign that your page is too long—and it's time to break the content into multiple screens, instead.

By the way, your headings should describe what's coming up in the following text. A heading does not have to be a complete sentence, although it can be. When in doubt, try to be as clear as possible. Avoid cutesy headings, such as the following for a section on how to string a guitar:

All Strung Up

Instead, just be straightforward about the content of the section:

How to String a Guitar

Yeah, it's not as witty (as if the first one was), but it's a lot more useful for your readers.

Creating Bulleted and Numbered Lists

When you think about making content easily scannable or grazeable, the key is to chunk it out into bits that can be absorbed in a short glance. With certain types of content, the best way to do this is by presenting it in a bulleted or numbered list.

Bulleted Lists

I love bulleted lists. It's very easy to grasp a list's contents just by glancing at the bullets or numbers. It's certainly a lot easier than trying to extract bits of content from a text paragraph.

Take this paragraph, for example, which is really just a collection of individual data points:

> In terms of performance, I really like the receivers from Cambridge Audio, Denon, Onkyo, and Sony.

Those data points are more easily grasped if you present them in list format (with a little rewriting for understandability). It looks like this:

> In terms of performance, I really like receivers from
>
> - Cambridge Audio
> - Denon
> - Onkyo
> - Sony

Notice how it's much easier to grasp the key data points (the four brands of receivers) than when they're just words in a sentence.

 Tip

There's probably no value in using a bulleted list if you only have a few data points. Two data points more easily fit within standard text; reserve your lists for when you have three or more points to get across.

You can also use bulleted lists to detail data originally presented in multiple sentences. Consider, for example, a paragraph where each sentence represents a separate data point, like this:

> The "south of the river" cities are a collection of thriving suburbs. Apple Valley is home to the Minnesota Zoo and a booming commercial strip down Cedar Avenue. Eagan hosts a number of large corporations, including Blue Cross. Burnsville is an older city, more established, but with several popular industrial parks. And Lakeville is more traditionally suburban, but with several big box retailers and a charming downtown area.

Turn each of these sentences into a bullet point and you have a more easily scanned list of data. It might look something like this:

The "south of the river" cities are a collection of thriving suburbs:

- **Apple Valley, home to the Minnesota Zoo and a booming commercial strip down Cedar Avenue**

- **Eagan, host to a number of large corporations, including Blue Cross**

- **Burnsville, a more established older city with several popular industrial parks**

- **Lakeville, more traditionally suburban but with several big box retailers and a charming downtown area**

Much easier to grasp, isn't it? The bottom line is that anytime you have a collection of items, consider breaking them out from the main text and putting them in a bulleted list.

 Tip

In lists where the bullet points are somewhat lengthy, consider boldfacing the subject of each bullet. For example, in our previous city list, you might boldface the names of each city.

Numbered Lists

We've already discussed the value of presenting step-by-step information to online readers. The best way to present your steps is in a numbered list. You know, step 1 do this, step 2 do that, and so forth. Although you can embed how-to information in text paragraphs, the numbered list format is much easier for online readers to grasp.

Take this how-to paragraph, for example:

To make porcupine meatballs, start by preheating your oven to 350 degrees. Mix 1 1/2 pounds ground beef with 2/3 cup rice, 1/2 cup of water, chopped onion, seasoned salt, garlic powder, and pepper. Use a tablespoon to shape the ground beef mixture into 1 1/2-inch diameter balls, and place the meatballs in an ungreased 2-quart shallow baking dish. Mix the remaining ingredients and pour over the porcupine meatballs. Cover and bake in a 350-degree oven for about 45 minutes. Uncover and bake the porcupine meatballs 15 to 20 minutes longer.

That's typical recipe presentation, but it requires the cook to read the whole thing. It's also easy to get lost in the middle and skip a step. A much better way to present this information is in a numbered list, like the following:

To make porcupine meatballs, follow these steps:

1. Preheat your oven to 350 degrees.

2. Mix 1 1/2 pounds ground beef with 2/3 cup rice, 1/2 cup of water, chopped onion, seasoned salt, garlic powder, and pepper.

3. Use a tablespoon to shape the ground beef mixture into 1 1/2-inch diameter balls.

4. Place the meatballs in an ungreased 2-quart shallow baking dish.

5. Mix the remaining ingredients and pour over the porcupine meatballs.

6. Cover and bake in a 350-degree oven for about 45 minutes.

7. After the initial 45 minutes, uncover the dish and bake the porcupine meatballs 15 to 20 minutes longer.

That's a lot easier to follow, don't you think?

Using Tables (or Not)

When you have large batches of complex data, there's no way to fit it all into a paragraph and have your readers understand what's going on. For some types of data, the only way to go is the tabular format—that is, data presented in a table.

If you're not familiar with what a table looks like, here's one. It's like a mini-spreadsheet, complete with column and row headings and cells that contain the important data points:

City	2000	2010	2020
Avon	50,000	75,000	85,000
Brownsburg	35,000	40,000	38,000
Carmel	75,000	85,000	90,000
Fishers	60,000	70,000	75,000
Greenwood	40,000	40,000	38,000

I'm not sure if there's a better way to present this type of complex data. The rigid format of rows and columns makes it easy to grasp the individual data points; the reader can go directly to the intersection of row and column to find a precise piece of data.

However, tables might or might not work for you on the Web. The problem comes in how you get a table onto the web page.

You see, there's no easy way to create a table with normal text; it has to be specially coded in HTML. That means you'll need to coordinate with your website designers to create the data table, put it in place, and make sure it looks pretty. If you don't have HTML coders handy (such as when you're creating a blog post), you might not be able to insert a table. Just take that into account.

 Tip

If you can't use a table in a particular instance, you probably want to go the bulleted list route. It's less than ideal, but it might be the only option available to you.

6

Firing Up Your Readers

Naturally, one of the goals of your online writing is to inform your readers about whatever it is you're writing about. In most cases, however, there's another, equally important goal—to inspire your readers to take some specific action.

If you're writing for an e-commerce site, that action might be placing an order for whatever it is you're selling. If you're writing for a hobbyist site, that action might be getting further involved in the hobby. Whatever the case, you want your readers to do something—and your copy needs to fire them up to do it.

To inspire readers to take the desired action, the copy you write must be compelling. It must capture the reader's attention and keep it for as long as necessary—that's no small chore given online readers' notoriously short attention spans. It must be persuasive enough to convince readers to do what you want them to do. And it wouldn't hurt if it made readers feel good about doing it, too.

This chapter is all about how to write copy that compels, copy that inspires, copy that persuades. It's about the various ways you can fire up readers with your words— and get them to do what you want them to do.

Figuring Out What Fires Them Up

Before you can fire up your readers, you need to know what it is that fires them up—that is, what specifically gets your readers interested and excited, and what inspires them to get personally involved.

This means thinking like the reader. (Or, if you're writing for an e-commerce site, what I like to call thinking like the customer.) Until you know for sure what your target readers find exciting and inspiring, you won't be able to excite and inspire them—except by luck. Rather than guessing, it's far better to get inside their heads, find out what turns them on, and then give them some of that. It's a much better approach than just guessing at it.

How do you get to know your readers better? Try talking to them. Not tweeting them or exchanging emails, but having an actual conversation. Ask questions; listen to their answers. Get to know them personally.

You can also observe your readers, either physically (in a group or focus group) or virtually (by tracking their online actions). This isn't as effective or efficient as forging one-on-one relationships, but it might be the only option available to some.

What you don't want to do is guess or assume. Assuming is particularly bad; when you start assuming that your readers act one way or another (typically that they act just like you), that is when you start going off the rails. Tell yourself that you have no bloody idea what your readers are really like (which is probably true) and move on from there. It's the only way to do it.

Engaging the Reader

To pull the reader into your copy, you have to talk directly to her. Not to some generic reader, but to a specific person reading your copy. You have to *engage* the reader to keep her reading.

Writing directly to the reader involves writing in the second person, not the third person. That means using the words such as "you" and "your" instead of "his" or "hers" or "their." Let me provide some examples.

In less-personal third-party writing, you might say something like this:

The user should now clamp the hose onto the pipe.

To present that instruction in the more direct second person, rewrite it as follows:

You should now clamp the hose onto the pipe.

Instead of saying this:

It's a great deal for them.

Write the following:

It's a great deal for you.

Always speak directly to the reader. Never speak obliquely to a generic audience. Avoid sentences such as this:

Our customers will enjoy it.

Who are your customers? They're individual people, so say that:

You will enjoy it.

Do you understand how this works? I know that you do.

Keeping It Short—and Making It Clear

We've already talked about the need for short copy online, but writing efficiently has the added benefit of more effectively engaging the reader. Short copy reaches out and pulls readers into the page; long copy pushes them away. You want to pull readers into your content, so do that by making your content easy to get into.

 Note

Learn more about keeping your copy short in Chapter 4, "Keeping It Short and Simple."

Clarity goes hand in hand with brevity. Not only must your copy be short and grazeable, it must also be very clear about the point that it's making. Remember, you shouldn't assume that readers know more than they do (another benefit of thinking like the reader, not writing for yourself), and you should, if you can, eschew jargon and industry buzzwords. Don't obfuscate; get to the point quickly and clearly to draw readers into your text.

And that's all I have to say about that.

Getting to the Point

Part and parcel of efficient writing is quickly getting to the point. Don't make the reader slog through multiple paragraphs (or pages!) to find out what you're writing about. Say it right up front, and be clear about it.

▶ *Caution*

There's no profit in obscuring your point to confuse people into reading further. It's okay to weed out inappropriate or disinterested readers early in the process. Don't waste their time.

Making Promises

To the point of getting to the point, one way to do this is to make a promise, and then deliver on that promise. Tell the reader what you're going to do for him, and then do it.

People like promises. They like people delivering on those promises even better. The promise draws the reader into the page or post; keeping the promise solidifies the relationship.

So if you're going to inform the reader about a given issue, promise to do so right at the beginning of the page or post. If you're going to deliver certain facts, say so. If you're going to make the reader's life easier in some way, tell the reader that.

Then all you have to do is deliver on your promises. If you promised specific information, give it to him. If you promised a solution to a given problem, provide that solution.

It's as simple as that. Promise the reader something useful, and then deliver on that promise.

Solving Problems

Readers also like having their problems solved. That's why many people come to the Web: to get solutions to whatever's ailing or vexing them. If you can deliver those solutions, you'll draw readers into your web page or post.

The best way to do this is to state the problem in the initial paragraph, along with the promise to solve that problem. Then, across the rest of your content, you provide the promised solution. The promise of solving the problem draws readers into the page; the solution delivers on that promise.

Telling a Good Story

The information you present should be engaging in and of itself, but the way you present that information also helps to pull readers into the content. To this end, consider everything you write as telling a story.

Facts are important, but facts alone are boring. You have to weave the information you present into a story, one that interests and engages the reader.

You see, people like stories. From the beginning of time, people have told stories that both informed and entertained their listeners (and readers). People get drawn into a story; they want to know what happens and how it ends. There's a built-in appeal when you can present your information as some sort of story.

All stories should have a beginning, a middle, and an end. The story needs to progress from start to finish in a way that moves quickly and keeps the reader guessing as to what comes next. It's a matter of moving the reader from point A to point B to point C, delivering them to a satisfying dramatic climax or factual conclusion. It's not just presenting a list of facts; it's weaving those facts into the fabric of the story.

Using Action Words

Engaging copy is vibrant copy. It stands up and demands attention through the choices of words used.

As such, your language needs to be lively, not dull. Choose words that move and excite, not those that lay flat on the page.

What are some of these "action words" that excite and inspire? Here's a list of 50 words that always work, no matter what topic you're writing about:

amazing	discount	guaranteed
attractive	easily	highest
authentic	excellent	immediately
bargain	exciting	improved
beautiful	exclusive	largest
big	famous	latest
colorful	free	outstanding
colossal	genuine	popular
complete	greatest	powerful

proven	sale	superior
quickly	secrets	terrific
rare	sensational	tremendous
reduced	sizable	unique
remarkable	special	unlimited
reliable	startling	valuable
revealing	strong	wonderful
revolutionary	successful	

 Tip

And don't forget the most powerful action word of them all: "you."

ACTION PHRASES

Certain combinations of words also serve to draw readers into your copy. You probably know some of these action phrases, such as **Act now**, **Limited time offer**, and **Order yours today**.

Many action phrases are specific to a given industry or operation. In the world of manufacturing, for example, **Reduced material costs** is a powerful phrase; to the rest of us, however, it doesn't mean much. This means you have to get to know the action phrases for your specific topic area—those phrases that excite your target audience—and use them.

Know, however, that some action phrases can be dangerously close to industry jargon, and as such should not be overused. Make sure the phrase actually means something and isn't insider doublespeak; avoid those phrases that are essentially meaningless.

Including a Call to Action

We'll end our examination of engaging writing at the literal end—the part that fits after everything else you've written. In most instances, the last thing you write is just as important as the first thing, because it's the part that encourages the reader to take action of some sort.

This is called the *call to action*, and just about everything you write should have one. Unless you're writing because you like the sound of your own (written) voice, you want the reader to do something based on what you've written.

I can think of few instances where writing does not have a call to action. If you're writing marketing copy, you want the reader to make a purchase. If you're writing an opinion piece, you want the reader to adopt your way of seeing things. If you're writing about a hobby, you want the reader to get more involved with that hobby. If you're writing how-to instructions, you want the reader to actually do the task you're writing about.

In short, just about everything you write should encourage the reader to take some further action.

The first step in constructing a call to action is knowing what it is you want the reader to do. That sounds simple, but it often isn't, especially in the corporate environment. It's common for every involved department to have its own opinion on what a website or blog is supposed to accomplish. You need to work through these competing desires to determine the one single action that is supposed to result from the given web page, blog post, or whatever.

That's because a call to action is singular. You don't have *calls* to action; you have a single *call*. That is, you can't ask your customers to provide their contact information, visit their local store, and invest in your company's stock. You can ask them to do one of these things, but not all. Asking for more than one action is confusing and will result in no action.

The call to action actually helps focus your writing on the item that you're constructing. It also provides a means to measure your effectiveness. If people do what you ask them, you're successful; if they don't follow your call to action, you've failed.

How do you write a call to action? By asking the reader to do a particular thing. If you want the reader to ask for more information, say **Click here for more information**. If you want the reader to leave contact information, say **Please fill out this form for us to contact you**. If you want the reader to attend a meeting, say **We look forward to seeing you on Monday night**. If you want the reader to buy something, say **Click here to make your purchase**. It's as simple as that; be as simple and direct as necessary.

This means, of course, that you want to use simple and direct language. Use action words such as **call** and **order** and **buy** and **subscribe** and **donate**. Don't be pushy, but don't be wimpy about it, either. Tell them what you want in language that gets the point across.

🔍 *Tip*

It also helps to create a little urgency in your call to action. Give the reader a deadline in which to act (**Limited time only; Sale ends May 31st**); you might even want to consider bribing the reader with some sort of gift or discount for acting early.

Remember, if you don't ask readers to do something, they won't do anything. And where's the value in that?

7

Finding Your Voice

Consider two different websites presenting similar information. One site presents its information in a dry, just the facts, ma'am fashion. The other site presents the same information but with a fun, slightly snarky spin. It's the difference between what's acceptable on the CBS Evening News versus what flies on The Daily Show; both outlets present the same information, more or less, yet each also has its own distinguishable personality.

When much of the information you present is already out there from other sources, how do you distinguish your online presence? You do it via the writing style you employ. The words you choose and the way you use them create your own personal voice on the Web—and that voice contributes to the image you project to your readers.

How do you shape your online voice—and what kind of voice should that be? The answer is different for every writer and every website, which is why voice is so important.

Giving Your Content a Personal Voice

If all you do is present generic information in a straightforward manner, your website or blog will be indistinguishable from dozens, if not hundreds, of similar sites. To make your site or other online vehicle stand out, however, you have to give it its own unique personality.

You establish your online personality from your content choices, of course, but also from your writing style—the words you use, your grammatical choices, and so forth. Your writing can be stiff and formal, loose and casual, or anything between. What style you choose should reflect and define the attitude and personality of your company or website.

 Tip

Your website's personality should be reflected in all the elements found on the page—layout, color scheme, images, typefaces, and so forth. You don't want flippant content married to staid graphics or vice versa; you want every element of your site reflecting the same style and approach.

What is style? It's the combination of everything you write, the words you choose, the language you employ, even the grammatical choices you make. This includes the tone or attitude you project. Is your writing serious or whimsical? Is it smart or tuned more for the masses? Is it snarky or straightforward, ironic or earnest, deadly serious or broadly humorous? And does that tone match well with your content?

You see, your content can be authoritative or practical, trendy or timeless, academic or casual. You frame the content with your writing style; the voice you project tells readers how to regard that content.

How do you create your online voice? It's almost all about the language choices you make. For example, if your style is personal and conversational, use shorter words, less formal verbiage, and a fair number of contractions; also use the words "you," "we," and "our" a lot. If your style is more academic or professional, use longer words, more industry jargon, and more formal language.

Your voice is also set by the rhythm of your writing. A professional voice will include longer and more complex sentences; a conversational voice requires shorter sentences that have more of a bounce when read. If you want to speak with an authoritative voice, avoid trendy phrases and slang; if you want to have more of a hip, young voice, slang away, dude—and feel free to use contractions and sentence fragments.

▶ *Caution*

Don't attempt to use slang or trendy language if you're not tied into that culture. There's nothing more embarrassing than a 50-year-old white guy in the suburbs trying to write for a hip, young, urban audience; you can always tell, bro.

Choosing the Right Style

How do you decide what's the right style and voice for your online content? It depends on the image you want to project, the type of content you want to deliver, and the audience you're trying to reach.

✉ *Note*

It's important to know that there's no one right or wrong style for your online writing. The same content can be presented in different voices, each reflecting the individual writers or companies behind the words. As long as your voice reflects who you are and who you're speaking to, you're okay.

Match Your Style To Your Image

Let's look at the image thing first. The style you employ communicates to readers what your site or brand is all about—and it should reflect that image.

For example, if you're a serious person or writing for a serious company, you should use a serious style. If your company is a bit more whimsical (think Ben & Jerry's), then your style should be a bit looser. The style should reflect the image you have or want to project.

What you don't want to do is have your style conflict with your personal or corporate image. A big, serious financial company such as Wells Fargo would probably lose customers if its site resembled something out of Monty Python.

However, there are lots of different ways to do serious. Staying with the Wells Fargo example, the company uses a more personal voice on its website (using the words "you" and "your" a lot) that ties into the warm, nurturing image it's trying to project. I'm not sure I believe that warm image (I do my banking with those bloodsuckers, so I should know), but at least the company's voice is consistent with its messaging.

> ✉ *Note*
>
> When the image you project clashes with the style you employ, readers experience *cognitive dissonance*—the discomfort that comes from trying to hold two conflicting ideas simultaneously. It's like watching Richard Nixon on *Laugh In*; the one just doesn't fit well with the other.

Match Your Style to Your Content

The voice you use in your writing should also, to some degree, match the content you're presenting. Detailed financial content, for example, is best presented in a straightforward, professional style. Do-it-yourself content for home hobbyists can be presented with a lighter touch.

Think about it—you don't want to present serious information in an unserious fashion. As an extreme example, anyone reading the online obituaries is likely to be shocked and offended by irreverent humor on the page; they expect a serious, reverent style. Along the same lines, you also don't want to treat lighter content too seriously. It's a matter of matching content with tone and not having one conflict with the other.

Match Your Style to Your Audience

Finally, your writing style should be one that makes your readers feel comfortable. Your voice should be the same voice that your readers use when talking about the topic at hand.

For example, if you're reaching out to young mothers, don't employ a dry corporate style; instead, talk in warm, familiar language. Likewise, if you're targeting the corporate market, don't go all hip hop in your verbiage. You have to match your style to what your readers expect.

When setting the tone, you also have to take into account reader standards, in terms of profanity, sexual references, even mentions of religion and politics. As an example, most people wouldn't expect to find (and might be offended by) casual profanity on a serious news site, but would be fully accepting of that same profanity on a college humor site. You need to understand your readers' standards and voice your content accordingly.

Your voice, then, needs to express who you are (or what your company or site is) and what information it is you offer; it also needs to reflect and appeal to the audience you're trying to reach. Use language that matches well with your topic or product and that is familiar to your target audience. It's all a matter of choosing the right words—and using them in the right way.

> ✉ *Tip*
>
> The style you choose should also be consistent from page to page and across all online vehicles. If you want to project a fun image, and do so on your site's home page, don't confuse visitors by switching to deadly serious style when you get to the individual product pages. If your email messaging projects a youthful image, don't go all gray flannel suit on your blog. Pick a style and stay with it, or risk confusing your readers.

Employing a Professional Style

The best way to understand voice and style is to examine a few different approaches. To that end, let's take a look at the two stylistic extremes found most often on the Web—professional versus personal styles.

We'll start with a professional style—one you might employ if you're writing for an industry organization, big corporation, or the like. To some extent, a professional style is an impersonal style, designed to distance the company from its customers to some degree.

When you employ a professional style, it's not you talking; it's the company or the product or the content. To that end, professional writing is *not* warm and cuddly; it's factual and to the point. Say what you need to say, and nothing more.

When to Use a Professional Style

You can employ a professional voice for any type of writing; it's not just limited to big corporate stuff. I think it's best suited when you want to come off as an authority on any given topic.

For example, if you're writing for a hobbyist website and want to position the site as the foremost authority on that topic, you should use a more professional voice. On the other hand, if you want that hobbyist site to fit within an active community of users, a more personal style would be appropriate.

Naturally, when you're presenting legal or financial or dry corporate content, a professional voice is essential. You would not want to present that information in a casual style; if it's professional content, a professional voice is required.

How to Employ a Professional Style

As noted, professional writing starts with professional content. You're probably going to be presenting a piece of information that's fairly straightforward, a set of facts that needs to be conveyed in an authoritative manner. (You're setting forth the facts, not inviting debate.)

This means remaining somewhat formal and avoiding a personal approach. Write in the third person; don't use the first person "I" or "we," and don't address the reader personally. (No "you" and "your.") Don't use humor or insert anecdotes into the text; just present what you need to present in a clear and concise manner. Avoid the passive voice, and minimize the use of contractions. You shouldn't employ slang, but you can probably get away with common industry jargon, depending on the audience.

In terms of the content itself, it needs to be as buttoned down as possible. If you convey a given piece of information, tell readers where that information came from. That means using citations and references, even (depending on the type of document) footnotes and endnotes. Don't insert opinions; keep to the facts of the matter.

The result should be a straightforward piece of writing, with a clear presentation of important content. It should not be confused with personal communication or an opinion piece; it should read as authoritative and professional.

Here's an example:

> Unique information about customers is not collected, except when customers specifically and knowingly provide such information. Information such as time of day, browser type, and IP address are saved with each query. That information is used to verify the customer's records and to provide more relevant services to users. For example, the customer's browser language may be used to determine which language to use when showing search results or advertisements.

Using a Personal Style

For many websites and blogs, you want to be more personal than professional. That means using a voice that speaks directly to and engages your readers.

In many circles, this is referred to as employing the author's voice. It certainly is a more conversational approach than what you read in most professional writing.

When to Use a Personal Style

I'll be honest with you; most online writing employs a conversational voice. This is especially true with blogs, which are often personal diaries, and with social media, which thrives on personal interactions. But many websites also benefit from having a personality, which comes from employing a conversational voice that connects directly with visitors.

Certainly, any personal vehicle you write for should employ your own unique personal style. So if you have your own website or blog or do any posting to social media, let your personality shine through.

In addition, if the company or brand or product you're writing for wants to make a personal connection with its customers, by all means employ a more conversational style. You can't personally connect with customers while maintaining a professional aloofness; get personal, let them get to know you, and make that direct connection.

How to Write Conversationally

The key to using a personal voice is to write conversationally—that is, write as if you're talking directly with the reader. That means using the words "me," "I," and "our" when talking about yourself, and the words "you" and "your" when addressing the reader. Treat your text as if it's a real conversation.

Writing conversationally also means using more casual, less formal language, in terms of both construction and word choice. Use shorter sentences and shorter words, get comfortable with contractions, feel free to use sentence fragments, and be a little less grammatically strict. (But not too much so, okay?)

 Tip

Conversational writing is less absolute than professional writing. Where professional writing is very strict about a thing being exactly what it is, conversational writing often qualifies statements—using words and phrases such as "often," "sometimes," "a bit," and "more or less."

The way I approach conversational writing is to literally have a conversation. Conversational writing should mimic verbal conversation, so fire up your tape recorder and start talking into the microphone. What you say can easily be transcribed into the written word.

You should also feel free to inject your personal observations and opinions. Tell the reader what you think or relate your own experience. While you're at it, offer an aside or two to let readers know that you're a real human being and not computer-generated text.

The goal in using a conversational style is to establish a personal relationship with the reader. You're not keeping readers at arm's length, as you do with more professional writing, but rather embracing readers and making them feel as if they're among friends.

Let's take the example we used for professional writing, stiff as it was, and destiffen it with a more conversational voice:

We do not collect any unique information about you without your permission. Every time you make a query, we save certain information, such as time of day, browser type, and IP address. That might sound a little scary, but we only use information to verify your records and to provide more relevant services to you. For example, we may look at your browser language setting to determine which language to use when we show you search results or advertisements.

Note the differences in sentence length, use of "we" and "you," and even the personal aside at the beginning of the third sentence. It still presents the same information, but in a warmer and more welcoming fashion. The reader gets the sense that he and the writer are in this together; he's being talked *with*, not *to*.

WHAT'S *YOUR* VOICE?

Ideally, especially when writing for personal purposes, your writing should sound like you. That is, it should sound the way you talk and think; it shouldn't be fancier or more formal that you are in normal day-to-day conversation.

That means if you talk somewhat formally, you should write pretty much the same way; don't write all hip and groovy if you're really a stiff. Conversely, if you're a fun, hip, happening kind of guy, keep your writing fun and hip, as well. You don't need to go overboard, of course (there's some value in subtlety and discretion), but let your writing reflect your normal personality.

Equally important is to be consistent with your voice, especially over the course of multiple entries, such as on a blog. Readers will sense something's up if your voice sounds different from one post to the next and might even think it's a different author doing the posting. Keep it true to yourself and consistent over time.

Now, using your personal voice isn't necessarily the way to go when you're writing for someone else's site or for a company. In those instances, your writing should have the voice of the other person or company. That means becoming familiar with previous materials so that you can mimic the corporate style, assuming the company has one. You're a hired gun and have to do the job asked of you.

But when you're writing for your own site or blog or newsfeed, let people know it's really you doing the writing. Use the same language you use in everyday conversation; address the reader directly and bring the reader into your confidence. It's as simple as creating a one-to-one conversation, but in print.

8

Incorporating Visuals

When it comes to conveying complex information, sometimes pictures work better than words. It often helps to see how something looks or works, rather than have it explained in text. This is especially true online, where users' attention spans are short and getting shorter. Online readers want information at a glance, and there's nothing more glanceable than a picture.

As a text person, how do you incorporate visuals into your work? It's a matter of determining what type of image works best, finding or creating that image, and getting it inserted into the web page, blog post, or other vehicle.

Why Visuals Are Important

As the old Rod Stewart song goes, "Every picture tells a story." There's something to that; a compelling visual can help to get across a point that might otherwise require a paragraph or more of text.

It's true that some things are better or more easily seen than described. I can wax poetic about the beauty of a mountain lake, but you'll get the point quicker if I just show you a picture of it. (Figure 8.1 should prove that point.) Same thing with some how-to content; it might be easier to show a diagram of how the shelves fit in a DIY bookcase than to write reams of detailed (and, to some, confusing) instructions.

Figure 8.1   *How many words would it take to describe this beautiful mountain scene?*

In addition, it's important to note that not everybody learns the same way. You might prefer getting your information from text (in fact, that's likely, given that you're a writer), but other people are visual learners. These folks need to see something in front of them, in picture format, before they truly grasp it. You'll never reach visual learners with an all-text approach; instead, give them your content the way they best respond.

Finally, incorporating visuals into an otherwise all-text page or blog is also good design. Visuals help to break up what would otherwise be a large block of static text and make the page more appealing and inviting to readers. For example, compare the web pages in Figures 8.2 and 8.3; the first employs an off-putting all-text approach; the second is much more inviting visually.

In Praise of the Brill Building Professionals

Lots of so-called critics like to dismiss the pop music of the pre-Beatles '60s as trite and easily forgettable, a regrettable detour from the harder rock 'n' roll of the Elvis '50s that was put by the wayside when the British true believers invaded American shores in 1964. I, however, disagree.

You see, the story of popular music in the 20th century is written, in large part, by professional songwriters -- the very folks who produced those oft-dismissed early '60s tunes. Professional songwriters apply their craft to the three-minute song, writing memorable words and melodies for other musicians to perform. The key word here is "professional" -- these are folks who know their craft and put out quality product on a consistent basis. None of that introspective bleeding heart emo crap intoned against a strummed chord or two; we're talking tunes with real melodies that anyone could sing along with.

In the first part of the 20th century, professional songwriting in America was concentrated in that area of New York City on West 28th Street, between Broadway and Sixth Avenue, commonly called Tin Pan Alley. (The name came from writer Monroe Rosenfeld, who likened the cacophony of so many songwriters pounding on so many pianos to the sound of beating on tin pans.) Songwriters, together and in teams, churned out their compositions in factory-like style; the best of these songs got sold to music publishing companies, and were then issued as sheet music (before the explosion of the record business) or picked up by one of the major singers of the day. Sometimes these Tin Pan Alley tunes ended up in vaudeville productions, Broadway plays, or Hollywood movies. The best of the best endured, and became classics.

The best songwriters of a generation filtered through Tin Pan Alley. George M. Cohan, Irving Berlin, Cole Porter, George and Ira Gershwin; all were professional songwriters for hire. Their songs were sung by the top singers of the day—Fred Astaire, Bing Crosby, Frank Sinatra, Mel Torme, Ella Fitzgerald, Tony Bennett, Nat 'King' Cole, and the like. Their songs were professional compositions, the work of trained musicians who were masters of their craft. They featured pretty melodies, sophisticated chord progressions, and mature, often witty, lyrics; they were written by adults, for adults.

By the 1950s, Tin Pan Alley and the New York music business had moved uptown—to that stretch of Broadway between 49th and 53rd streets. The hub of this activity was 1619 Broadway, in an eleven-story edifice called the Brill Building.

The Brill Building was built in 1931, during the height of the Great Depression. Some of its first tenants were music publishers, including Famous Music, Mills Music, and Southern Music. By 1962 the building was home to more than 150 music companies, and this concentration of companies made the Brill Building a kind of "one stop shop" for aspiring musicians.

The entire music process was contained in that one building. You could write a song on one floor, sell it to a publisher on another floor, have an arrangement

Figure 8.2   *An all-text web page—great words, but visually boring.*

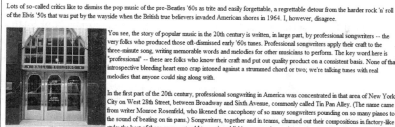

In Praise of the Brill Building Professionals

Lots of so-called critics like to dismiss the pop music of the pre-Beatles '60s as trite and easily forgettable, a regrettable detour from the harder rock 'n' roll of the Elvis '50s that was put by the wayside when the British true believers invaded American shores in 1964. I, however, disagree.

You see, the story of popular music in the 20th century is written, in large part, by professional songwriters -- the very folks who produced those oft-dismissed early '60s tunes. Professional songwriters apply their craft to the three-minute song, writing memorable words and melodies for other musicians to perform. The key word here is "professional" -- these are folks who know their craft and put out quality product on a consistent basis. None of that introspective bleeding heart emo crap intoned against a strummed chord or two; we're talking tunes with real melodies that anyone could sing along with.

In the first part of the 20th century, professional songwriting in America was concentrated in that area of New York City on West 28th Street, between Broadway and Sixth Avenue, commonly called Tin Pan Alley. (The name came from writer Monroe Rosenfeld, who likened the cacophony of so many songwriters pounding on so many pianos to the sound of beating on tin pans.) Songwriters, together and in teams, churned out their compositions in factory-like style; the best of these songs got sold to music publishing companies, and were then issued as sheet music (before the explosion of the record business) or picked up by one of the major singers of the day. Sometimes these Tin Pan Alley tunes ended up in vaudeville productions, Broadway plays, or Hollywood movies. The best of the best endured, and became classics.

The best songwriters of a generation filtered through Tin Pan Alley. George M. Cohan, Irving Berlin, Cole Porter, George and Ira Gershwin; all were professional songwriters for hire. Their songs were sung by the top singers of the day—Fred Astaire, Bing Crosby, Frank Sinatra, Mel Torme, Ella Fitzgerald, Tony Bennett, Nat 'King' Cole, and the like. Their songs were professional compositions, the work of trained musicians who were masters of their craft. They featured pretty melodies, sophisticated chord progressions, and mature, often witty, lyrics; they were written by adults, for adults.

By the 1950s, Tin Pan Alley and the New York music business had moved uptown—to that stretch of Broadway between 49th and 53rd streets. The hub of this activity was 1619 Broadway, in an eleven-story edifice called the Brill Building.

The Brill Building was built in 1931, during the height of the Great Depression. Some of its first tenants were music publishers, including Famous Music, Mills Music, and Southern Music. By 1962 the building was home to more than 150 music companies, and this

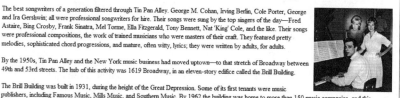

Figure 8.3   *The same article, made more visually interesting with a couple of pictures.*

HOW MANY WORDS IS A PICTURE WORTH?

Yeah, I know the old saying, "a picture is worth a thousand words," but I'm not totally hip with that. I think pictures can be useful, but I'm a copywriter, a text kind of guy, so I'm not sure about that thousand words bit. Although some subjects can be presented solely visually, even a great picture often needs a little accompanying description.

So I would never, ever try to tell a story with only pictures. (Even the *Easy* series books I write for Que, which are for visual learners, have a fair amount of descriptive text.) Images can convey big ideas, but you still need words to fill in the details.

Remember that one of your primary writings goals is to make a topic easily understandable to the reader. You should use whatever tools are at your disposal—even those tools that don't involve words and letters.

Choosing the Right Type of Visual

The word "image" encompasses a number of different types of visuals—photographs, illustrations, cartoons, charts, infographics, and more—all of which have a different impact. How do you decide *which* type of graphic to use with your content?

I can't pretend to describe every use of every type of graphic image, but I can offer some general advice and suggestions—which I do in Table 8.1. (Remember: tables are good for presenting some forms of complex information.) Use this as a guide.

Table 8.1   Uses for Different Graphics

Type of Graphic	Good for	Bad for
Clip art	Borders (repeating the image)	Just about anything remotely professional
Line drawing	Step-by-step content, detailed schematics	Representing real-life objects
Photograph	Representing real-life objects, portraits, and the like	Technical examples
Chart	Visualizing simple or complex data	Representing non-numeric content
Infographic	Visualizing multiple pieces of data about a single topic	Detailed numeric analysis

Type of Graphic	Good for	Bad for
Animation	Simulations, explaining ideas and services	Representing concrete situations
Video	Demonstrations, how-tos, product overviews, interviews, testimonials	Any situation where you don't want the text overshadowed

What you want to do is match a specific type of visual to the content you're presenting. The visual should help illustrate the story you're telling without detracting from the text you're presenting. A good match between text and visual ends up being more than the sum of its parts; a bad match causes people to stop reading.

 Caution

Which visual you choose might depend on other factors, such as what's available and for how much. Websites on a budget might not have the money for custom visuals or even for purchasing stock photos for online reproduction. In all situations, you have to use what you've got.

Using Clip Art

Let's start with the use of clip art, like the kind found in Figure 8.4. Clip art consists of ready-made illustrations that you can easily insert into a web page or other document. Word processing programs, such as Microsoft Word, typically come with built-in clip art libraries; you can also find a lot of clip art for free on the Web.

Tip

Most clip art is available royalty free, which means you can use it just about anywhere without paying anything.

There are several problems with using clip art online, however.

First, most clip art looks cheap and generic. Much of it is even comical looking. It's not the sort of thing you want to use with a more professional website or blog; it cheapens your image and makes your site look unprofessional.

Figure 8.4 *You'll see this piece of clip art a lot around Halloween.*

In addition, because clip art is free and freely available, the best of it gets used quite a bit—to the point of overuse. When you find the same piece of clip art on multiple websites and blogs, it has overstayed its welcome. You don't want your site to look like or be confused with other sites; you want to establish your own unique image, which means using your own unique artwork.

So despite (or perhaps because of) its low cost and widespread availability, I wouldn't recommend using clip art with your online writing. You can do better.

Using Line Drawings

A line drawing is an illustration, not a photograph. (Figure 8.5 illustrates the difference.) As such, a line drawing can be as detailed or as sketchy as you like. It can be a fairly accurate representation or one that takes some artistic liberties with the subject.

Line drawings can be used for artistic effect or to accurately represent a detailed object. In the first instance, consider the stylized portraits of columnists on the *Wall Street Journal* website, shown in Figure 8.6. They could have used regular photographs, but that's not the *Journal's* style. By using illustrations, they create a distinctive look and feel for their content.

Figure 8.5 *On the left, a photograph; on the right, a line drawing. See the difference?*

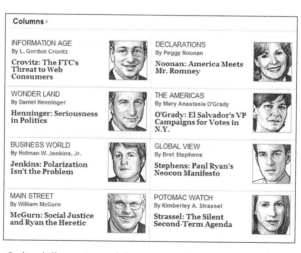

Figure 8.6 *Stylized illustrations of the paper's columnists on the* Wall Street Journal *website.*

As for showing detail of an object, look at Figure 8.7. This illustration details how to connect a cable box to a television set. Yes, you could have shown photographs, but they wouldn't have been as clean or as easy to understand as this simple line drawing—which makes this an ideal visual to accompany text instructions.

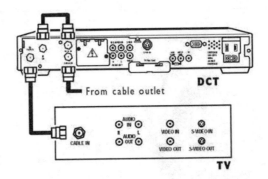

Figure 8.7   *An illustration that details how to connect a cable box to a TV set.*

Where do you get line drawings? Well, you'll probably have to generate them internally. That means using an in-house artist or hiring an outside illustrator. That effort (and the accompanying cost) is one of the drawbacks of using illustrations—although it's worth the expense if your readers need to see that sort of technical detail.

Using Photographs

Okay, line drawings are great for showing technical detail, but for most other situations, nothing beats an attractive photograph. This is why you see so many of them on the Web.

You can include photographs on your web pages, in your blog posts, in your email communications, even attached to your social media posts. You can use photos of people or things or of people doing things. You can even, if it's your desire, include photos of cute kittens and babies.

 Note

Although it's best to upload your own copies of image files to your website, you can also embed photos found on other websites—assuming you have permission to do so, of course. Learn more in Chapter 9, "Utilizing Links and Outside Content."

If you're going to use photographs to accompany your writing, make sure they're both appropriate and of an acceptable quality. It's better to forgo the use of a photograph than to use a bad one. There's not much point in using a photo of something that has little or nothing to do with your subject. The photo has to have meaning, to somehow enhance the text. If it's just taking up space—well, there's something to be said for adding visual interest, but it's better if your visuals actually supplement your text.

Where do you get photos for your online projects? You can take them yourself, of course, and that's a good option for many. You can also purchase photos from stock photo libraries, of which there are many online. For example, Figure 8.8 shows a stock photo accompanying an article on the Salon.com website; it helps to set the tone for the article and adds that elusive visual interest to an otherwise all-text page.

Sunscreen: Worse than cigarettes?

An astonishing new campaign from the tanning industry finger-points at -- believe it or not -- doctors

BY MARY ELIZABETH WILLIAMS

(Credit: mangostock via Shutterstock)

Sucks to be you, tanning industry. Sure, people are still using tanning beds, but with melanoma rates on the rise, you're being restricted from peddling your golden promises to adolescents in several states. And now Pennsylvania is considering requiring you to post warnings about the dangers of your services. These days, you're more associated with leathery New Jersey moms than the glow of good health. No wonder you're so pissy lately.

Figure 8.8   *A stock photo accompanying an article on the Salon.com site.*

You can also use public domain photos and photos from Flickr and other photo sharing sites that are licensed for commercial use. Just make sure that the permissions for a given photo cover your particular usage; don't take a photo licensed for personal use and use it on a commercial website.

 Caution

What you don't want to do is steal photos (or other images) from other websites. If you don't have permission to use a photo, don't; you can probably find something similar elsewhere.

TIPS FOR BETTER ONLINE PHOTOS

When it comes to shooting or choosing photos to accompany your online content, the wrong photo can compromise the quality of your text. To that end, here are a half-dozen or so tips for finding photos that complement rather than distract from your text:

- **Use quality images:** That means photos with good lighting and contrast and without obvious flaws, such as red eye. Great-looking photos make everything around them better.

- **Don't make 'em guess:** Along with the advice to use quality images, you should also use easy-to-understand images. That is, go for realistic rather than artistic; people need to know what it is they're looking at and not have to guess at it.

- **Crop to best effect:** Space on a web page is at a premium, so you don't want to waste it with unimportant visual elements. Crop any given photo so only the most relevant part of the image is displayed—and all the useless stuff isn't visible.

- **Avoid clichéd and overused images:** This is a particular problem when using stock or public domain images. Who wants to see another photo of a stack of dollar bills when you're writing about something financial, or two people shaking hands if you're writing about some new deal? Try to find some fresh ideas instead of reusing stale ones.

- **Reduce the resolution:** High-resolution photos are wasted on the Web; they look no better than low-res photos and take much longer to download. Visitors don't want to wait forever for a page to load, so keep the resolution low and your visuals user friendly.

- **Don't overuse images:** Just because you can add photos to your text doesn't mean you should. You want no more than a 75/25 ratio between text and images on a page; add too many photos and your text content begins to take a backseat. (Plus, the more photos you have on a page, the longer it takes to load—which is a definite no-no.)

Just remember that most people will look at a picture first and text second, so the images you choose need to be both relevant and of appropriate quality. Bad or irrelevant photos will reflect poorly on your content.

Using Charts

A visual doesn't have to be a photograph or a drawing. It can also be a chart or graph. Using an appropriate type of chart is a great way to convey complex numeric information in a single glance.

What kind of information can you communicate in a chart? Just about anything, from sales numbers to demographics to how many dogs and cats there are in your community. If it involves numbers, you can express those numbers in chart form.

There are lots of different types of charts you can use, from pie charts and line charts to bar charts and bubble charts. (Figure 8.9 shows a few chart types.) Different types of charts are better for presenting different types of information, so you want to make sure you choose the right chart type for your specific data. Table 8.2 will help you make an informed decision.

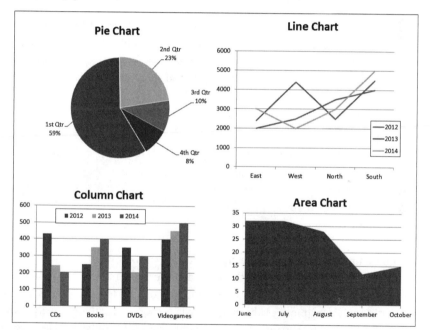

Figure 8.9   *Pie, line, column, and area charts.*

Table 8.2   Best Uses for Various Chart Types

Chart Type	Good for	Bad for
Area	Showing data over time with an emphasis on accumulated totals	Comparing one item to another

Chart Type	Good for	Bad for
Bar (horizontal)	Comparing multiple items at a fixed point in time	Comparing data over time
Column (vertical)	Comparing data over time	Comparing items at a fixed point in time
Line	Showing data over time, with an emphasis on trends	Comparing one item to another
Pie	Showing proportional relationships with each part represented as a percentage of the whole	Showing any data changing over time

You can probably create your own charts, using either Microsoft Excel or PowerPoint; enter the appropriate numbers into a spreadsheet grid and then select the type of chart you want. From there it's a matter of formatting the chart for best effect, in terms of fonts and colors and angles and such.

 Tip

When creating a chart for the Web, it's okay to be colorful; people expect a bit of color online. You should, however, choose fairly large fonts and keep the accompanying callouts short and simple. The goal is to make the chart scannable and each element easily read.

That doesn't mean, however, that a chart is always the best way to present numbers. If your chart is too complex, the individual elements might be too small for people to read easily, especially on small computer or smartphone screens. Or the information might be more easily explained via text or a table than visually; that's sometimes the case. In any instance, choose your charts carefully to make sure they work for you and not against you on the page.

 Tip

For best visibility, a chart should probably take up at least half a normal screen page.

Using Infographics

Then there are those new-fangled visuals, called *infographics,* that contain all manner of embedded information. Infographics are very trendy these days and have a lot of appeal to data-hungry users.

As you can see in Figure 8.10, an infographic lets you present multiple pieces of data in a single, easily scanned visual. Well, easily scanned if you don't mind scrolling down the page; most infographics are much taller than they are wide. That's because of all the information they contain in multiple graphs and images. It's really a way of combining multiple visuals into what appears to be a single visual.

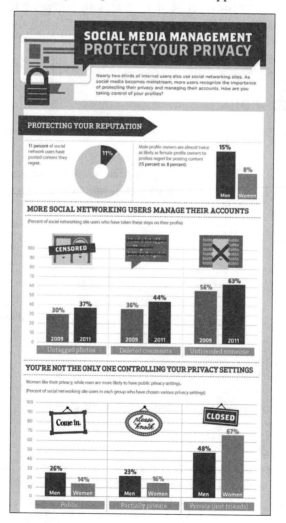

Figure 8.10   *An infographic (well, part of it, anyway; it's a long one) from ZoneAlarm.*

Infographics are pretty popular these days, especially when it comes to visual social networking like some people do with Facebook and Pinterest. An interesting or entertaining infographic can go viral; lots of people will pass it around in their Facebook feeds and Pinterest pinboards.

Because of this potential viral ability, a lot of companies are adding infographics to their websites. I'm not sure that's a great idea; they take up a lot of space and totally overwhelm the page. Personally, I think infographics are better suited to blog posts and social media, where they can tell the entire story and not replace valuable text-based content.

In any instance, if you use an infographic, make sure it presents relevant and accurate information. There's a real temptation to present as many fun facts as possible, but if the information isn't useful, people won't scroll all the way to the bottom—let alone share it with their online friends.

Using Animations

If pictures are good, then moving pictures should be even better, right? In some instances, that is true.

Let's look first at animations—moving illustrations, as it were. Animations can be useful, or they can be totally superfluous. Unfortunately, there tends to be more of the latter online.

 Note

On the Web today, most animations are referred to as Flash animations, because they're constructed using Adobe's Flash technology. That might change over time, especially with the adoption of HTML5, but for now when you hear the term "Flash animation," we're talking about most web-based animation.

Here's a good use for animation: demonstrating how a device or process works. By animating illustrations, you can show how something works over time. That's a good thing.

Here's a bad use for animation: funny cartoons. Unless you're a professional cartoon animator or run a comedy site, forget those cute or funny animations. They don't serve any useful purpose—and online space is too valuable to waste.

▶ *Caution*

Most people find Flash animations annoying at best. In my experience, most are unnecessary and serve no purpose other than to get in the way of me finding the content I'm looking for. Don't use animations for a showy effect; employ them only when they serve a necessary function.

Should you use animations to accompany your text? When appropriate, yes. That means if you have a process or service to demonstrate, by all means animate the process. But if you just want to move some images or text around the page to look cool, don't do it. That's not a useful purpose; it's just annoying.

▶ *Caution*

Not all devices can play back Flash animations and videos. For example, Apple's iOS is not compatible with Flash technology—which means your fancy animations won't play at all on iPhones and iPads.

Using Videos

Finally, we come to the topic of videos—little movies you embed in your web pages or blog posts. Like animations, videos can be both very good and very bad.

On the plus side, videos can help demonstrate a product or show viewers how to do something. Videos are great for how-to presentations, cooking demonstrations, and the like. They're also a good way to present interviews and testimonials; it's always best to hear kind words from the horse's mouth, as it were.

Videos can also add an entertaining element to a blog or website and are very popular in social media. Tread carefully, however; you don't want to be entertaining for entertainment's sake. Add a video to your text not because you need to inject a little fun into things, but because it serves a real purpose. The video should amplify the text you write, not draw attention away from it.

▶ *Caution*

Because most people like to watch movies more than they like to read, a video can easily overshadow your text content. In fact, if you embed a video on your web page, it might be the only thing visitors take the time to view; the medium is that powerful.

In my experience, the most effective online videos either educate, inform, or entertain the viewer. If you have a video that does that in service to a given project, it might be worth including it. If the video simply entertains without providing other relevant use, that's another thing.

So if a video is the best way to present certain information, great. But if you really want people to read your words, don't distract them with videos; save the videos for when moving images are the better approach.

 Note

Learn more about the best kinds of videos for different audiences in my companion book, *YouTube for Business: Online Video Marketing for Any Business, 2nd Edition* (Que Publishing, 2011).

9

Utilizing Links and Outside Content

The World Wide Web is just that—a web of interrelated content. When reading a web page or online article, readers expect to find links to related content on other websites. This sort of linkage makes the original text more useful, by expanding it to include additional information found elsewhere.

Adding links to your online copy is both necessary and challenging. Done right, you enhance the value of your content. Done wrong, you either annoy readers with too many links or lead them off your site, never to return.

How do you best add links and other outside content to your online content? That's what this chapter is all about.

How, When, and How Often to Link

When you add links from your text to other content on the Web, you enable readers to enhance their reading experience. You can lead readers to additional details, background information, related content, even just stuff you think they'll find interesting.

How to Add a Link

You can add links to words, to headings on a page, or to photos and other images. Figure 9.1 shows what a typical text link looks like—that old familiar blue underlined text.

> In anticipation of my upcoming book, **The Ultimate Digital Music Guide**, I've started a new **Ultimate Digital Music Guide Blog**. I post to it whenever I damned well feel like it, about anything I damned well feel like writing about -- music-related, that is. I hope you find it an interesting read, and also hope you purchase the accompanying book when it's released this July!

Figure 9.1   *Click the blue underlined text to follow the link.*

Most web page editing programs make it easy to add links to selected text; heck, Microsoft Word even has a Hyperlink button you can use to insert web links. It's typically a simple matter of selecting the link text—technically called the *anchor text*—on your page or post, and then entering the URL of the page you want to link to.

 Note

A link to another web page is called a *hyperlink*.

You can also add optional ScreenTip text that displays when a reader mouses over the anchor text on the page, as shown in Figure 9.2. If you decide to add ScreenTips to your links (to be honest, few web writers do), they should include informative text about what you're linking to, such as a description of the linked-to page or content.

> Though the verdict marks a final decision in this trial, there are still a few things in the air when it comes to the aftermath. Apple needs to file a chart that identifies the products it wants to keep off store shelves (the above ruling should give you some idea) -- paperwork that's due by Monday. There's also a hearing set for September 20 to discuss those potential bans.
>
> Amended Verdict Apple Samsung | Apple, Samsung to argue sales bans in court on Sept. 20 -- Friday, Aug 24, 2012 |

Figure 9.2   *Mouse over a link to display the ScreenTip text.*

There's a real art in deciding which text should contain a given link to other information. You can link to a single word, a part of a sentence, a complete sentence, even a whole paragraph. For that matter, you can embed links in bulleted or numbered list items, and even in section heading.

Know however, that the less anchor text there is for a given link, the cleaner the page will look, and the clearer it will be to readers what to click. Choose the right words in your text that best reflect and point to the content you're linking to.

For example, let's say you have the following sentence that links to an article on the CNN website:

The legal implications of this strategy could affect the company's bottom line, as detailed in this CNN article.

You could select the entire sentence as anchor text, but that's probably a bit too much. A better strategy would be to select **as detailed in this CNN article** as the anchor text. Even better, make only **CNN article** the anchor text; it's short and to the point and very clear about what you're linking to.

 Caution

> If you turn an entire paragraph (or more!) into anchor text, readers will be turned off by the profusion of blue underlined text and likely not click anything at all.

By the way, one thing you see a lot of on the Web are the words **click here** used as anchor text. Although this might seem an obvious thing to do, it's actually redundant; web users know to click an underlined link and don't need to be told to do so. Instead, make the relevant text the anchor text, and eschew the use of the phrases "click here," "click for more," and the like.

What to Link To

You can link to just about anything you find on the Web. You can link to web pages, articles, blog posts, images, videos; you name it.

In general, you want to link to content that supplements your core content. That might be any of the following:

- An article from a major news site that adds detail to your content
- A Wikipedia article (if you trust the veracity of that site) that explains a concept or item you're discussing

- A relevant blog post from a respected blogger that also discusses what you're writing about
- A company's home page or product page
- A related review on another website
- A chart or infographic that details the current topic
- A video that demonstrates what you're writing about

For example, if you're writing about your opinion of a local restaurant, you might link to that restaurant's website, its reviews on Yelp, or a similar review website. If you're writing about your favorite performing artist, you might link to that artist's website or one of her videos on YouTube. If you're writing about an upcoming election, you could link to election coverage on a major news site or even a specific candidate or party's website.

▶ Caution

Nothing annoys readers more than clicking on a link that's no longer live or that leads to a wrong or non-existent web page. Always check your links before your writing goes live—and follow up as necessary to keep the links fresh over time.

When (and How Often) to Add Links

Links add depth to your content, in a sidebar sort of way. Instead of inundating readers with additional or background information right here right now, you provide a link to that information that readers can pursue at their leisure. By linking to the additional info, you avoid distracting the readers and interrupting the flow of your text.

You should add links when there is relevant but not directly pertinent information that might be of interest to the reader. If the information is necessary to complete the understanding of your text, it should be included within the core content, not linked to. And if the information isn't relevant, there's no point in linking to that, either, is there?

However, you don't want to go crazy with your links. If you include too many links on a given web page, the reader will see nothing but blue underlined text, which will depreciate the value of any individual link—and also make it very hard to read your main content. (See Figure 9.3 to see what I mean.) In addition, if you include too many links on a page, you'll end up losing a lot of readers to those linked-to pages.

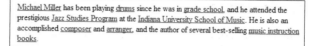

Figure 9.3 *This block of text contains too many links; it's confusing to the reader.*

It's better, then, to include only those links that add important depth to your core content. Try to include no more than one link in any given sentence; heck, limiting it to a single link per paragraph isn't a bad idea. The links you choose should distinguish themselves for the value they add to your text; as with most things, it's a matter of quality over quantity.

In other words, show a little restraint, okay?

WHEN *NOT* TO LINK

Just because you can link to something, it doesn't mean that you should.

Although you can add real value to your content by selective linking to other sites, remember that every time someone clicks one of those links, he leaves your site. And some percentage of people who click away won't return.

If you don't want readers to leave your site, then you shouldn't include *any* links within your text. You certainly don't want readers to click over to a competing website and buy their products. You also don't want readers to discover that a linked-to site has more or better content than you offer, and thus never return to your disappointing site.

That said, banning all links from your text might not be feasible or even be the best strategy; remember, online readers expect links as part of the web experience. To that end, you need to carefully choose *where* within your text to add your links.

For example, if you want people to read an entire paragraph before linking to another site, don't include the link within the paragraph. Instead, insert a new sentence after the paragraph that functions as the anchor text. That way people won't click away until they've read the full paragraph. It's not as draconian as completely excluding all links, but it does help focus readers on your content for as long as possible before they click away.

Embedding Images and Other Content from the Web

Linking is the most common method of connecting to other content in the World Wide Webisphere, but it's not the only way to do it. You can also embed content that you find elsewhere into your web pages, blog posts, and social media updates.

How Embedding Works

When you embed an item onto your web page, that item is still hosted at its original location. Your web page loads as normal, then the image or video or whatever is loaded from that other site into the web browser that's displaying your page. If the item you're embedding is changed on that other site, the changes are also reflected when the item loads onto your page. If the item is deleted on that other site, it will no longer appear on your page.

The nice thing about embedded content, from the perspective of readers, is that it doesn't appear as a link they have to click, but rather as the content itself. That is, the image or video or whatever is literally embedded in your content; it appears in line with the surrounding text.

For example, Figure 9.4 shows a YouTube video embedded on my own website. The video is "live," in that readers can play it from my web page just by clicking the Play button. Readers are not sent to a different website to view the content.

Figure 9.4   *A YouTube video embedded on an independent web page.*

What Can You Embed?

Images and videos are the most commonly embedded content. It's easy enough, if you know HTML coding, to insert the URL for a given image or YouTube video into the underlying code of a web page or post. It's not as easy as creating a hyperlink, though, which is why fewer people do it. But if you have access to technical staff, they can do it for you.

Note

You can also copy images from other sites and paste them into your web page. This is not a live embed; the copy and paste process breaks all connection to the current version of the copied content.

Text is less frequently embedded but more frequently copied. That is, you copy the text from another website or blog and then paste it directly into the content on your own website or blog. It's not "live" like an embedded object, but it certainly is borrowed.

Should You Embed Content from Other Sites?

The concept of borrowing somebody else's content for your own purposes is questionable for a number of reasons.

First, it's passing off someone else's content as your own. This is especially problematic when you copy text from another site and paste it into your site without attribution. That's plagiarism, which, while not illegal, is unethical. It's the sort of thing that'll get a student a failing grade on a term paper or a reporter kicked off a newspaper, if discovered. Besides, it's just not right to steal (excuse me, "borrow") some other writer's work; it really is like cheating on a test.

 Note

Plagiarism is the act of using another person's work without proper acknowledgement of the original source.

Second, copying or embedding images and videos might indeed be illegal. We're talking about copyright law here (or we will be, in the following section of this chapter), and it's breaking the law to use copyrighted material without explicit permission or proper compensation.

Let's look at a couple of examples:

- You're writing a blog post about famous singers, and you copy Ella Fitzgerald's bio from Wikipedia and paste it directly into your text without attribution. This is the plagiarism thing writ large, and it's a big no-no. Don't do it.

- You're writing a blog post about famous singers, and you copy Ella Fitzgerald's bio from Wikipedia and paste it into your site, but provide proper attribution about where it came from. This gets around the plagiarism angle but still is lazy writing. I'd advise against it.

- You're writing a blog post about famous singers, and you link to Ella Fitzgerald's bio on the Wikipedia site. This is perfectly acceptable. Good form, my friend!

- You're writing a blog post about famous singers and embed a photo-graph of Ella Fitzgerald from the official Ella Fitzgerald website. (Yes, there is one; it's at www.ellafitzgerald.com.) This is not good; you don't have permission to do this, and you might in fact be engaging in a copyright violation. Don't do this.

- You're writing a blog post about famous singers, and you embed a video of Ella Fitzgerald that you found on YouTube. This is actually okay because YouTube gives blanket permission to embed any public video on its site and even provides the embed code to do so. It's a good use of online resources.

Bottom line: it's okay to link but not always okay to copy or embed other content. In fact, I'd advise against copying any text content and embedding any copyrighted images. YouTube is the notable exception here, because it actively encourages embed-ding of its videos, but beyond that, stick with your own original content as much as you can. If you need to go beyond that to content elsewhere on the Web, link to it.

Understanding the Legalities of Linking and Embedding

So embedding is problematic, but linking is fully acceptable online behavior. Are there any limits or rules that apply to the links you create?

Linking Is Legal

Linking is perfectly legal behavior, even if the site you link to doesn't really want you linking to it. There have been instances of certain websites asking other sites not to link to them, but even though those requests might have come from the site's legal representatives (and look legally scary), they don't have legal force. That is, although you might want to cede to a site's request to sever your links, just to be a good neighbor, you don't legally have to do so. Linking is not illegal; you're not actually using another site's content when you create a link. So feel free to link to your heart's content, no lawyers necessary.

Do you need to get permission to link to another site? Nope. Not at all. There's nothing stopping you from linking to anything on the Web. That's what the Web is about, after all.

Embedding...Not So Much

Embedding other sites' content, however, is less legal. Assuming that the content on the other site (images in particular) is copyrighted and not licensed for free public distribution, and that you do so without explicit permission or compensation, your embedding or copying that content on your site is infringing on the owner's copyright. That is, you're stealing the content—literally. And stealing is against the law.

Let's put it another way: you can't use another person's or site's content without permission. And even if you get permission, you might have to pay for it. You don't have this problem if the content is in the public domain or has been licensed for a particular use (either commercial or noncommercial, depending). But if the content has not been thusly licensed and you haven't contacted the site owner about using it, you had better not embed it on your site; you'll be legally liable for damages.

What about fair use, you might ask? If you're quoting a line or two from another site as part of review or reference, and you properly cite that site, that's allowable under the fair use doctrine. Copying whole paragraphs from another site, however, is not. Nor is copying content from another site without attribution. In other words, you can't try to fool readers into thinking that borrowed content is your own; that's not fair use.

✉ *Note*

Fair use is an exception to copyright law that permits limited use of copyrighted material without requiring permission from the copyright holders. The keyword here is "limited"; fair use typically applies to short excerpts of a work for the purpose of review, criticism, commentary, news reporting, and the like. So, for example, if you quote a line of dialog from a film in your review of that film, that's fair use. If you instead appropriate an entire scene from someone else's film in your own film script, there's nothing fair about that use.

Should You Worry?

To be honest, it's unlikely that anybody's going to sue an individual who embeds a picture or other content on a personal blog or website. I'm not saying it can't happen, just that it likely won't; you're too small a fish to bother with. Companies are more likely to bring out the legal beagles when there are bigger fish to fry, such as when a big commercial website uses content without permission.

That doesn't excuse unauthorized copying or embedding from smaller websites and blogs, of course; there are lots of other issues that argue against this, including the likelihood that you'll lose credibility if your readers discover you've "borrowed" material from elsewhere. But it's likely you can get away with a little unauthorized use if you're too small for anyone big to notice. It's not necessarily a chance you should take, but it's one you probably could.

10

Optimizing Your Copy for Web Search

One thing that truly distinguishes online copy from traditional print copy is that online copy gets read by more than just your readers—your human readers, that is. Online copy also gets "read" by the indexing software used by Google and the other online search engines. This software helps determine how high your page or post or whatever ranks in the search engine results. (Obviously, you want to rank as high as possible to attract as many human readers as possible.)

So when you write your online copy, you need to take the search engines into account and optimize your copy so that it ranks higher instead of lower. That means that you're writing for both human beings and machines. For many writers, that is a new and unique challenge!

Because just about everything online can show up in these search results, you need to optimize all your online content for search. This search engine optimization (SEO) isn't only for web pages; you also need to optimize your blog posts, press releases, and even social media updates. It's all about making your content as searchable as possible.

How Online Search Works—and Why It's Important

Because search engines drive so much traffic to most online content, you want to ensure that your site or blog or whatever ranks as highly as possible in the results for all the major search engines. This activity is what we call *search engine marketing* (SEM), and it involves optimizing your content to rank higher in these search results.

Why High Rankings Are Important

Why is a high ranking in the search results important? It's all a matter of being found.

First, if you don't show up in the search results at all, your content won't be found—period. If nobody knows your page or post or whatever is there, they can't visit it. Unfound pages means unread content.

Beyond that, just showing up in a Google search index isn't good enough. You need to rank as high as possible in the search results for a given query to stand out from all the competing content. Most people don't click past the first page of search results; in fact, most people don't scroll through that entire first page.

This means that you want your content to rank somewhere in the top 5 or 10 sites that pop up when someone searches for a given topic. Any lower and the number of visitors you attract decreases significantly.

How Search Results Are Ranked

Before you start optimizing your content for the search engines, you need to know just how Google, Yahoo!, and Bing rank their results. What makes a search engine rank a particular page high in its search results and a similar page much lower?

Although each of the major search engines has its own particular algorithm for ranking the pages in its search index, they all follow similar methodology. That is, similar factors are important to ranking high with all the major search engines.

Because Google is far and away the most popular search engine on the Web, it's instructional to look at how that site ranks its results. When doing so, keep in mind that Google, like its competitors, attempts to serve its users by ranking the most important or relevant pages first, and ranking less-relevant pages lower in the results. It does so by applying a complex algorithm based on three primary components:

- **Text analysis:** Google looks first for words on a page that match those words in the search query. But it goes beyond simple text matching because it's also looking at how those words are used. That means examining font size, grammatical usage, proximity, and more than a hundred other factors to help determine relevance to the query. Google also analyzes the content of neighboring pages on the same website to ensure that the selected page is the best match.

- **Links and link text:** Google then looks at the links (and the text for those links) on the web page, making sure that they link to pages that are relevant to the searcher's query. Links that go off to pages unrelated to the query help to bring down a page's ranking.

- **Inbound links:** Finally, Google tries to determine a page's importance by counting the number of other pages that link to that page. The theory is that the more popular a page is, the higher that page's ultimate value. Although this sounds a little like a popularity contest (and it is), it's one that actually works. Bottom line: the more pages that link to a page or post, the higher the ranking.

Tip

Although the number of inbound links you receive matter, it's also important *which* pages are linking to your site. Google figures that links from pages more closely related to your page's topic should mean more than random links from unrelated pages. So, for example, if your website is about vintage automobiles, a link from an auto parts website would result in a higher rank than a link from a site about hospital supplies. With this in mind, it's likely that a page with fewer, but higher-ranked, pages linking to it will rank higher than a similar page with more, but lower-ranked, pages linking to it.

Understanding Search Engine Optimization

To improve your search engine rankings, you need to optimize your content for these very same search engines. This process, not surprisingly, is called *search engine optimization*, or SEO.

There are lots of details, but in general, SEO requires you to focus your content to best match the terms or keywords that your target readers are presumably searching for. You have to identify the keywords they use in their queries and then include those keywords in your copy—as well as behind the scenes in your page or post's HTML code.

✉ *Note*

> SEO is part and parcel of what is called search engine marketing (SEM). SEM can also involve search engine advertising, through Google AdWords and other similar programs.

SEO also requires you to organize your content in such a way that search engines can more effectively determine its actual subject matter. That also affects web page design; there are design techniques that can improve your search ranking and those that can cause the search engines to ignore you completely.

Effective SEO, then, requires you to write in a way that works for the search engines while still being understandable to and effective for your human readers. That can be a bit of a balancing act, as you'll soon see.

BIG BANG FOR SMALL BUCKS

If you're thinking in marketing terms, SEO is one of the most efficient tools in your bag. It's a relatively low-cost way to increase traffic and generate revenue.

Key to the cost conversation is the simple fact that you can't buy placement in search engine results; Google, Bing, and the others don't allow that. The results you achieve are totally organic—that is, your results are based on the true worth of your content, nothing less and nothing more.

The only cost you incur, then, is the cost of your SEO efforts. This might be zero, if you do your own in-house SEO, or it might be a little more than that, if you employ an SEO consultant to work over your entire website. In any instance, the cost of SEO is a lot less than the cost of purchasing search advertising via Google AdWords—and much, much more effective.

What you get then, is big bang for your bucks—which makes SEO a great leveler on the marketing playing field. A small firm with good SEO skills can rank higher in Google's search results than larger competitors with bigger budgets. It ultimately doesn't matter how big the company or its web marketing budget is; SEO is more about smart marketing than it is about the bucks.

This is why SEO represents a major component of the online marketing mix for most companies, large or small. It's not the only thing you need to do to market a business online, but it's definitely the most important thing.

What Search Engines Look For

We previously discussed how Google and the other search engines rank their search results. That methodology—text analysis, outbound and inbound links—is in the service of determining what a given piece of content is all about and how that content relates to the search at hand.

With that in mind, there are a number of things the search engines look for in your content. As you might suspect, these happen to be the very things you'll want to optimize your content for search.

Keywords

A search engine doesn't yet have the capacity to read sentences and paragraphs and understand what it reads. That's one advantage we humans still retain over the machines; we're capable of cognitive understanding.

Google and its brethren, then, have to employ machine-based processes to try to emulate understanding of web-based content. Unfortunately, those processes aren't terribly advanced. Current technology enables a search engine to pull specific words and phrases from a given piece of text, but that's about it; the search engine has no way of knowing how well those words and phrases are used and to what end.

To determine what's important on a page, then, search engines look for *keywords*. A keyword is a word or phrase entered as part of a search query; the search engine tries to find a given keyword on the matching web page or post, and then determines how important that keyword is to that content.

 Note

In SEO terminology, a keyword can be either a single word or a multiword phrase. For example, both **guitar** and **acoustic guitar** can function as keywords on a guitar-based website.

The search engine does this by noting where on the page the keyword appears and how many times it's used. A page with a keyword buried near the bottom will rank lower than one with the keyword placed near the top; a single use of a given keyword will rank that page lower than a similar page that uses the keyword repeatedly in the text. Now, this isn't a foolproof way of determining importance and appropriateness, but it's a good first stab at it.

For example, if someone is searching for "golf" and your web page includes the word "golf" in a prominent position—in the first sentence of the first paragraph, let's say—your page is a good match for that particular search. If, on the other hand, you have a page about sports in general that doesn't include the word "golf" at all, or includes it only near the bottom of the page, the search engine will determine that your site *isn't* a good match for that searcher. It doesn't matter if you have a big picture of Arnold Palmer at the top of your page (search engines can't read images, unfortunately); unless you use the keyword prominently and relatively often, you won't rank highly for that particular search.

So the major search engines, when they examine your content, are going to look for the most important words—those words used in the title or headings, those words that appear in the opening paragraph, and those words that are repeated throughout the piece. The more prominently you include a word in your content, the more important a search engine will think it is.

▶ *Caution*

Giving prominent placement to the *wrong* words can hurt your search rankings. For example, if your page is about sports but you, for some reason, include the words "dental" and "molar" multiple times on the page, it will likely be viewed as a page about dentistry. This not only drives the wrong visitors to your page, but also lowers your search ranking in general because you're now one of the less-useful dentistry pages listed.

HTML Tags

A search engine looks not just to the text that visitors see when trying to determine the content of your page, but also to the page or post's underlying HTML code—specifically, the *metadata* in the code. Now, this is all a bit technical and might or might not be something you, as the copywriter, have control over. I can guarantee, however, that your technical staff knows and cares about this and can probably use your informed input.

I won't go into all the technicalities here. Just know that your tech staff or web designers might come to you for a list of keywords for them to use in the HTML code. If they do, give them the list. And if they don't ask you, give them the list, anyway; you don't want them making up their own keywords, do you?

Links

As mentioned previously, Google and the other search engines also look at the links from and to your content. For the outbound links, you need to take this into account when determining which external pages you link to and the anchor text you use for each link. For the inbound links, that's less a copywriter's responsibility than someone elsewhere in your marketing department; you can try to convince relevant sites to link to yours.

Optimizing Your Site's Content

I could write about the various tricks and tools that some SEO experts swear by, but I don't swear by them so I won't go there. When it comes to effective SEO, there are no tricks; it's all about providing the most useful and relevant content to your readers. That's right, the most effective thing you can do to improve your search ranking is to improve your content. Everything else you do is secondary; when it comes to SEO and improving your search ranking, content is king.

What Is Quality Content?

How do the search engines define quality content? Pretty much the same way you and I do. It's content that fills readers' needs, and relates to and answers the questions at hand.

Quality content is useful content. It's informative, and it's accurate. It's grammatically correct, and it's punctuated properly and reads well. It's original, it's lean and mean, and it's on point. It is relevant to the topic at hand, and most important, it is authoritative.

▶ *Caution*

In most cases, quality content is *not* overtly promotional or commercial in nature. Your content needs to inform the reader without being self-serving; it needs to serve a useful and practical purpose, not one that talks only about yourself or the product you're offering.

In short, quality content distinguishes your web page or post from competing pages. When a visitor says, "I learned something important there," you know you have quality content. If a visitor instead says, "I'm not sure why I bothered visiting that site," you know that your content is lacking on the quality front.

Tip

The quality of your content is also somewhat dependent on the *quantity* of your content; the more text you include, the more likely it is that you're covering that topic in depth. To that end, some search engines place an emphasis on text length; they assume that a long web page has had more effort put into its creation, and thus is more likely to be of higher quality. That might not always be true, but it's something for you to consider when you're writing—and balance it against your readers' desire for shorter pages.

Why Does Quality Content Matter?

Quality content matters because it's all about delivering relevant results. All the major search engines want to provide searchers with sites that best answer their users' queries; they don't want to serve up sites that leave their users still asking the same questions.

There are other reasons for improving your online content, too. First and foremost, the better and more relevant your content, the more satisfied your readers will be. You should want to create the most useful, authoritative content possible on the topic at hand; you should not be willing to settle for offering second-rate content to people who can quickly and easily click away from your content to other sites that offer something better.

In addition, the better your content, the more likely it is that other sites will link to it—and, as you recall, these inbound links are important to your search ranking. If your content disappoints, other sites won't link to you; if your content excels, you'll get a lot of links without having to ask for them.

Note

Experts dub content that attracts links from other quality sites as *linkworthy*. If your content is just like all the rest out there, it's not linkworthy— that is, there's no reason for other sites to link to it.

Providing Authoritative Information

All this talk about creating quality content is fine, but just how do you go about doing it? The first thing you need to do is provide authoritative information.

It's simple to say that you want your content to be so complete that users won't have to visit anywhere else online to find out more about the topic at hand. Include every piece of information that's relevant, make sure that you answer any questions your readers might pose, and you establish yourself or your site as the leading authority on the topic.

Then there's the matter of *relevant* content. If you do a good job figuring out what particular information your target audience is looking for, your content can and probably should be more concise than a competing site that throws in everything but the kitchen sink. In other words, offering targeted information is often a better approach than being unnecessarily comprehensive.

The key, then, to providing authoritative information is knowing what that information should be—which is a function of knowing what your target reader is looking for. It all gets back to my concept of *thinking like the reader.* You have to know what readers want to know—what information they're looking for, and how they're looking for it. When you can provide exactly the right information, you become the authority on that topic.

Writing Engaging Copy

Now we come to the softer side of authority—how you present that information. We're now onto the familiar topics of writing style and how to write engaging online copy.

There's demonstrable benefit, beyond appealing to English teachers, of employing good writing. Although you could present everything you know about a given topic in a series of short bullet points, that isn't very engaging to the reader; in fact, some search engines (such as Google) might see the lack of complete sentences as a form of *keyword stuffing* and actually lower your search ranking. So there's a lot to be said for presenting your information in a grammatically correct, properly punctuated, engaging fashion.

 Caution

Keyword stuffing is a technique that inserts multiple instances of a keyword onto a page—often using hidden, random text—in an effort to increase the keyword density and thus increase the apparent relevancy of a page. Most search engines today view keyword stuffing as a kind of search-related spam and employ sophisticated algorithms to detect the technique.

Bottom line: facts alone don't make for quality content. You have to present your facts in a way that is readable and easy to follow—just as you do in any medium.

Crafting SEO-Friendly Content

Your online content not only has to be authoritative and engaging, it also has to be presented in such a fashion that search engines notice it. This means making your content SEO-friendly—which might be a new skill for you.

Just what is SEO-friendly content? Here's a list of things that can make or break the way search engines interpret your online content:

- **Use words, not pictures:** Today's search engines look only at the text on a web page, not at a page's images, videos, Flash animations, and the like. In fact, they really can't see nontext items; at best, they can read the accompanying description in the item's HTML, but they certainly can't look at a picture and tell you what it is. This is why you want to present your most important content in good old text format and save the images to pretty things up for the humans.

- **Include keywords in your copy:** When you're presenting your core concepts, make sure you work in those keywords and phrases that your potential visitors will be searching for. If a keyword doesn't exist in a page's copy, most search engines won't return that page as part of the relevant search results.

- **Repeat keywords and phrases—naturally:** It's not enough to include your most important keywords and phrases once on a page. You need to repeat those keywords and phrases—but in a natural manner. It can't look as if you're keyword stuffing; the words have to flow organically in your text.

- **Make the important stuff more prominent:** Whether we're talking keywords or core concepts, the most important information on a web page should be placed in more prominent positions, where it will be more easily found by search crawlers. This might mean placing the information in one of the first two or three paragraphs on your page; it might also mean placing key concepts in your page's headings and subheadings.

- **Break up the copy:** It's always a good idea to modularize the content you place online; I've talked at length throughout this book of the benefits of "chunkifying" your content. Well, short, chunky content is also key to effective SEO. Instead of presenting a long train-of-thought block of text, break up that block into short chunks; each chunk should be introduced by its own prominent heading or subheading. Make it easy for both readers and the search engines to find the key information on your page.

- **Length matters:** Although I'm an admirer of concise copy, especially for human readers, some search engines actually reward those sites that have more words per page. On average, today's top search engines seem to have a preference for pages with content in the 1,000-word range. But that's just an average. For Google's top 10 search results, the average number of words per page is about 950; for Yahoo!, it's closer to 1,300 words per page. So it might be okay to go a little longer, as long as you don't overdo it.

Remember, though, that the way you present your content is secondary to the content itself. You have to start with authoritative content and then work from there.

Working with Keywords

To some degree, all SEO revolves around the use of keywords. Whether you're talking about the content on a page or the code that underlies that content, you use keywords to give your content and code more impact.

It's vital, then, that you learn how to create a list of keywords relevant to your readers—and how to include them in the content you create. It all starts with learning how to *think like a reader*; you need to get inside searchers' heads to determine which words they're using in their queries.

Performing Keyword Research

The art of determining which keywords to use is called *keyword research*, and it's a key part of SEO. When you know which keywords and phrases your target readers are likely to use, you can optimize your content for those words and phrases; if you don't know how they're searching, you don't know what to optimize.

Some sites conduct extensive (and expensive) market research to determine how their target audiences are searching. Other sites just wing it and try to guess what the top searches are. I don't recommend either approach; there are simpler and more effective ways to get smart about keywords.

Case in point: several companies offer keyword research tools that compile and analyze keyword search statistics from all the major search engines. You can use the results from these keyword research tools to determine which are the most powerful keywords to include on your site.

These keyword research tools work by matching your content with keywords relevant to that content; they've already searched through hundreds of thousands of possible keywords and phrases on the most popular search engines and mapped the results to their own database. You enter a word or phrase that describes what your site has to offer, and the research tool returns a list of words or phrases related to that description, in descending order of search popularity.

The more popular keyword research tools include the following:

- KeywordDiscovery (www.keyworddiscovery.com)
- Wordtracker (www.wordtracker.com)
- WordZe (www.wordze.com)

These tools don't come cheap; expect to pay about $35 to $70 *per month* to subscribe. But if you don't know enough about your readers, it's money well spent.

Determining the Right Keyword Density

After you've generated a list of keywords, you now have to use those keywords in your content. We'll start by examining how—and how often—you should include keywords in your page's copy.

First, know that the more often you use a keyword in your body text, the more likely it is that search crawlers will register the keyword—to a point. Include a keyword too many times, and crawlers will think you're artificially "stuffing" the keyword into your phrase with no regard for the actual content. If you're suspected of keyword stuffing in this fashion, don't be surprised to see your search ranking decrease—or your page disappear completely from that search engine's search results. (As I've mentioned, search engines don't like keyword stuffing.)

Thus you need to determine the correct keyword density for your content. What is an optimal keyword density? That depends. If you have a lot of different keywords on a long page, you could have a density of 20% or more and still rank fine. If you have only a handful of keywords on a short page, a 5% keyword density might be too much. The key is to make sure your content is readable (to human beings, that is); if it sounds stilted or awkward because of unnecessary keyword repetition, chances are a search engine will also think that you're overusing your keywords.

 Note

Keyword density is the number of times a keyword or phrase appears compared to the total number of words on a page.

Writing Keyword-Oriented Copy

So what's the best way to incorporate keywords into your site's content?

It all starts with good, old, solid copywriting—with a twist. You need to provide readable, compelling copy for your visitors while incorporating all the necessary keywords and phrases that matter to the search engines. You don't want to sacrifice one for the other; never make your page less readable just to cram in another keyword. Go for readability first, and then incorporate the keywords as you can.

One way to improve both readability and search optimization is to break your copy into small sections or chunks of text, and then introduce each section with a heading or subheading. As we've discussed, search crawlers look for keywords in your heading tags; headings also help readers identify important sections on your page. So chunking up your text with shorter sections and more frequent headings benefits both your human and machine audiences. Two other good places to include keywords are in your piece's first and last paragraphs. Not only do search crawlers look more closely at the beginning and end of a page and tend to skip the middle, readers often look to the first and last paragraphs to find key ideas and then get a summary of the content presented. It's just like writing a newspaper article; it's the first and last paragraphs that are most important.

When you incorporate keywords and phrases into your text, you should do so in a natural fashion—while using the word or phrase verbatim. So if your key phrase is "windmill farm," you have to use that exact phrase, and in a way that doesn't sound forced. This is a definite copywriting challenge, but one that can be met.

So that's your challenge—write copy that is appealing to human readers but that also means something to the search engine software. When in doubt, err on readability; if your human audience thinks it's good, the search engines will likely come to the same conclusion.

11

Writing Web Pages

Great web pages combine user-friendly design with engaging text. If the writing is bad or inappropriate—too long, too demanding, too stiff—you'll have a bad web page, even if the design is first rate. (Conversely, bad design can make great text unreadable, too.)

Good writing is good writing, whether it's for a web page or an email newsletter, so all the advice so far in this book applies directly when you're writing for web pages. But web pages have some unique characteristics you need to take into account when populating them with text—including the size and shape of the page itself, as well as the need to optimize each for search.

Writing for the Browser Window

Throughout most of your life, whatever you've written has been displayed in portrait format, most often on an 8.5" × 11" piece of paper. You're used to writing for a container that enables (actually, encourages) easy scanning from top to bottom.

Writing for the web is different. Although a web page, when fully scrolled, might resemble a long page of paper, as shown in Figure 11.1, web browsers (viewed on widescreen computer monitors) force readers to see only a small window to the page at any given time. And that window typically isn't in portrait format, but rather slightly landscaped, which defeats any easy top-to-bottom scanning, such as what we're all used to. (Figure 11.2 shows that same web page—well, part of it—as viewed on a web browser.)

Figure 11.1 A full—and lengthy—web page. (Actually, it's my personal page; you think I'd know better, wouldn't you?)

Figure 11.2 *The top part of my web page that you see within a standard browser window.*

This has several implications for your writing. First, you should try, whenever possible, to fit your *entire* content into a single browser window page. This means trimming your content to the bare essentials and then linking to additional content. This is the web equivalent of putting everything "above the fold" in the newspaper business, and doing so really focuses your writing. (Figure 11.3 shows how the Boy Scouts of America does it; everything fits within the standard browser window.)

Figure 11.3 *The Boy Scouts of America (www.scouting.org) site fits all the home page's content into a single browser window.*

If you can't fit all your content into a single browser window, at least fit the most important stuff above the fold. That includes all the navigational links to additional content on the site.

The key is to keep linking to additional content, rather than forcing readers to scroll, scroll, scroll down a super-long page. It's a way of breaking your content into short chunks—which is important in all your web copy.

Keeping It Short for Scanners

About that chunk thing: as I've preached throughout this book, you need to keep your copy short and chunky so that web readers can easily scan it. Experts have found that web users are more likely to browse a web page for relevant words and phrases (keywords, in other words) than read all the words on a page in depth. That's scanning, folks, not reading.

Way back in 1997, usability guru Jakob Nielsen conducted a study and found that 79% of web users scanned web pages, whereas only 16% read word-by-word. These scanners ended up "reading" only 20% to 28% of the words on any given page.

If you're a serious wordsmith, that information might be demoralizing, but it's just the way it is. You can put in endless hours finely honing your crystalline prose, but those unwashed heathens on the Web won't bother to read them all. Instead, web users are scanning for specific information; they're not interested in your style or phrasing.

You can bemoan this fact, or you can accept it and work with it. I suggest the latter approach.

If you want to make the most of how people "read" web pages, you need to create easily scannable text. You can do this by

- Incorporating essential keywords and key phrases throughout the text
- Adding headings that both break up the text into smaller chunks and highlight key concepts
- Keeping paragraph length to no more than three sentences whenever possible
- Writing short sentences composed of short words
- Using bulleted and numbered lists whenever possible

Keep it short, keep it clear, keep it concise. That's good advice for any online writing, especially when creating web page copy.

Tip

One way to keep your paragraphs short is to limit yourself to one idea per paragraph. A concise and meaty paragraph is better than a long and rambling one. (The same advice applies to sentence construction: include just one idea per sentence and avoid compound sentences.)

TABLES: YES OR NO?

One way to present complex information in an easy-to-scan fashion is to employ tables. In fact, I suggested as much previously in this book; tables are great for presenting large quantities of complex data.

The problem with using tables on web pages is that they don't always display properly. You have to remember that not all users have the same size computer screen, nor do they all size their browser windows the same. The result is that one user might view web pages at 1400 pixels wide, another at 800 pixels, and a third at just 500 pixels.

Because browser width is not set in stone, you never know how much page space you have to work with. You might construct a table that looks good on a widescreen display at 1400 pixels, but that table gets squished or truncated for users viewing at 800 pixels.

In fact, tables of any significant width become pretty much unreadable on tablet screens (in portrait mode) and on smartphones. On those devices, you're better off presenting the information in a standard bulleted list.

The bottom line is that you need to preview any tables you use on a number of different devices at different browser widths. This probably means using narrow tables, if at all. Remember, the goal is scannability—which falls by the wayside if half your table is pushed off the side of the screen.

Organizing Your Content Hierarchically

Because web page visitors might only see only the first screen of information on a page, you want to make sure that the first screen contains the most important information. That means you should employ the tried-and-true inverted pyramid style, where you start with the conclusion and work your way down through additional detail. If a visitor reads only that first screen, the person will at least get the gist of what you're talking about.

Linking for Scannability

One of the things readers scan web pages for are those blue underlined links. In fact, our eyes go directly to those blue links; there's something about them that draws your attention.

This means that you need to include a fair number of links in your web page copy. The links shouldn't be random, of course; they need to serve the purpose of linking to additional information, either elsewhere on your site or on another site on the Web.

Remember, it's the blue underlined anchor text that people are drawn to, so use it appropriately. Turn your most important keywords into anchor text, then link them to further content on another page. Readers will immediately scan those keywords, figure out that the page contains what they're looking for, and then start to read it in more detail.

Embracing SEO

In the previous chapter I discussed the importance of search engine optimization (SEO), so I won't repeat myself here. I will, however, point out the best ways to optimize your web pages for search.

Use Those Keywords—In the Right Places

Keywords are incredibly important in the cause of SEO. All search crawlers look for the keywords and key phrases on a page and use those keywords not only to determine the content of a page but also to directly match user search queries.

That means you need to insert your most important keywords into your web page copy. Even better, insert those keywords *early* in the copy, so they appear higher on the page—the first paragraph is ideal, if you can swing it. Even better, link some of those keywords to additional content, either on your site or elsewhere on the Web; keywords used as anchor text rank higher than those in plain text.

By the way, you should also employ keywords in the headings in your text. That's because the search crawlers assume that heading text reflects the major content of a page, and they look there for keywords.

Put the Most Important Stuff First on the Page

I know, I just got done saying this in the context of fitting content in the web page window, but a proper hierarchical approach is also important for SEO. That's because search crawlers start at the top of a page and then read downward—and, like human readers, they might not read the entire page.

It's essential, then, to put the most important elements at the top of your page, in the main headings and initial paragraphs. A search crawler will see your leading content and register it as important; content lower on the page will be registered as subsidiary, if it's noted at all.

Use Headings and Subheadings

Another way to tell a search engine that something is important is to include it in a heading or subheading on the page. The machines aren't that different from us puny humans in that regard.

That's because a page's heading tags (in the underlying HTML code) are singled out by most search crawlers, in the assumption they highlight the most important content of your site. So you need to use headings to separate and highlight content on your page and to highlight your most important keywords and phrases.

Use Text, Not Pictures (or Videos or Flash)

Here's something you might not have known: search crawlers read text on a page, not anything else. They don't read images, they don't read Flash animations, they don't read videos. Every element on your page other than text is essentially invisible to search crawlers. It's only the text that matters.

This is important if your website designers insist in presenting important content via nontext elements. The most glaring examples of this are sites that use nothing but Flash animation on their introductory pages, which not only annoys many users but causes most search crawlers to skip completely over those pages—and, perhaps, the rest of the site.

The reason this is bad is that a complete Flash page is basically a blank page as far as the major search engines are concerned. If the page is completely in Flash, the search engines have no idea what the page is about. If there's no text to read, the crawlers think that there's nothing there.

The same thing goes with pages that rely on images or videos for the bulk of their content. A search crawler can't look at an image or view a video; not only can it not be captivated by the beauty of an image, it has no way of determining what the image is. Again, an image-only page appears blank to the search crawlers.

So the first thing you need to do is overrule those designers who want to Flash up your site and take a back-to-basics, text-based approach. You don't need to get rid of all images, animations, and videos, but they need to be downplayed on the page—and supplemented by well-written, descriptive text. (You know, the stuff you're hired to do.)

Don't Over Optimize

With this emphasis on optimizing for search, you might be tempted to over optimize a page. That is, you might end up inserting too many keywords, or use them in a way that interferes with the page's basic readability.

That's not good. Although you need to be aware of the search engines, it's the writing that comes first. Remember, you're writing for humans, not for the machines!

Keywords are important, but they're not the most important thing. Your copy has to be readable, which means you can't just insert keywords because you need to insert keywords. Keywords have to be used organically; they have to be integral to the surrounding copy. Use them when you can, not because you have to.

You also need to avoid overusing keywords. Repeating the same keywords throughout a block of copy not only reads poorly, but can be construed by the search engines as keyword stuffing, which can lower your search ranking.

Take, for example, the following paragraph:

> Our umbrellas are much more durable than competing brands of umbrellas. We construct our umbrellas from only the finest umbrella materials. Umbrella customers around the world choose our umbrellas over other types of umbrellas. Look for our umbrellas at an umbrella merchant near you!

Can you spot the keyword in this paragraph? Of course you can (spoiler alert: it's *umbrella*); the thing reads as if it were written by a machine for a machine. This is the type of writing to avoid.

Instead of mechanical repetition of a select few keywords, employ those keywords when they make sense—and use them judiciously. There's no benefit at all in stuffing your copy with the same words over and over. Neither the search engines nor your human readers will reward you for this.

KEYWORDS IN HTML CODE

This isn't a book for web designers or HTML coders, but as the guy who's probably responsible for managing your site's keywords, you need to know that keywords can—and should—also be employed in your site's underlying HTML code. That's because most search crawlers scan specific HTML tags for information they use in indexing a page. Insert your keywords and phrases into these tags, and you'll improve your site's results for that search engine.

The most important tags to focus on include the following:

- **<TITLE>:** This tag defines the text that appears in the title bar of a web browser; the title should present your page's official name and provide a glimpse to its content. It's also an effective place to use your chosen keywords, because the page title is one of the first places that search crawlers look to determine the content of your page. For this reason, include your most important keywords and phrases into your page's title, via the **<TITLE>** tag.

- **<META>:** This tag defines several individual attributes, conveying so-called metadata about your page. The two primary **<META>** attributes are **DESCRIPTION** and **KEYWORDS**. The **DESCRIPTION** attribute is where you put a short description of the page's content, using your favorite keywords. The **KEYWORDS** attribute is nothing more than a list of key-words that some search engines (but not Google, unfortunately) use to catalog all the keywords on a page.

- **Header tags:** The HTML standard lets you use six different levels of headings, from **<H1>** to **<H6>**, in descending order. Search crawlers look in these tags for content information, which makes them a good place to employ important keywords.

You don't need to know the HTML coding involved in all this; leave that up to your web designers or technical staff. You do need to know which keywords are most important, however, and supply the relevant text for each of these tags when asked. (Or just give it to 'em if they don't ask.)

12

Writing Online Articles

There's a lot of news to be had online, which means there's a lot of article writing going on. Although a lot of online articles are identical to their print brethren (many sites simply repurpose stories originally published in print), there are also a lot of articles written specifically for the Web.

Because print and online media are so different in terms of how they're consumed, I'm a big believer in writing articles specifically for online use. When you do so, the way you write changes—as does, in many instances, what you write.

What Online Articles Do Best

You can find all sorts of articles online. Some are straight breaking-news articles, such as what you find at CNN (www.cnn.com); some contain more specific industry news, such as the tech stories at CNET (news.cnet.com); others are softer in nature, such as the parenting news at *Parents* magazine online (www.parents.com).

In general, online articles mirror other types of online writing in that they're more concise than traditional print articles. Shorter article length pretty much rules out in-depth reporting and analysis; for this reason, most online articles stress immediacy over introspection.

The bottom line is that online articles are better for reporting breaking news than they are at providing detailed insight. Websites tend to focus on what's hot right now and leave the analysis to weekly or monthly print magazines.

That doesn't mean that you can't find in-depth reporting online, but you're going to find more of the shorter, immediate stuff. If you focus your efforts on writing concise breaking-news stories, you'll be heading in the right direction.

Writing Engaging Headlines

One thing that's vitally important for online articles is the thing that readers see first: the headline. Just like in print, tantalizing headlines get readers interested; boring, matter-of-fact headlines cause people to turn the page.

What this means is that you need to make your title reach out and grab the reader's attention. A dull title will cause readers' eyes to gaze over; an engaging title will do just that—engage the reader and get him reading.

Short Headlines Rock

The first step in creating an engaging title is to keep it short. Long titles, just like long articles, turn readers off. Short titles are easy to scan and get right to the point.

Take for example, this headline:

Dozens of Riders Stranded for Up to Two Hours on Malfunctioning Ride at Minnesota State Fair

Okay, that's informative enough, but it's way too long. Some of that info can wait until the body of the article. A better approach would be something like this:

Broken Ride Strands Dozens at Fair

(Note that I also replaced the more direct word "broken" for the more obtuse "malfunctioning." Simpler is always better in the world of headline writing.)

Engage the Reader

Your title also has to clearly state what the article is about and how it affects the reader. Think about benefits versus features here; tell readers why they'll benefit from reading the article. (And do so in as few words as possible.)

> ▶ *Caution*
>
> Avoid cutesy or clever titles in your online articles. That sort of thing might work in the print world (depending on the publication), but it's death on the Web. Online readers don't have time for your supposed humor; it's better to get right to the point and be clear about what's coming up in the article.

Optimize Your Title

Finally, you have to keep search engine optimization (SEO) in mind when creating your title. Try to throw a couple or three keywords into your title, if you can. The search engines look specifically at title text when determining page content; the presence of the right keyword can move your article up several places in the search results.

For example, if you're trying to attract gardeners to a given story, you probably want to include the keywords **garden** or **gardening** in your article title. Instead of writing this:

Ten Tips for Hardy Perennials

You need to rewrite the headline to include your keyword, as follows:

Ten Gardening Tips for Hardy Perennials

Make Every Word Count

This all argues in favor of making every word of your title count. You really have no space for wasted words; your title must be concise, informative, immediate, and action oriented (and include those keywords, of course). Tell the reader what the article's about and how it affects him, and do so in such a way that he just can't turn away. That's a winning title.

Keys for Better Online Article Writing

As to your articles themselves, everything you've learned so far about online writing applies.

Shorter Is Better

First and foremost, you need to keep it short. Online articles, while longer than most blog posts or social media updates, are still shorter than their print siblings. You have to present your information as concisely as possible; otherwise, readers will tune out before the article is over. When in doubt, try to keep it to 800 words or less.

 Tip

If you absolutely, positively must write a longer article (some topics demand it), break up the article into multiple sections on successive web pages, rather than presenting it as one long, scrolling mess.

Make It Scannable

You also need to make your article scannable. Write short paragraphs, short sentences, and short words. Just because it's an article doesn't mean that online readers will be any more inclined to read the whole thing than they would any other type of online writing.

That also means using nontext elements to present information when possible. That could be pictures, charts, bulleted lists, tables, you name it—anything to help the reader get more in a single glance. (Adding a little visual interest doesn't hurt, either.)

Don't Bury the Lead

Content organization is every bit as key in an article as it is in writing copy for a web page. Put the most important facts up front in the first paragraph, then fill in the details later. In journalistic terms, that means you shouldn't bury the lead; don't make readers hunt for what most interests them.

Adapt Your Writing Style

In terms of writing style, some consider web articles something of a cross between print and broadcast writing. That is, online writing needs to be tighter and punchier than print writing, but also more detailed than the simple, declarative sentences employed for broadcast copy. Naturally, the active voice is preferred.

That said, online readers have little patience for personal asides and other content that doesn't contribute directly to the narrative. They're not reading your article in the comfort of their easy chairs; they're sitting in front of a glowing screen with other reading options just a click away. Don't try to interject interesting but nonessential content; what might work well in print feels like unnecessary filler on the Web.

EDITING AND PROOFREADING: NECESSARY BUT SELDOM DONE

Here's one big difference I see between online and print articles: In print, you see few grammatical and spelling errors. Online, you see a lot. Really. A ton.

I'm talking about things such as incorrect use of words—"there" versus "they're," for example. Missing articles, such as "a" or "an" or "the." Misspellings. Wrong or missing punctuation. And more.

You want to know why online writing comes off as being so imprecise? Because it's too immediate. That is, the time between writing and posting is often measured in seconds. In the print world, there's enough time between the writing and the printing to allow for a few more sets of eyes to examine the text. Online, with the need to post immediately, there's simply no time for such niceties as copyediting and proofreading.

The result is that many online articles go live without being edited or proof-read. You get a run through a spell checker, but that's it. Any mistakes in the original text don't get caught, and thus get exposed to the world at large.

Careful readers, then, see a lot of mistakes in online articles. The web versions of major publications look to be more poorly edited than their print cousins—which they are, if they're edited at all. I suppose online publications save a few bucks by not employing editing and proofreading staff, and maybe online readers are more forgiving of such mistakes, but to me, personally, it's just embarrassing.

If you know your work won't be edited before it's posted, you need to do your own bit of proofreading. Sit back in your chair, take a deep breath, and read through your article carefully. Look for mistakes; heck, it might even be worth your while to print out a copy and take it to another location for perusal. If nobody else is going to catch your errors, you'll have to catch them yourself. Otherwise, it's you who'll be embarrassed by the result.

Don't Forget the SEO

One last thing about writing online articles: web articles are indexed for search, just as regular web pages are. That means someone searching Google for a given topic is just as likely to see your article in the search results as they are a whole website devoted to the topic—provided you've optimized your article for search.

You need to do the same SEO for each article you write as you would for your web page copy. That means doing all the following:

- Create a list of keywords on which readers are likely to search.
- Include those keywords in your article—the more important ones in the early paragraphs.
- Use the most important keywords more than once over the course of the article—but don't overuse them to the point of keyword stuffing.
- Include the most important keywords in the title of the article.
- Link to other relevant content from within your article.

However, if you face a conflict, you need to focus on readability over SEO. Quality content will get ranked higher, and that should always be your priority.

13

Writing Blog Posts

The blogosphere is an interesting little cul-de-sac on the Internet. It's not the World Wide Web, although it operates there. It's not social networking per se, even though blog posts regularly get passed around and commented on by communities of users. Blogging isn't exactly journalism, either, although some journalists are bloggers and some blogs are journalistic in nature.

Blogging can be an effective way for you to reach your target audience—if you do it right. The best blog posts both inform and engage readers; the worst posts are overtly promotional and self-serving, little more than minimally disguised advertisements or press releases.

If you want to engage your readers, you have to learn how to write effective blog posts. It's not quite like writing online articles—although they're similar in many regards.

Getting Personal

One common definition of a *blog* is that it's a website on which an individual or group of users record their personal opinions. Looking at it this way, a blog is like a personal diary where one or more writers vent their thoughts of the day.

But blogging is more than just proffering personal opinions—although there are plenty of personal blogs out there. These types of blogs offer a channel for individuals to vent their thoughts and views about politics, religion, sex, or the cost of ground turkey at the supermarket.

For our purposes, we're talking about more professional blogs, which can still be hosted by a single individual or by larger entities. For example, many businesses host their own blogs, which they use to promote their products and brands. You also find a lot of blogs that review music, movies, television, books, restaurants, consumer products, local attractions—you name it.

All these blogs have in common their personal viewpoints. That is, blog posts are seldom anonymous third-person recitations, but first-person accounts and opinions. Even company-owned blogs (the best of them, anyway) feature lively posts written by the company's employees, rather than dry statements crafted by the company's PR department.

The best bloggers, whether they're writing for themselves or for a larger publication or company, add their own insights to whatever issue they're addressing. These blogs are informed with the blogger's personal experience and values, which puts a unique spin on the core content. It's not just the facts, ma'am; it's the facts as the blogger sees them.

This makes blogging somewhat unusual among mainstream online publications. A blog post is like an online article, but with a more personal slant. It's one place where you can interject your personal opinions into your writing.

Establishing a Personal Style

Because blogging is more personal than other forms of online writing, it calls for a more personal writing style. A dry, impersonal style won't cut it; your blog posts need to reflect your own personal style as much as possible.

That means infusing your posts with your own personal language. Unless you happen to be a machine, that means employing a casual style. You need to keep the writing light and the style warm and inviting. (Unless, that is, you're deliberately seeking to provoke, in which case you can move the style needle from warm to hot, as appropriate.) In short, your blog needs to have its own personality.

Blog writing also requires that you be somewhat free with your opinions. Few successful blogs offer only a collection of facts. The best blogs supplement those facts with the blogger's opinions. That's why many people read blogs: to make a connection with a (presumably) informed individual.

To make sure readers know that it is an individual they're reading, you need to write in the first person. Use the words "me," "mine," and "I" as liberally as you deem fit; avoid "we" and "our," which sound a bit Big Brotherish in the blogosphere. And write as simply and as directly as you can; like all online readers, blog readers tend to scan rather than read in-depth.

So let your blog readers know what you think about the topic at hand in your own unique voice. Just don't be wordy about it.

 Tip

Blog posts don't have to be text only. You can include pictures and videos in addition to your main text, both of which can help to inject your personal style to the post.

Focusing on the Title

The first thing people see when accessing a blog is the title of the most recent post. In fact, when scrolling down a blog page to view older posts, readers scan the titles, not the posts themselves. This emphasizes the importance of creating engaging titles when you write your blog posts.

You approach blog post titles the same way you approach titles for other online articles. The title must be short and punchy, and use action words and phrases to convey the main point of the post. Remember, most people will read only the title, whether on your blog or on a page of search engine results. If they can't figure out what the post is about from the title, you're not doing your job.

You also need to include your most important keywords in your title. I'll talk about blog search engine optimization (SEO) later in this chapter, but for now know that the search engines crawl blog post titles looking for keywords and phrases—so your title needs to include a few, if you can. You can't pack too many keywords into a title, of course, so you have to choose judiciously. But titles are what count most when search engines are indexing blog posts, so fitting in the primary keywords is essential.

All this rules out single-word titles, by the way. I'm all for stylistic obfuscation, but a post titled **Thoughts** doesn't tell me anything about what those thoughts are about. Better to use the title **Thoughts on the Upcoming Election**, or even better,

Why I'm Voting Republican (or Democratic or Whig or whatever). Just say what the post is about in as few words as necessary.

 Tip

Although there are no practical limitations on the length of a blog post title, search engine results pages will show only the first 65 characters or so of a post title; anything past that 65-character mark gets truncated. So you can go long if you want to, but a lot of people won't see the words at the end.

Engaging Readers with Your Introductory Paragraph

After the title, the next most important piece of your post is the introductory paragraph. It's true; first impressions matter, especially in the blogosphere. You might get their attention with a catchy title, but you'll hook them with the first sentences you write.

The first paragraph not only introduces the topic du jour, it also serves to draw readers deeper into the blog post. You need to make your main point here, and then lead readers further to learn more.

Keeping It Short—But Not *Too* Short

Past the introductory paragraph, you need to continue exploring the topic you just introduced. The succeeding paragraphs should elaborate on your main point, add necessary details, argue your point, and explain your conclusion. This is your space to personally expound on whatever it is that you're excited or concerned or disturbed about.

How long it takes you to do this depends a lot on the subject, your personal style, and the confines of the specific blog. More detailed topics require a more detailed examination, and thus result in longer blog posts. A more verbose writing style will add more words to a post, whereas a dryer style will result in more succinct posts. But this all might be topped by the demands of the blog host.

Now, if you're the host of your own blog, you can determine what's the right post length. But if you're writing for another company or publication, they might define post parameters for you and other writers. If the blog host says to keep your posts under 500 words, then you better do so; if they say the sky's the limit—well, knock yourself out, pal.

However, the nature of online reading argues in favor of shorter blog posts, whenever possible. Remember, online readers have notoriously short attention spans, and they tend to scan text rather than read all the words. Surveys report that on average, readers stay just 90 seconds or so on any given blog. How many words can *you* read in a minute and a half? You get the point.

I'd advise using the same general rule for blog posts as for other online articles. Keep your posts under 1,000 words each, if you can, and ideally under 500. Much longer and your readers will start dropping like those proverbial flies.

 Tip

You probably want to "break" longer blog posts so that the entire post doesn't appear on the main blog page, thus making it harder for the reader to scroll through all the posts. Break a long post after the first two or three paragraphs and let the reader click to view the rest of the post "after the break."

On the other hand, there's such a thing as having a post that's too short. A blog post of just a sentence or two is better considered as a tweet or Facebook status update. (Social networking is the heart of brevity.) Blog posts can and should be longer than a 140-character tweet; there's an expectation of some depth in the medium. I can't really give you a hard and fast minimum, but if you can't get it up to 200 words or so, what's the point?

POSTING FREQUENCY

How often should you blog? That's a good question, and for businesses somewhat strategic. If you post too often, you could overwhelm readers with unwanted information. If you don't post often enough, your blog will appear stagnant and irrelevant. You need to strike a happy medium.

For most blogs, the optimal posting frequency is somewhere between once a day and once a week. It kind of depends on what actual news and information you have to convey, as well as the strength of the relationship you have with your readers. Obviously, the more you have to say, the more often you can legitimately post. And the more your readers become fans, hanging on your every word and action, the more often they'll want to hear whatever it is that you have to say.

If you regularly blog more than once a day, you're probably going to start boring your readers. At some point, they're going to look at all the posts you make and say, "Who cares?" I'm not sure exactly where useful information turns into useless blather, but you want to be somewhere on this side of that point.

On the other hand, if you post less than once a week, even the most loyal readers will forget you're there. You need to stay in front of them, and that means putting something out there on a somewhat regular basis. If your last post was a month ago, you just won't appear serious about this whole blogging thing. Your readers will feel abandoned, and that's definitely not what you're going for. If you can't post more often than that, you're better off not having a blog at all.

So aim for posting daily, or every few days. That leaves something new out there just about every day for your followers to read; it keeps their interest without overwhelming them—and demanding too much of their time.

Optimizing Your Blog and Posts for Search

If you want newbies to find your blog, you need to optimize it for search. That's right, most people find new blogs—and interesting blog posts—by searching Google, Bing, and Yahoo! If these search engines can't find your posts, neither can new readers.

SEO for blogs is a little different from SEO for web pages, or even for online articles. You actually have more optimization to do—of both your posts and of the blog itself.

Optimizing the Blog Template

The first thing to pay attention to is your blog's template, which defines how blog posts are displayed. The template also contains the content that surrounds the blog posts themselves—the blog title and description, as well as everything displayed in the blog's sidebar.

As with traditional websites, keywords are important to optimizing your blog. After you decide on the keywords and phrases that reference the main topics of your blog, you need to insert those keywords within your blog's descriptive text— which, ideally, should appear high on your blog page, probably directly underneath the name of the blog. It's these keywords that search engines look for when they're indexing blogs; the more prominent and more relevant the keywords, the higher your blog will appear in the search engine's results.

 Tip

Your blog designers should also place important keywords in the template's relevant HTML code, particularly in the template's **<TITLE>** tag, **<META>** tags, and in all alternative image text.

Optimizing Individual Posts

You also need to optimize each post on your blog for search. That's because it's the posts (and the posts' content) that shows up in those search engine results.

Start by including important keywords in the title of each blog post. This is even more important than with traditional websites because many news readers and content aggregators display only the titles of blog posts.

Next, focus on the content of each post. As with other online content, it's important to weave keywords into the post text, especially in the first paragraph. You'll also want to include the requisite links to other blogs or websites and incorporate keywords into the links' anchor text.

Finally, make sure you apply labels or tags to each of your posts. (Most blog hosts and editors let you add labels and tags separate from the post text.) These tags are one of the ways that readers find content on your blog, but they're also useful to any search engine trying to determine your blog's content. Assign each keyword or phrase as a separate label or tag. These labels are also internal links to your post and that increases the number of links, which is always a good thing in terms of SEO.

▶ *Caution*

Don't forget to proofread your writing before you post it to your blog. Most blog-editing software will check your spelling, but not your grammar, punctuation, and word usage. You're the only thing stopping an error-ridden blog post from hitting the Internet.

14

Writing Social Media Updates

Social networking is the latest and greatest online phenomenon. Chances are that you or your organization have actively embraced social networking, probably in the form of Twitter and Facebook. That's probably a good thing; social networking is a great way to connect with your fans or customer base.

It even seems easy; the posts are so short that anyone can write them—right? Not necessarily. In my experience, it takes more talent and discipline to write something short than it does to write it long; editing for length is harder than just blathering on.

With that in mind, welcome to the wonderful world of writing for social media. It's definitely not as easy as it looks!

Understanding How Social Media Work

Social media are those websites, services, and platforms that people use to share experiences and opinions with each other. These new media are differentiated from traditional media because of their two-way, conversational nature. Traditional media (newspapers, magazines, radio, television, and the like) utilize one-way communication; these media broadcast their static messages to the widest possible audiences, but the audience doesn't communicate back. Social media, on the other hand, are interactive, encouraging two-way conversations between parties.

There are many forms of social media today, only some of which require actual writing. Everybody divides them up a bit differently, but I tend to see them in this fashion:

- Social networks, such as Facebook, LinkedIn, and Pinterest
- Blogs
- Microblogging services, such as Twitter and Tumblr
- Media sharing sites, such as Flickr and YouTube
- Social bookmarking and news services, such as Delicious, Reddit, and StumbleUpon

The first four types of social media require the creation of content, either in text or visual form. In contrast, social bookmarking sites are all about sharing existing content and seldom, if ever, require your writing skills.

✉ *Note*

Social media can also include social review sites, web-based message forums, and any number of topic-specific websites that create their own online communities. In other words, anyplace online where social interaction occurs has the makings of being a social medium.

A BRIEF HISTORY OF SOCIAL MEDIA

Social media isn't really a new concept; aspects of today's social media have been around since the late 1970s. In fact, today's social media can be seen as a mashup of features that other online media have offered for years—message forums, instant messaging, email, media sharing, and the like. So it's not what they do that's new; it's the way they bring it all together into a single site or interface.

If you consider a social network as a kind of virtual community, you can see the history. In my mind, the concept of online virtual communities dates to the earliest dial-up computer networks, bulletin board systems (BBSs), and online discussion forums, including The Source, The WELL, CompuServe, Prodigy, America Online, and Usenet. These proto-communities, many of which predated the public Internet, offered topic-based discussion forums and chat rooms, as well as rudimentary forms of private electronic communication.

Other components of what is currently considered social networking developed in the 1990s and 2000s. The concept of topic-based website communities, as typified by iVillage, Epicurious, and Classmates.com, arose in the mid-1990s. Blogs emerged around the year 2000, and photo-sharing sites, such as Flickr and Photobucket, became a part of the Internet landscape in the early 2000s.

Modern social networks first arose in 2002, when Friendster combined many of these online community features into the first large-scale social networking site—and introduced the concepts of "friends" and "friending" to the social web. Friendster enjoyed immediate popularity (more than 3 million users within the first few months of operation), but was soon surpassed by MySpace, which launched the next year.

In 2004 we saw the launch of what would become the king of all social media, Facebook. Initially called "Thefacebook," Mark Zuckerberg's little networking site was designed primarily for college students. Sensing opportunity beyond the college market, however, Facebook opened its site to high school students in 2005, and to users of all ages (actually, users above the age of 13) in 2006. This broadening in Facebook's user base led to a huge increase in both users and page views, which led to Facebook surpassing MySpace in April 2008. Today, Facebook reigns supreme in the social media space with more than 1 billion active users—a truly staggering number.

Keeping It Short

Social networking is all about short communications. It's more like texting than it is blogging or email; get your message across quickly and then get out of the way for the next update.

There Are Limits...

The need to be concise is most apparent with Twitter, which has a ridiculously short 140-character limitation. Other social media aren't quite as draconian, but that doesn't mean you have the liberty to post page-length screeds. Users of social networks don't have the time or patience for long posts, which is why you need to be as concise as possible.

Figure 14.1 shows a typical Twitter post (called a *tweet*); it's short to the point of being cryptic, given the use of questionable grammar, acronyms, and the like. Figure 14.2 shows a similar post from Facebook; because Facebook doesn't have the same strict character limit, you see more standard grammar and fewer spelling compromises.

Figure 14.1   *A typical tweet on Twitter—painfully short.*

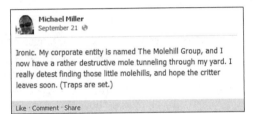

Figure 14.2   *A typical Facebook status update—not quite as limiting, but still concise.*

Note, however, that no social medium encourages full-paragraph dissertations. Oh, you *can* write bloglike posts on Facebook, but only the first part of the post will show in the news feed and few if any followers will click through to read more. The nature of the social network demands short, single-thought posts, and that's what you need to provide.

Say One Thing, and One Thing Only

The key phrase here is "single thought." A social media post needs to do and say one thing, not two or three. If you have two things to say, do two posts. Limit your posts to a single topic and a single point—and, if you can, a single sentence. (Okay, two or maybe even three sentences are okay, as long as they're short.)

What do you do if you have multiple points to present? Simple: break that information into multiple posts. This works nicely into the dictate for frequent posts; if you can turn a single long post into two or three shorter ones, that creates more activity for your feed, which is a good thing.

Take, for example, the following long and multisubject post:

Several new products are now shipping. First is our new XL9 weed killer, guaranteed to neutralize all extraneous unwanted growth from your lawn.

Then there's Mole-No-More, designed to drive those pesky nuisances from your
yard. Finally, check out our new TurboLawn fertilizer, designed to maximize
grass growth in your entire lawn. Stock up today!

Now, this post might work just fine on a blog, but it's way too long and complex
for social media. Instead, break it up into three separate posts (and spread the posts
out on your schedule), like this:

Now shipping: XL9 weed killer kills unwanted growth.

Now shipping: Mole-No-More drives pests from your yard.

Now shipping: TurboLawn fertilizer maximizes grass growth.

That's three posts for the price of one, and each one more focused and powerful
than the original. Think single thoughts, and post accordingly.

▶ *Caution*

Along the same lines, you don't want to include more than a single thought
in any one sentence; social media does not welcome such complexity.
Avoid semicolons, dashes, and all other enablers of compound sentences.
If you have two clauses or thoughts to get across, put them in two separate
sentences.

Remove Excess Verbiage

When it comes to posting for social media, it takes a lot of work to trim things
down to an acceptable length. This is especially challenging when trying to cram a
long message into Twitter's 140-character confines, but something you need to do
for Facebook and other networks as well.

As just noted, you start by limiting each post to a single idea. Then, it's a matter of
subjecting your original copy to a dispassionate triage and slicing out all the dead-
wood you can find.

What sorts of things can you cut from your posts? Here are some suggestions for
things you can remove:

- **Unnecessary modifiers:** For example, instead of saying **very unique**,
  the single word **unique** is sufficient. Instead of saying **currently
  unavailable**, just say **unavailable**.

- **Unnecessary phrases, especially those at the beginning of a sentence:**
  These phrases not only increase your word count, but also push the

key information into the middle of the sentence, where it's less impactful. For example, instead of saying **If you want to advance in the job,** say **To advance in the job.** Instead of **The first thing you need to do is start packing,** say **Start packing.** Instead of **You can choose to turn left** with **You can turn left,** or even just **Turn left.**

- **Redundancies:** Sometimes we also say the same thing, too. When faced with the words **and, too, also, in addition,** or **as well,** pick just one per sentence.

- **Connectors:** Instead of spelling out the word **and,** use the **&** sign or a comma. For example, instead of saying **We reduced bulk and lowered costs,** write **We reduced bulk & lowered costs,** or even **We reduced bulk, lowered costs.**

🔍 *Tip*

Another way to condense social posts is to freely employ contractions. For example, instead of spelling out **cannot** use the contracted **can't**. You can also abbreviate to your heart's content; **ed** is just fine for **education**, and **ex** is good for **example**.

Use Simpler Language

Word choice is important when posting to social media. You might prefer fancy language as a style issue, but longer words are not only harder for the reader to scan, they also eat up valuable character count. Pull out your thesaurus and start looking for shorter alternatives.

For example, instead of saying **explanation,** say **answer.** Instead of saying **challenge,** say **test.** Instead of saying **additional,** say **extra.** Instead of saying **mixture,** say **mix.**

Bottom line: the advice I've been giving throughout this book is even more important for social media. Write short paragraphs. With short sentences. And short words. Okay?

Setting the Tone

Given the brevity required, what kind of writing style should you employ for your social media posts?

First, you might not have much leeway in terms of style. When you're writing a 140-character tweet, you might not be able to employ the necessary adverbs and adjectives that lend tone to your content. This is news headline time, folks, with not a descriptor in sight.

But that's not fair; a good writer can inject tone into the shortest of passages. It's a subtle thing, but it's doable if you make careful word choices and employ the right inflection of language. It's about writing with an attitude, really.

Given that social network postings are meant to encourage social interactions, a personal style is probably the way to go. You don't want to be too stiff or professional; write the way you talk, without being wordy. It's okay (necessary, really) to use contractions, buzzwords, well-known acronyms, and the like. Sentence fragments are allowed.

Employing a personal style doesn't necessarily mean that your posts should be personal—especially if you're writing for an employer or a third party. In this type of scenario, you're representing a company or organization and have to assume that persona. Your writing can still be conversational, however; you need to come off as friendly and helpful, but not necessarily opinionated.

▶ *Caution*

Don't make your posts overly energetic; avoid shouting at the reader with unnecessary action words, exclamation points, ALL CAPS, and the like.

Engaging Readers, Socially

The style you employ is in service of engaging your social network followers. Your writing has to be direct but also encourage some sort of response. You want your followers to "like" a post, to comment on it, or to share it with their online friends. Sharing is the ultimate goal; the more a post gets passed around, the more viral it becomes.

How do you engage your social networking followers? There are a number of approaches to take, including the following:

- **Ask a question:** People are compelled to answer questions, so ask away. For example, if you're posting for a bakery, ask followers which is their favorite type of muffin. If you're posting for an auto manufacturer, ask followers what their first car was. If you're posting for a clothing retailer, ask readers what they think about a given piece or style.

- **Be helpful:** Provide concrete advice about a problem. Readers will appreciate your help and share it with others.

- **Tease the reader:** You probably don't have room to tell the complete story in your post. Give the reader a taste of what you have, then link to the rest of the story on your website or blog. Encourage clicking the link to learn more.

- **Share a personal experience:** Readers love to hear personal stories and like to comment on them.

In other words, do whatever you can to not only inform your readers, but inspire them to respond or take action. Social networks are not broadcast media. (Well, they end up being that for a lot of users, but that's not their intent.) They're supposed to literally be social media—media that encourage and facilitate social interaction. That interaction starts with the posts you make, so make the most of them.

What to Post?

You know your social media posts should be short, and they should be engaging. But what, in general, can you post about?

When you're posting for a business or organization, you can employ several strategies. For starters, you can use your posts as promotional notices, kind of like press releases to your social followers. That means updating your followers about new products and services, company events, and the like. Pretty straightforward stuff.

You can also use your posts to relay favorable notices and reviews, announce upcoming events, and even run contests and sweepstakes. For that matter, you can use social posts to share useful or interesting content, such as YouTube videos or customer photos.

If you're a restaurant, for example, you can post your daily specials as status updates on your Facebook page or Twitter feed. If you run an auto repair shop, post about common service procedures. If you're a landscaping business, post about seasonal landscaping and gardening issues. If you run a design firm, post about some of your more interesting projects. You get the idea.

The key is to use your social posts to inform and engage your community. Point out interesting trends, repost comments from fans and reviewers, take the opportunity to ask your fans what they're interested in. Try to encourage comments and reposts. Make it interesting.

 Tip

How often should you post on Facebook or Twitter? Some people and companies post daily, some weekly, some hourly. I'm a fan of regular updates, but not too regular. Posting several times a day—well, you can overdo it, especially if you're posting just to post. Daily posts might be better, as long as you have something truly genuine to post about. Let your content dictate your posting schedule—and then spread your posts out over a certain time period, rather than just dumping them all out there at once.

Writing for Facebook

Facebook is the largest social network today, by a wide margin, and thus is likely to be the most important social media you write for. Let's look at some of the things you can do to maximize the effectiveness of your Facebook posting.

Short Posts are Better

Facebook doesn't have a set character limit for its posts. (Well, it does—63,206 characters, which I'd classify as "large enough.") Because of this flexibility, might Facebook users think they can post whatever they want, no matter how long it is. That is not the case. Facebook users have the same propensity for scanning over reading, which always argues in favor of shorter posts.

In addition, if you're using Facebook's mobile app, it truncates posts of a certain length. No surprise, not every reader clicks the Continue Reading link (shown in Figure 14.3).

Figure 14.3 *Facebook's mobile app truncates longer posts—which means you need to write shorter ones.*

So even though you can write longer posts on Facebook, it doesn't mean you should. In fact, shorter posts are better—they fit more easily into readers' news feeds, they're more easily scannable, and they're more direct and more powerful. You don't have to stick to the same 140-character limit you have on Twitter, but keeping it to 250 characters or so isn't a bad idea.

You can increase your effectiveness by being even more concise. Buddy Media (www.buddymedia.com) researched retail brand pages on Facebook and found that posts of 80 or fewer characters received 66% more engagement than longer posts. Posts of 40 or fewer characters engaged 86% of readers. If nothing else convinces you that you should write shorter posts, these stats should.

Don't Forget the Links

Unless you're conveying only simple information, every post you make to Facebook should include a link to something. That can be a link to a page on your website, to a post on your blog, to an online article, to another website, whatever. But Facebook users look for and click these links, so you're bound to disappoint if you create linkless posts.

Also, because links in Facebook posts are rather obvious (as you can see in Figure 14.4), don't bother including the standard Click Here or Click for More Information text. Readers will see the links and will click if they want. You don't need to prompt them.

Figure 14.4   *A Facebook post with a link to another web page.*

🔍 *Tip*

Links in Facebook posts typically include thumbnail images, which add visual appeal to your posts.

Utilize Images

Facebook started out as pretty much an all-text social network. Over time, however, images have intruded—to the extent that the vast majority of Facebook updates today include images of one form or another. (Figure 14.5 shows a typical post with an embedded photo.)

As with other forms of online content, images help to draw readers' attention, give visual interest to the content, and help to illustrate the content. Make sure you choose an image that complements and supplements your post content; you can get readers' attention with the visual but still want them to read the text.

Figure 14.5   *A Facebook post with an embedded image.*

Keep It Personal

As noted previously, you want your Facebook posts, as well as all your social media posts, to employ a personal writing style. With Facebook, however, it pays to go beyond simple tone and to write directly to a single person. That is, you want each reader to think you're posting just to him, not to a larger group. Keep that single reader in mind and speak directly to him—just as if you were sending a private message.

Use Proper Punctuation and Grammar

Finally, remember that Facebook isn't Twitter (which we'll talk about next). You have the space to include proper punctuation and grammar and to avoid unnecessary abbreviations and acronyms. Your writing should still be concise in terms of word choice and sentence length, but you don't have to write as if you're sending a text on your phone. Use all the keys on your keyboard, even the symbol ones.

How proper does your Facebook punctuation need to be? The thrust here is to be informal without being blatantly incorrect. That means it's probably okay to use contractions and some acronyms, at least those that will be familiar to a general audience. (Always remember that your Facebook audience is a general one, not one that's industry-specific.) Some would argue with me, but I also think it's acceptable to use sentence fragments on occasion, if you do so willfully and intelligently.

Put another way, a Facebook post isn't as formal as a blog post, but not as informal as a tweet. Dial it in somewhere between those goalposts.

Writing for Twitter

Now to Twitter. Twitter is not technically a social network; rather, it's a microblogging service. The heck with the technicalities, however; everybody treats Twitter much the same way as they do Facebook and other full-blown social networks.

What Twitter does is enable the broadcasting of short text messages to a group of followers. You post a tweet and anyone subscribing to your feed sees it. Because a tweet is much like a text message, at least in terms of length, it often receives immediate attention—and can then be shared with others, via a process dubbed *retweeting*.

How do you compose effective tweets? It's a bit different from any type of writing you've done before.

Keep It Short—No, Shorter Than That, Even

Twitter imposes a 140-character limit on its tweets. If you compose a 141-character tweet, only the first 140 characters will get transmitted. There's no leeway.

 Tip

You might want to keep your tweets even shorter than the allowed 140 characters. If you want your tweets to be retweeted (and who doesn't?), keep them to 120 characters; the extra 20 characters give retweeters space to add their own comments to yours.

Because of that 140-character limitation, tweets do not have to conform to proper grammar, spelling, and sentence structure—and, in fact, seldom do. It is common to abbreviate longer words, use familiar acronyms, substitute single letters and numbers for whole words, and refrain from all punctuation—just like you do when texting from your cell phone.

For example, you might shorten the sentence **See our new Friday specials** to read **C R new Fri spcls**. It might not make sense to you now, but it will to your tweeps.

▶ *Caution*

Try not to over abbreviate your tweets. If someone has to spend several seconds deciphering what you wrote, you just lost them. Use sensible abbreviations, and when it doubt, spell it out.

Shorten Those URLs

The 140-character limitation presents a challenge when you want to include links
to your website (or other websites) in your tweets. Entering a link is as simple as
typing the URL, but long URLs might not fit. To that end, consider using a link-
shortening service, such as bit.ly (www.bit.ly), to create shorter URLs to better fit
within Twitter's limitations.

When you include a URL in a tweet, you don't have to say so. That is, skip the
"click here" language and just add the link to the end of the post. So instead of
writing something like this:

> **Ford releasing new line of pickups. Click here for more: bit.ly/TAalis**

All you have to write is this:

> **Ford releasing new line of pickups. bit.ly/TAalis**

Remember, no unnecessary verbiage; Twitter followers know to click links.

Mention Other Users

Links aren't the only things you can insert in your tweets. You can mention other
Twitter users in your tweets and make their names clickable. To do this, type an "at
sign" (@) before the user's name, like this: **@username**. Clicking a referenced name
displays that user's Twitter profile page.

Use Hashtags

You can also enter the equivalent of keywords, called *hashtags*, in your tweets.
A hashtag is a word that is preceded by the hash or pound character, like this:
#hashtag. When you add a hash character before a specific word in a tweet, that
word gets referenced by Twitter as a kind of keyword, and that word becomes
clickable by anyone viewing the tweet. It also helps other users find relevant tweets
when they search for that particular topic. Clicking a hashtag in a tweet displays a
list of the most recent tweets that include the same hashtag.

Why include hashtags in your tweets? It's a great way to have your content show up when someone searches Twitter for a specific topic. For example, if you want to appeal to someone searching about golf clubs, include the hashtag **#golfclubs** in your tweet. To show up in search results about airplanes, include the hashtag **#airplane**.

> **✉ Note**
>
> A hashtag has to be a single word—which means you often combine several words in a phrase into a single-word hashtag. For example, use the hashtag **#michaelmiller** when writing about me, Michael Miller. (Hashtags are also not case sensitive.)

You can include hashtags in the body of your tweet or at the beginning or end of the tweet. Some claim that putting hashtags at the beginning improves search results, but to me that lessens the readability of the tweet itself—and readability is still king. I'm okay with including hashtags in the body of the tweet, in place of the regular word or phrase. (Figure 14.6 shows how this works.)

Figure 14.6   *A tweet with hashtags in the text.*

Include Images—Sort Of

One thing you can't add to a tweet is a picture; by default, Twitter is a text-only service. However, certain third-party applications, such as TwitPic (www.twitpic. com), enable you to include links to photos within your tweets. Upload a photo to TwitPic and it creates a tweet with a link to that picture hosted on TwitPic's site. It's easy and fairly common.

Writing for Other Social Networks

I've focused this chapter on the two largest social media: Facebook and Twitter. But they're not the only social networks out there; chances are you'll be asked to write for some of the others, too—which might include Google+, LinkedIn, and Pinterest. (Even though Pinterest is a more visual social network, each image on the site is accompanied by a brief text description.)

The advice I give for Facebook applies for all of these social networks. (Twitter is the odd bird in this bunch, with its all text, 140-character limitation.) So if you're writing for Google+ or LinkedIn or whatever, keep your posts short, add some sort of visual interest, and include a link back to your website or blog. And don't forget to engage your readers!

ONE POST FOR ALL?

If you're composing posts for Facebook, why can't you use those same posts for your Twitter feed? Well, you can; there's no rule that says what you post on Facebook has to be different from what you tweet about on Twitter or send to Google+.

Integrating your social media messaging makes the task of social networking a bit more efficient. This is especially so when you employ a cross-network posting tool, such as HootSuite or TweetDeck; these tools let you compose one message and then send it to multiple social media.

Just because you can cross-post to multiple social networks doesn't mean you should, however. There are some definite downsides to consolidating all your social media posts.

Consider length, for example. If you default to the lowest common denominator in terms of length (Twitter's very short posts), you're missing out on the opportunity to elaborate more fully on Facebook. Or, going the other direction, if you compose a post acceptable to Facebook, it's going to be too long to tweet on Twitter.

Twitter is also an issue when you consider things like hashtags. I've seen too many updates in my Facebook feed that obviously started life as tweets; they include those Twitter-specific elements like hashtags and @-sign mentions, which mean little to casual Facebook users. If you want to maximize your posts for the technical Twitterverse, you're going to confuse the Facebook proletariat.

Then there's the frequency thing; not all media are suitable for the same posting frequency. For example, Twitter is conducive to more frequent posts (several a day), whereas you probably don't want to post quite that often on Facebook. If you try to post once for all media, you'll either post too frequently for some or not frequently enough for others.

For that reason, I'm not a big fan of sending the same posts to multiple media. I think you can send similar *messages* to all viable networks, but each message needs to be massaged for each specific site. What works for Twitter isn't best for Facebook, and vice versa.

15

Writing Email Newsletters and Promotions

Email might play second fiddle to the more glamorous social media, but it's still an integral part of the Internet today. Email is the preferred means of corporate communication, and it's also a very effective means of marketing and promotion. You need to know how to write effective email copy to be a successful online copywriter.

Interestingly, I find email copy to be the most traditional of all forms of online copy. In many ways, email copy is much like traditional direct mail copy; you don't have to worry about optimizing for search, length isn't too big an issue, and you're striving to invoke a direct response from the reader.

Still, there are lots of unique aspects to writing email copy—and different types of email copy you can write. Let's take a look.

Composing the Subject Line

Whatever type of email you're composing, you have to include a subject line. The subject is one of the most important components of the entire piece; it's the first thing—maybe the only thing—a recipient sees when she opens her email inbox.

What Subject Lines Must Do

An effective subject line convinces the recipient to click to read the full email. An ineffective subject line inspires the reader to bypass or delete the email—or worse, gets the entire email flagged as spam.

For your subject line to work, it has to do multiple things:

- **Attract the attention of the recipient:** In other words, it has to somehow stand out from all the other message subjects in the recipient's inbox. Given that most folks receive dozens if not hundreds of emails a day, this is not an easy task.

- **Convey the content of the message:** A subject line, by definition, needs to describe the subject of the email communication. It's a summary, a title, and a peek into what the reader can expect to find inside.

- **Convince the recipient to open the email:** Most email programs display only a list of message subjects. Not only does a subject line have to stand out in this list and convey the content of the message, it has to inspire the recipient to click and read the full email. Being interesting or informative isn't enough; it has to be convincing as well.

If your subject line works, the recipient opens the email and starts reading. (This then gets into writing effective body copy—but you have to get the reader's attention with the subject line first.) If your subject line fails, the recipient doesn't click it and doesn't read your email; your interaction with the customer is effectively over, and you haven't gotten your message across.

How, then, do you create an effective subject line? There are a number of best practices you can and should employ. Let's look at a few.

Be Concise

Subject lines must be short. Long subject lines will get truncated in most email inboxes. For best results, keep the subject line at no more than 50 characters, including spaces.

Tip

> One way to keep a subject line short is to use common abbreviations and symbols, such as the ampersand (&) for the word "and."

For example, anyone reading this 70-character subject line:

Important shareholder news regarding fourth-quarter earnings shortfall

might only see the first 50 characters:

Important shareholder news regarding fourth-quarte

The first part of the subject line is so verbose that readers don't even get to the actual news. In this instance, you probably want to rewrite the subject to remove unnecessary words (the recipient is presumably a shareholder, so we don't need to say that; the word "regarding" is both too fancy-schmancy and not really functional); and use an acceptable abbreviation ("Q4" for "fourth-quarter"). The result is much more impactful:

Important news: Q4 earnings shortfall

That's a lot more likely to get you to click, isn't it?

In addition, writing a short subject line has the benefit of making it easier to scan. Recipients don't read all the subject lines in their inboxes; they only scan the subjects for what looks important or interesting. A short subject line not only scans better, it can often look more urgent than longer lines.

 Tip

> There are no hard-and-fast rules for how to capitalize subject lines. You can use title case (initial caps on all words) or sentence case (capitalize the first letter of the first word only); it's up to you. Just be consistent about it—both within a message and across all messages from you or your company.

Put the Important Stuff First

While you're writing concisely, you also need to write hierarchically. That is, you need to put the most important information first.

Given that you have 50 characters to work with, this means frontloading your most important message into the first 30 characters or so of the subject line. Not only does this guarantee that readers first encounter the most important concepts, it also ensures that the keywords in your subject won't get truncated if a reader configures his inbox with a narrow subject column.

For example, instead of writing this:

Sunday is fun day—all rides 50 percent off

Switch things around to put the important stuff first, like this:

50% off all rides this Sunday

(Also note the switch from **percent** to **%** and the loss of the unnecessary "Sunday is fun day" trope.)

Describe the Content

In all these discussions on how to create effective subject lines, let us not forget that the purpose of the subject is to describe the message that follows. Yes, it has to grab the recipient's attention and stand out in the inbox, but in doing so it must tell the recipient what's in the message body. If the subject doesn't do this basic task, it's next to useless.

However, you have to describe the message content in a way that is appealing and engaging, using words that add up to fewer than 50 characters. Those are just the rules of the game. The point of the game is to describe the content—nothing more, nothing less.

So if you have a message that announces an upcoming new product release, should you use the following attention-getting but vacuous subject line?

Exciting announcement from the Boylston Company!

Or should you write something more descriptive, like this?

Boylston announces revolutionary new lawn trimmer

I don't know about you, but I'd be more inclined to read the latter than the former. It tells me exactly what I want to know—even if I don't open the message. Don't bury the lead; put the important news right up front.

Caution

Legally, at least in the United States, the subject lines of all commercial emails must accurately and directly reflect the message content. That's part of the CAN-SPAM legislation designed to reduce the amount of spam email.

Use Language Appropriate to the Reader

When you're composing a subject line, keep the target audience in mind. You can—and, in fact, should—employ language that is familiar and appropriate to the reader. So if your audience is conversant with a particular technology, feel free to use appropriate tech buzzwords and acronyms in the subject line. If your audience is experienced in a given industry, use that industry's conventions and phraseology. They'll know what you're talking about—and you'll establish your email as legitimate by your use of "insider" terminology.

Create a Sense of Urgency

Remember, you want readers to open and read your email. As such, the subject line must convey a sense of importance and urgency that compels recipients to read more.

It's useful to tell readers why they must read the email now and how reading the email will benefit them. It helps if you can explicitly or implicitly convey the timeliness of the content, something that tells readers that there's an expiration date to the information within and they need to read it *now*.

There also needs to be an implied sense of loss if the message isn't read. Make the reader think she'll miss out on something really important if she doesn't click and open the email. However you do it, you have to convey a good reason to read the full message.

 Caution

Some words in a subject line are bad, in that they flag spam filters. You should avoid spam-related words and phrases such as **free**, **cheap**, **win**, **buy**, **save**, **breaking news**, **low prices**, and the like. In addition, NEVER USE ALL CAPS IN A SUBJECT; that's a sure-fire flag for spam, as is the use of exclamation marks (!) and dollar signs ($).

Writing Email Newsletters

There are two main types of commercial email that you might be asked to write: email newsletters and promotional emails. We'll tackle the first one first.

Short Stories; Lots of Links

An email newsletter is an email version of a traditional printed newsletter—sort of. Where a printed newsletter might contain multiple pages with stories of various lengths, an email newsletter typically is much shorter and with much shorter articles. The "stories" in most email newsletters more resemble short blog posts than they do print articles; they're one or two paragraphs long with a link to more information on your company's website. The goal is not to be comprehensive in coverage, but to drive traffic back to a master website or blog.

That doesn't mean that an email newsletter shouldn't be informative; if we prioritize the content hierarchically, the reader can still get a lot of information in those one or two paragraphs. You just don't include all the messy details. Leave that for the linked-to page on your website.

Include Timely Content

To be valuable to the reader, the content in an email newsletter must be informative, but it also needs to be timely. You don't want to put month-old news in a newsletter; if it's that old, it ain't news anymore. This speaks as much to a newsletter's schedule as to its content, but know that there's an expectation for a newsletter to contain recent and relevant information.

Expect Knowledgeable Readers—with High Expectations

When writing for an email newsletter, it's important to keep the reader in mind. Because email newsletters are subscription vehicles, you know that the reader is interested enough in a company or organization to proactively subscribe to receive the newsletter. That means you're writing for engaged readers who are already predisposed to like and follow a company or brand. That's good; they're already on your side, before you write a single word.

That also means you can assume some familiarity on the part of the reader with the sponsoring company or brand. You don't have to sell the reader on the company; in fact, it's likely they know the basics and want to learn more.

Because your readers have personally signed up to receive the newsletter, they have some expectations about what they're going to receive. You need to know this up front; you have to meet those expectations (in terms of both content and style) before you start writing. If you can, familiarize yourself with past newsletters as well as reader responses to those missives; you should also read the solicitation offer that inspired readers to subscribe, just to see what they thought they were going to receive.

Create Compelling Headlines

An email newsletter can be either plain-text (like the one in Figure 15.1) or HTML-based with graphic elements (like the one in Figure 15.2). In the old days, some email programs wouldn't display HTML emails, making text-based newsletters more practical. Today, however, just about everybody can receive and read HTML emails, so there's little reason not to go this route.

```
========================= Good Experience - 7 Dec 09 =========================
                              By Mark Hurst
              Sign up: http://goodexperience.com/newsletter.php
=============================================================================

Monday, December 7, 2009

   - New "Uncle Mark" and several other goodies
   - For more reading...
   - 3 job posts: CA, NV, NJ
   - How to post a job
   - Fun Stuff

   -------------------------------------------------------------------------
      New "Uncle Mark" and several other goodies
   -------------------------------------------------------------------------

   I'm happy to announce several new goodies you might enjoy:

   1. The new Uncle Mark guide is finally up - my seventh annual guide
   to consumer technology and gift picks. Thanks to everyone who emailed
   wondering where it was, and sorry for the delay :)

   Uncle Mark 2010 covers new territory in these sections...
   - two devices you might not know
   - phone
   - a few good iPhone apps
   - camera
   - games you should know about
   - a new gft pick for kids
   - items for new & expecting parents
   - everyday tech tools
   - other "essential" items

   Download Uncle Mark 2010:
   http://unclemark.org/unclemark2010.pdf
```

Figure 15.1 *A plain-text newsletter, from Creative Good (www.creativegood.com).*

Whichever approach you take (and you might or might not have a say in this), you need to focus on the headlines for the stories in your newsletter. Remember, people scan newsletters the same way they scan everything they read onscreen, so you have to assume that most readers will read no further than the headlines. The headline for a story needs to both convey the content of the story and entice the reader to read the story. If the reader doesn't read it, at least he got a little bit of info from the headline; if the headline was compelling enough, then he probably read the rest.

As such, headlines should be treated much like subject lines. They should be short and concise, action oriented, and engaging. A good headline pulls the reader into the story; a mediocre one gets ignored.

Figure 15.2   *An HTML newsletter from the AVS Forum (www.avsforum.com).*

Tip

Nothing annoys me more than opening some sort of commercial email communication I no longer want to receive and not finding a way to easily unsubscribe. It might be painful, but you need to prominently display an "unsubscribe" link in every email newsletter you deliver. Make it easy for people to quit receiving your emails; if they don't want to hear from you, there's no point in sending them more stuff they don't want.

Writing Effective Promotional Emails

The next type of email you might be called upon to write is the promotional email. This is the online equivalent of a direct mail solicitation; the goal of the mailing is to get the recipient to buy something.

As such, promotional emails are more direct than newsletters, and more single minded. There needs to be a clear call to action and a prominent "click here" ordering mechanism. You don't want to leave potential customers hanging; make it easy for them to place an order.

Keep It Short and Chunky

Like everything you write for online consumption, promotional email copy needs to be short and chunky. Don't write a two-page email if a one-pager will do the job. (For that matter, don't write two paragraphs if one will do—you know the drill.)

You need to make the email copy easily scannable. That means short paragraphs, short sentences, and short words. Present complex information in bulleted and numbered lists. Use lots of headers to break up the copy and lead into different sections. Front load the content by putting the most important information first.

If at all possible, keep the email focused on a single topic. Don't try to sell two products in a single email; limit the email to a single promotion, if you can. (Management won't always agree to this, unfortunately.) Include only the most necessary information in the email and link to your website for more details.

It's really like writing for the Web, except more so. Keep it brief and focused and you'll get better results.

Use Actionable Language

Promotional emails are like direct mail pieces in that they want the customer to do something—most typically, purchase the product or service being promoted. As such, you should take your cues from direct mail copywriting.

Probably the most important thing, in terms of your writing style, is to use concise and actionable language. That is, use lots of action words—verbs that tell readers what you want them to do.

What are good action words to use in your email copy? Here's a short list:

- act
- boost
- buy
- create
- discover
- enhance
- extend
- hurry
- improve
- increase
- join
- learn
- order
- purchase
- read
- reserve
- save
- see
- take

There are more, of course, but these will get you in the right frame of mind. You want to prod readers a little, push them toward doing whatever it is you want them to do. Don't beat around the bush here; be direct about the desired action by employing these action words.

 Tip

Although your copy needs to be direct, it also needs to be personal. You're writing to an audience of one, not of many. That means you can be appropriately informal in your writing style. Write in the second person and use lots of "you" and "yours" in the copy; avoid saying "we," "I," or otherwise talking too much about yourself.

Invite Action

The action words you use should lead directly to a desired action—and that means including a specific call to action in the email.

Put simply, you need to tell people what you want them to do. Don't leave it hanging; don't give them options. Tell readers directly what they should do next. If you don't, they won't do it.

The call to action should be direct and clear. Don't complicate things with multiple calls to action; give them one thing to do and no more than that.

You also need to make sure that readers notice the call to action. That means placing it in a prominent position in the email and highlighting it as much as possible. You can put a call to action at the very top of the message if you like; you can also include the same call to action in multiple positions, just so nobody misses it.

You should make it easy for the reader to complete the call to action. That means including a link back to your website and maybe even a toll-free phone number to call. The action needs to be simple and understandable; the more complicated you make it, the fewer conversions you'll get.

And that's the bottom line about promotional emails. Everything you write is in service to the sale. Every sentence, every word should drive the customer toward spending hard-earned money on your product or service. It's not a subtle thing; you want customers to buy something, and you want them to do it now. That's the goal of your copy and don't forget it.

DON'T SPAM

In spite of what some users might think, promotional emails are not spam. Spam is an *unsolicited* commercial email; the emails you write are sent with the recipient's permission. That is, legitimate promotional email is permission marketing, in that the recipient at some point in time has given permission for you to send out your email messages. It's spam only if you email people without their prior permission.

To some people, that might be a fine line. They might have forgotten that they checked that particular option on your website, or maybe another site kind of tricked them into giving permission. Still, legitimate email is opt-in email; even though it might eventually become unwanted, it is not technically unsolicited.

And you don't want to trick people into signing up for something they don't want; that would make you a spammer, and nobody likes spam. Really, nobody. Not the recipients who find this junk email overrunning their inboxes, nor Internet service providers who find their bandwidth eaten up by the huge number of unwanted messages, nor other advertisers who find their legitimate emails marginalized by all the spam messages for Canadian drugs, "performance enhancing" products, and the like.

Legitimate marketers don't engage in spam, and they reject any connection to the junk email industry. They go to great lengths to stress the opt-in nature of their mailings and feature large and noticeable Unsubscribe links in their mailings, so that anyone who no longer wants to receive emails can be removed from future mailings. Legitimate email marketing is all about giving consumers emails that they want and expect to receive.

I assume this is what you're doing—writing copy for legitimate opt-in emails. If you're not sure whether your activities are spamlike, just don't do anything that would annoy you as a consumer. You don't want to receive emails in your inbox that you don't want; tailor your email activities accordingly.

There are actually lots of rules and recommendations for what you can and cannot do regarding commercial email, most of which are detailed in the CAN-SPAM act passed by Congress in 2003. You can learn more at the FTC's website (www.ftc.gov); go there and search for **CAN-SPAM** to access all available information.

Following Through with Your Landing Page

Here's one more thing about writing email newsletters and promotional emails: your job doesn't stop with the email itself. You want to drive people back to your website (for more information or to make a purchase), so you need to coordinate your email copy with the content of the linked-to landing page.

 Note

A *landing page* is a specific page on your website that is linked to from an email message, online press release, or other online vehicle.

The link from the email to the landing page should be a constant process and a consistent experience. Use the same language on the landing page that you do in the email, as well as the same images and visual design. Think of it as continuing the conversation; you start talking in the email and finish up on the landing page.

To that end, the landing page should be unique to a specific email newsletter or promotion. If the email is selling a particular product, the landing page should be all about that product. It shouldn't be a general product-line page, and it most definitely shouldn't be your company's home page. The landing page needs to be a continuation of the email that drove the reader there, and thus needs to be specific to whatever it is the email is about.

For this reason, I recommend that you, the copywriter, be responsible for both the email copy and the copy for the landing page. Think of it as two parts of the same assignment and structure your work accordingly.

16

Writing Online Ads

Not all online copy is obliquely promotional; some of it is explicitly so. That's right, we're talking about online advertising, which is as directly promotional as it gets.

There are lots of types of advertising online, but the bulk of what you see falls into the category of text-only ads. This means, of course, that copywriting skills are of much value if your company or organization is doing any online advertising at all. Although online ads are often very short and very direct, without a lot of words, you still need to write that ad copy, which should be part of your job description.

Understanding Different Types of Online Advertising

You can find lots of different types of ads on the Web. Although the simple four-line text ad might be the most popular, you might also be called on to write copy for display ads, interstitials, and more—so it pays to know what's out there.

Text Ads

They're small. They're unobtrusive. And there are lots of them. I'm talking about online text ads, which are the most prominent type of online advertisement today.

Text ads are most often found on the results pages of the major search engines—Google, Yahoo!, Bing, and the like. These ads are typically listed alongside or on top of the organic search results, as shown in Figure 16.1, and labeled as such.

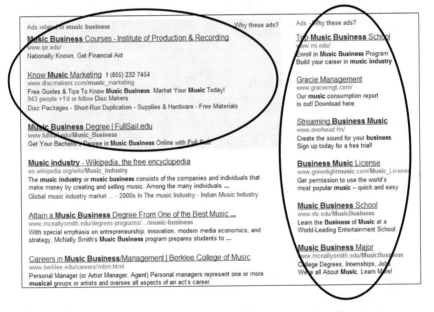

Figure 16.1   *Text ads at the top and side of a Google search results page.*

Text ads can also appear on third-party websites. In most instances, these third-party sites are part of the ad network run by the major search engine. So if your company advertises with Google's AdWords network, your text ads will appear on Google's search results pages and on websites that belong to the AdWords network. (Figure 16.2 shows a block of AdWords text ads on a third-party website.)

How To Become A Blogger
Learn how to build an audience with
Online Blogging and Journalism.
www.FullSail.edu/blogging

Online Marketing Degrees
Prepare for a career in Marketing w/
flexible online classes!
postuniversity.com

ITT Tech - Official Site
Convenient Schedules, Over 130
Locations. Browse New Programs.
www.ITT-Tech.edu
                              AdChoices ▷

Figure 16.2   *A block of text ads on a third-party website.*

Even though these ads are all text, there's not a lot of writing involved; the typical ad consists of three or four short lines of text and no images. The first line is a clickable headline, followed by one or two lines of body copy, and then a final line consisting of the target URL. Short but sweet, these ads are; you have to write some powerful and efficient copy to encourage customer clicks.

Most online text ads are pay per click (PPC) ads, meaning that the advertiser doesn't pay anything for placement; you pay only when someone clicks the ad. At that point, you pay the agreed-upon cost per click (CPC) rate. That is, you pay by the click, not by the view.

The vast majority of these PPC text ads are *contextual* or *context-sensitive* in nature. This means that the ad is served only to websites with content that is directly related to the ad's content—or, more precisely, to those keywords purchased by the advertiser. As an advertiser, this works to deliver more targeted impressions for your ads; if you're advertising running shoes, for example, your ad will be served to sites related to running or to shoes, not to sites about car stereos or financial services.

As noted, PPC text ads are also served to search results pages. In fact, this is the primary means of delivery; the major PPC ad networks are owned by the major search engines. So when you purchase a keyword for a PPC text ad, your ad will appear on search results pages when someone searches Google, Yahoo!, or Bing for that particular keyword.

Take the running shoes example again. You purchase the key phrase "running shoes" for your ad, and when someone searches Google for "running shoes," your ad appears on the subsequent search results page. Someone searching for "dental floss" won't see your ad; you get visibility only to those people looking for what you're offering.

These little four-line text ads might be unobtrusive, but they're ubiquitous. Advertisers large and small employ this type of PPC text advertising as a significant part of their online marketing plans. If you're responsible for your company's ad copy, you'll be writing a lot of these little ads.

✉ *Note*

Text ads are arguably the most efficient form of advertising available, online or off, because of their unique combination of targeted placement and results-oriented payment.

Display Ads

Display ads are the visual opposite of text ads—ads that display images, animations, even videos. Display ads can be big, like the banner ads you find at the top of many web pages, or small, like graphical versions of text ads. These ads are designed to attract the visitor's attention and, in some instances, to click for further information.

One of the benefits of display advertising is the variety available. For example, if you don't want your online presence relegated to a bland text ad, you can run a small image ad, like the one in Figure 16.3. This type of ad is the same size as a text ad, but conveys the advertising message in a graphical format; with most of these ads, the entire ad is clickable and PPC in nature.

Figure 16.3 *A small image ad—the same dimensions as a text ad but with an image.*

Larger display ads tend to be more popular among big advertisers. The best-known type is the so-called banner ad that stretches across the top of a web page, like the one in Figure 16.4. Display ads can also run along the bottom of a page or down either side. (A vertical display ad is called a *skyscraper*.) This type of ad can even sit in a box in the middle of a page.

Figure 16.4 *A horizontal display ad.*

Display ads are almost always graphical. Most incorporate images; some incorporate Flash animations or videos. Most are clickable, although if you're going strictly for image building, that might not always be a requirement.

What you don't get in most display ads is a lot of text. The effect is mainly visual; there might be a headline or brief line of text accompanying the visual, but the image is what counts in these types of ads.

Interstitial Ads

An interstitial ad is one that appears between web pages—that is, in the transition from one page to another. Sometimes the interstitial ad appears before a visitor can view a site's landing page; other times, the interstitial ad appears between two pages on a site.

In any case, interstitial ads interrupt a user's web browsing session. They must be seen (or clicked away from) before a visitor can view the page she wants to view. As such, they're sure to be seen—and just as likely to be hated. Use them with caution, as most web surfers find them quite irritating.

Not surprisingly, that very same irritation, due to the forced viewing, is what some advertisers like about interstitials. Love 'em or hate 'em, you can't easily ignore them.

The other thing that advertisers like about interstitials is that they provide a large amount of real estate to work with. You essentially have the entire page for your advertising message; you're not limited to a banner or a box.

This means that interstitial ads are likely to require more ad copy than normal display ads. Good for you!

✉ *Note*

Until a few years ago, you'd also likely encounter *pop-up ads* on some sites. These are ads that pop up in new browser windows, and they're highly annoying. For this reason, all newer web browsers incorporate pop-up blocking technology, which has led to the demise of this particular ad format.

Writing Effective Copy for Text Ads

Text ads, then, are the most popular type of advertising on the Web and the type you're most likely to be required to write copy for. With that in mind, let's look at what it takes to write effective copy for these text ads.

In most ad programs, a text ad (like the one in Figure 16.5) consists of four lines of text, as follows:

Figure 16.5   *A four-line PPC text ad.*

- The first line is the headline or title with a relatively short character count. (For Google AdWords ads, it's 25 characters max.)
- The next two lines contain the body of the ad, often a product description, which can hold more characters (but still not a lot; AdWords limits you to 35 characters per descriptive line). These two lines of text sometimes run into each other, so it's advisable to consider them a continuous long line.
- The final line displays the URL of the site where you're driving traffic.

How do you best fill these components of a typical text ad? Read on and I'll tell you.

Writing a Compelling Headline

The most important part of any text ad is the headline. This is because some ad formats on third-party pages display *only* the title and URL, skipping the two description lines. This means that your headline has to do the heavy lifting; it has to grab potential customers at a literal glance. Although you can fill in more details in the next two lines, the headline pretty much has to stand alone if necessary.

Even when the complete ad is displayed, as it is on most search results pages, the headline is still the most important element. It's the first thing that people see. A good headline will draw them to read the rest of the ad, but a bad headline will turn them off completely.

For this reason, you have to write a compelling headline for your ad. It should attract the attention of potential customers and compel them to click on the ad. It's the equivalent of a carnival barker—"Click here, click here!"

Naturally, the headline must inform customers of what you're selling or trying to accomplish; in this aspect, it needs to be informative. But the headline should also trigger a specific customer behavior, in most instances a click through to your chosen landing page.

A good headline includes action words that grab the user's attention: words like "free" and "sale," "new" and "more," "discover" and "bargain." These words cause users to read the rest of the ad or click the headline to learn more.

Writing Compelling Copy

It's not just your headline that should be compelling. The two lines of descriptive or body text should also persuade potential customers to click through to your landing page.

To this end, you should use words that appeal to the customer's emotions. People want to be excited or comforted or entertained; your copy should fulfill these emotional needs.

 Tip

The most effective PPC ads include specifics—percentages, dollar amounts, product names, and the like. For example, you can show users how to **Save $10**, **Increase profits by 25%**, or buy something for **$19.99**.

In addition, your copy needs to solve a problem or answer a question the customer might have. What does the customer need to do that your product does? That's the solution to push in the body of your ad.

Persuasive ad copy tells consumers how to save money, how to get something done, how to learn something important, how to do something better. You do this by using certain action words that invoke emotion and enthusiasm in potential buyers. These words include the following:

- bargain
- bonus
- cheap
- discover
- enhance
- free
- learn

- limited time (savings or offer)
- sale
- save
- special (offer)
- tips
- tricks

Because you have only two short lines of copy to work with, you don't have space to talk about your product's features. Instead, you must focus on the benefits—that is, how the customer will benefit from buying what you're selling. If you're selling a weight-reduction aid, don't talk about its unique chemical compound; tell people that they'll "lose weight fast." Tell readers what's in it for them.

You also need to set your product off from the competition. To that end, play up your unique selling proposition—the thing that sets you apart from competing products. What makes your product better or different from everything else out there? That should be clear in your copy.

Including a Call to Action

Because most text ads link to the advertiser's website, you want the potential customer to do something. We're not talking generic image advertising here; text ads should result in a specific action—that you need to ask for.

To that end, your ad copy should include a strong call to action. You have to ask customers to do something before they'll do anything at all.

What's a good call to action? Here are some common ones:

- Browse our site
- Buy now
- Download your free trial
- Get a quote
- Join us today
- Learn more
- Order now
- Read our brochure
- Request more information
- Sign up
- Start now

Notice what's *not* on this list: the phrase "click here." Asking someone to click your ad is not a good call to action for a number of reasons. First, it's implied in all PPC ads; the title is a hyperlink, after all. Second, most ad networks don't like it, and it might reduce your quality score—and your ad placement—if you include it. Third, clicking isn't really what you want users to do; you want them to get more information or buy now or something similar. Focus on that.

Remember, you want customers to do something specific, beyond just clicking the ad—and you have to tell them what that is. Without a call to action, your ad is just a bunch of words on the page.

Including Targeted Keywords

The headline and descriptive copy should also contain one or more of the keywords you've associated with the ad. Anyone searching for a given keyword is going to be more inclined to click an ad containing that keyword than one that doesn't.

That's because people look for the keywords they've queried when they're viewing search results. If someone searches for "toboggan," he's going to scan the search results page for the word "toboggan." He's more likely to click an ad that contains that word than one that doesn't; there's the implication that an ad that contains "toboggan" in its headline or copy is relevant to his search.

So including keywords in your headline won't necessarily help your ad get displayed more, but it will improve your click-through rate. And that's desirable.

Writing Efficient Copy

It's important to remember the character limitations inherent with most text ads and to work within those limitations. You definitely don't have room for excessive verbiage; you might not even have room for proper grammar and complete sentences. Your writing has to be short and to the point to get your message across in the minimum amount of space.

So don't even think about putting puff words ("lowest" or "best") or unnecessary punctuation (! or *) in your text ads. There simply isn't space to waste on these unnecessary words and characters.

What is okay is to use space-saving characters, such as the ampersand (&) for the word "and." You can also use widely understood abbreviations and acronyms, where appropriate.

The whole point is to put forth a compelling message in a minimum amount of space. But then, you're used to that by now, aren't you?

Considering the Right URL

The final line of most text ads is the URL. As with the other lines of copy, the URL line is limited in length.

This length limitation effectively rules out displaying individual pages or directories on your site; you pretty much have room to display your home page URL and nothing more. For example, although you might want a specific page, like this:

www.molehillgroup/books/webwordsthatwork.html

There's probably not enough space to display the entire path and page name. Instead, you want to display only the site's home page URL, like this:

www.molehillgroup.com

 Tip

> If you have an overly long domain name, there might not be enough free characters to display the entire URL. In this instance, you might need to establish an alternative, shorter domain instead.

But here's where it gets interesting. Even though you *display* the home page URL (as the anchor text), the accompanying link can be to any individual page on your site. That is, readers see only the displayed URL; they do not see the actual destination URL. So you can display that www.molehillgroup.com URL while linking to the individual product page deeper into the site. When customers click the short URL link, it takes them to the landing page you specified.

 Tip

> Some of you might be wondering if you can use URL shorteners, such as Bit.ly, to shrink long URLs in your ads. I'd recommend against it. First, the URL you display should be a memorable one, not the gibberish produced by a shortener. Second, you don't need to shorten the actual link URL because no (or few) length restrictions apply. In short, there's really no need for URL shorteners in your text ads; save them for those tweets you make.

DON'T FORGET THE LANDING PAGE

In the previous chapter, we touched on the subject of landing pages, in terms of how they relate to promotional emails. That is, if you're driving someone from an email to make a purchase, you need to link to a landing page on your website dedicated to completing the purchase.

It's the same thing for online advertising. Every online ad you create should link to its own unique landing page that elaborates on the short text in the ad and leads to a purchase opportunity.

The connection between your ad and the landing page is of utmost importance. That means that your landing page must discuss or display the product or service promoted in the ad. It probably shouldn't display any other products or services; you don't want to confuse the customer. Remember, potential customers click your ad to find out more about what the ad talked about. They expect to click to a page that follows seamlessly from what was discussed in the ad.

For this reason, your landing page needs to be consistent with your advertisement, both in terms of content and presentation. That means using the same terminology and writing style employed by your ad; talk about the same product in the same way.

That's why I always recommend that the same person who writes the ad copy be responsible for the copy on the landing page. It needs to be a holistic experience; both the ad and the landing page need to speak with the same voice. (I know, that's more work for you—but it's worth it.)

17

Writing Online Press Releases

We now turn our attention to public relations (PR), which is a lot different online than in traditional media. In fact, online PR is so different from traditional PR that I'm not sure existing press release writing skills get you very far when you're writing for an online audience.

Online press releases have more in common with email and web page copy than they do with traditional media-focused press releases. You're writing for a much different audience and with significantly different intent. If you're an experienced PR person, it's like learning to walk all over again.

How Online PR Differs from Traditional PR

PR is all about influencing people and generating word-of-mouth action. But who you influence and how is different when we're talking about online PR.

Old-school PR is all about influencing traditional media—newspapers, magazines, radio, and television. Online PR still needs to influence these traditional influencers, but it also targets a much broader audience—including Google and the other search engines.

Influencing the Influencers

First, you need to influence *online* influencers, who are a bit different from traditional media influencers. These folks include the following:

- Professional writers, columnists, and reviewers for commercial websites
- Personal and professional bloggers
- Twitterers and Facebookers with large and loyal followings
- Popular amateur contributors to various review and sharing websites

Of these influencers, only the first group—writers, columnists, and reviewers—are similar to your traditional media targets. The other influencers are likely not to be paid professionals; most aren't even trained writers. In fact, most of the influencers online are civilians, people who do what they do merely because they like to, not because it's a job. That makes for a bit of a different push in your press releases, as you might imagine.

Influencing the General Public

In addition, and more important, your online PR efforts often get seen directly by consumers. That is, your press releases go out into the ether and end up getting reproduced on this website or that blog exactly as you wrote them. A reposted press release can generate a huge number of views and lead a lot of valuable traffic directly back to your website, which means that you need to keep the consumer in mind when you're writing your online press releases. You can't rely on the target media to do any filtering for you.

Influencing Google

Your press releases are also likely to end up in the search results of people searching for the topic mentioned. Someone querying Google for "widgets" will see your press release for your new widget line in their search results. That's added exposure and lasting exposure; an online press release can show up in search results years after the initial post.

INTERACTIVITY AND ACCOUNTABILITY

Another key difference between traditional and online PR is the interactive conversations that develop online. Whereas traditional PR is pretty much a one-way effort, in that you put the press release out there and that's that, online PR is a two-way street. That's because a significant portion of your online PR efforts are targeted directly at customers, encouraging them to contact your company directly.

It's this two-way conversation that makes online PR so valuable. A successful online PR effort results in more than just a placement in a prominent publication; it drives measurable traffic and sales to your company's website.

Note the word "measurable" in the previous paragraph. That's also something new with online PR. Traditionally, you couldn't really measure the effects of your PR efforts; all you could track were articles that mentioned your company or product.

Online, you can go beyond tracking placements to measuring how effective each placement is. It's a simple matter to track clicks back to your site, and where those clicks came from. You can measure, with relative ease, which of your PR efforts produced the most concrete results.

This trackability has several benefits of its own. Obviously, a company can now determine which PR efforts are working and which aren't, and fine-tune its activities accordingly. But the company can also hold its PR people accountable—for sales, no less! This might be the first time in their careers that PR people have fiscal responsibility; it might be a bit of a shocker for them—and for you, if you're writing the press release copy.

Writing for Consumers

What's involved with writing an online press release? It's just like writing a traditional press release, but with a slightly different slant.

Target Benefits, Not Features

As you've just seen, an online press release differs significantly from a press release meant for traditional media consumption in that the target audience is different—much different. A traditional press release is targeted at editors and journalists, in the hope of interesting them in writing an article based on the content of the press release. In contrast, an online press release is targeted directly at the end consumer, not at the middleman; websites, blogs, and online publications will link to your press release, which will then be read as-is by prospective customers.

You might think this isn't a big change. Journalists and customers both read English, and in either case you're still writing about your latest product or promotional initiative or whatever. But the message you impart—and the way you impart it—is subtly different. When the target is the end consumer, you have to tell that person precisely what benefit this new product or initiative will have for him. It's less talking about the product's features and more about its benefits.

That doesn't change the basic nature of a press release, however. Even if the audience is the end consumer, a press release is not an advertisement or direct solicitation. It is, more or less, a news story, announcing something important to the target audience. In the case of online press releases, that something has to be important to potential customers; they find out about it by reading your online press releases, much the way they'd read a news article.

Bottom line, your press release needs to do more than just announce some new product or initiative. It needs to tell potential customers how this new product or initiative will benefit them. The news you impart has to be both interesting and useful to your target audience—or they won't read it.

▶ *Caution*

Because of this consumer orientation, you can't just put your old press releases online and expect them to be effective. You'll need to rewrite any existing press releases for online use with the target consumer in mind.

Speak Directly to the Public

You have to impart this useful information in a way that speaks directly to the general public or consumer, not to the editor or reviewer or other middleman. Because online press releases are likely to be posted verbatim, there's no other writer or reviewer that will filter the content or rewrite the press release for public consumption. The press release, as written, will be what the public sees; you have to change your writing style to directly address the end reader.

However, this doesn't change the basic writing approach. Online press releases, like traditional ones, are still written in the third person, like a news story. You don't say "we" and "our" (first person), nor do you say "you" and "your" (second person). You still write about your company from the third-person perspective to put a little editorial distance between the press release and the company. It lends a bit more authority to the story in the press release.

What does change is the thrust of the press release content. Instead of just announcing some *thing*, the story is how that thing will benefit the reader. It's all about benefits versus features with the news being the potential benefit to the reader.

For example, instead of writing

Miles Laboratories announces new offices in Hamfordshire.

You need to address the benefit to the public, as follows:

Miles Laboratories' new Hamfordshire office to create 300 new jobs.

Or, for something with a more product-oriented bent, instead of writing:

ShamPow announces new SuperX cleaner.

Rewrite the press release to focus on the product's benefits to potential customers:

ShamPow's new SuperX cleaner removes 50% more kitchen grime.

 Tip

You want your online press releases to use language that your readers are comfortable with. That means the language of your customers or general public, not that of editors and reporters in the industry.

Because you're speaking directly to a general audience, you'll want to keep your content concise and also somewhat lively. Remember, you're competing with other online content (in the form of articles, blog posts, social media posts, and the like), so make sure it captures the reader's attention—and doesn't lose it by carrying on too long.

 Tip

A press release, online or otherwise, should be used to announce something truly newsworthy. It's a kind of news story, after all, and if what you're announcing isn't really news, you're just crying wolf. Find a newsworthy event (that is of interest to the general public or your target audience) and then build your press release around it. Don't diminish the impact of your PR activities by releasing press releases for no real reason at all.

Watch the Grammar and Punctuation

Unlike some other forms of online writing (I'm thinking about you, Twitter), online press releases require precision in grammar and punctuation. These are official company pronouncements, and thus reflect on the company itself. A sloppily-written press release could cause readers to think poorly of the company, and avoid its products and services.

This means you need to follow all the rules of proper punctuation and grammar. Avoid sentence fragments and minimize contractions; shy away from industry-specific buzzwords and acronyms; and don't abbreviate words that don't need to be abbreviated. Write in a somewhat formal style (no personal stuff here) and properly place all your punctuation marks. Proofreading is recommended.

Include All Necessary Information

A lot of traditional press releases kind of tease the subject. The real intent is to get someone—a reviewer, a reporter, or an editor—to pick up the release and write a story about it. At that point, the reviewer/reporter/editor can contact the PR person to get all the necessary information.

With online press releases, there isn't that kind of third-party follow-up and elaboration. Online press releases go directly to consumers, and you really don't want a horde of would-be customers pestering your sole underpaid PR peon with their questions. Instead, you need to include all necessary information in the body of the press release.

As such, you need to include the same information in a press release that you would in a blog post or article—or product page on your website. Give customers everything they need to move forward in the purchasing process. If you can't cram it all into the press release, include links to additional information on your website.

Include a Call to Action

With consumers in mind, you also need to include a strong call to action in any product-related online press release. This is quite different from traditional press releases, which are more informative than directly promotional. Again, think advertisement or direct response, and you'll be headed in the right direction.

Because online press releases are likely to be read verbatim by potential customers, you want those readers to click through to your website for more information or to make a purchase. That means asking them to do so in an explicit call to action. Remember, you have to tell readers what you want them to do; you can't assume they'll just do it.

Include Consumer Contact Info

The different audience for an online press release means you need to include different contact information than you would in a traditional press release. You do *not* want to include the traditional PR contact number because you really don't want the general public calling your overworked PR staff; that doesn't serve either party well. Make sure all the contact information you include is consumer-oriented, so that you can quickly convert contacts into customers.

Which URL should you include in the press release? Although you want to mention your website's home page URL somewhere in the press release, it's better to link directly to a unique landing page that follows directly from the content of the press release. You want the movement from press release to website to be seamless—and trackable.

When you use a unique URL for the press release, it's easy for your web analytics folks to determine how much traffic each press release drives to your site and how many sales result. It's that new accountability we were discussing previously; do your job right and you'll see how big an influence your work is on product sales.

Consider the Format

Most traditional press releases, like the one in Figure 17.1, look similar. The company's name, address, and press contact information is at the top, followed by the words **FOR IMMEDIATE RELEASE** (yes, in all caps) and the release date. Then there's a headline, followed by several paragraphs of body copy—all written in the authoritative third person. The final paragraph contains a bit of boilerplate text about the company, and then there's # # # or – **30** - , both old-school ways of indicating the end of the thing. It's all so stuck in another world—one I'm not sure exists anymore.

When you're writing an online press release, throw this traditional format in your digital recycle bin. You need something fresher, more visually appealing, and more targeted at the end consumer. Here's what you need to do:

- Start with the headline, not the contact information.
- Move into the body copy, but organize it into short sections. Each section should be preceded by its own heading or subheading.
- At the end of the main copy, include a call to action—something along the lines of **For more information...** or **To order your copy...**, followed by a link to a specific landing page and/or a toll-free phone number.
- If you must, after the call to action include a brief background paragraph about your company.
- At the very bottom of the press release, include a short paragraph (okay, a sentence) along the lines of **For media inquiries, contact...** and then include a link to or the email address of your company's PR contact.

Contact:
Susanna Reed
Public Relations Manager
MyCo International
120 New Salvation Blvd.
Minneapolis, MN 55413
612-555-5555
sreed@myco.com

FOR IMMEDIATE RELEASE
December 5, 2012

Kelvin-Ready Technology Breaks Through Traditional Barriers To Accomplish A Wide Range Of Common Test Objectives

Minneapolis, MN – MyCo International Corporation, a global leader of Test Contactor solutions and services for the semiconductor industry, is pleased to announce the rebranding of its configurable FRYDO™ Test Contactor to better articulate the product's growing use for accomplishing more traditional test objectives.

Since first introduced in 2009, this Test Contactor has provided test engineers with unprecedented test objective versatility for their pad and leaded devices. When populated with only force contacts, it has all the high performance features of the industry-leading, standard FRYDO™ 200.

"This is the same, superior, flexible, configurable Contactor our customers have come to rely on," says Product Manager Fritz Zelig. "Only the name has changed to communicate what sets it apart from traditional Kelvin technologies. It's the one Contactor that quickly, easily, and efficiently configures for a variety of test scenarios."

MyCo International is the leading manufacturer of Test Contactors solutions and services for the global semiconductor industry including RF/Microwave and Precision Analog applications. MyCo is headquartered in Minneapolis, Minnesota with worldwide sales and support offices in California, Japan, Singapore and the Philippines. For more information, visit www.myco.com.

###

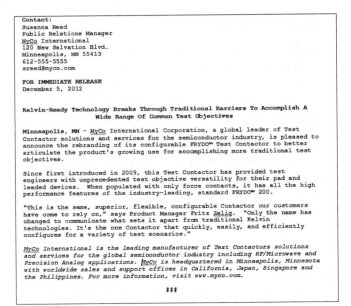

Figure 17.1 *A traditional print press release.*

Figure 17.2 shows how an online press release might look. Naturally, you're talking about creating an HTML document, or maybe a Word document, with all the necessary formatting to make it look pretty. Include inline images as appropriate.

New Solutions from ReefCo Make It Easy for Aquarists to Set Up Successful Reef Aquariums

GRAND FORK, CO— ReefCo, the leading supplier of chemical solutions for saltwater aquariums, announces a new line of chemical additives designed to simplify the setup process for new tanks. Aquarium owners will appreciate how quickly new tank setup becomes with the use of this new line of ReefCo products.

Saltwater Aquariums Can Be Challenging

When it comes to setting up reef aquariums, water quality matters. It's sometimes difficult for home aquarium enthusiasts to set up new reef tanks, given the delicate balance of pH, alkalinity, nitrates, nitrites, ammonia, and other chemicals. It can take weeks for a typical tank to cycle through the nitrogen cycle and build up the right levels of various kinds of bacteria.

ReefCo Simplifies the Setup Process

The saltwater aquarium setup process can be simplified through the careful application of stabilizing agents. ReefCo's biochemists have devised a series of chemical additives that stabilize a new tank's chemical conditions and eliminate the need for nitrogen cycling. The result is a ready-to-use aquarium just minutes after filling a new tank with water.

Four TankUp! Additives Prepare New Saltwater Tanks

ReefCo's TankUp line of chemical additives includes four unique products, each responsible for managing a specific chemical element in a new saltwater tank. These products include:

- pH Up!
- AlkaRight
- Nitrate Up!
- AmmoNo

"By providing the ability to stabilize a tank on day one, the TankUp line will bring more casual aquarists into the hobby," says ReefCo president Hal Myers. "We believe this is an industry-changing development."

Available at All Local Fish Stores

ReefCo's new TankUp! line of tank additives will be available at all local fish stores, as well as major pet supply chains such as PetSmart and Petco.

For More Information

Additional information is available on ReefCo's website, located at www.reefco.com.

About ReefCo

ReefCo (www.reefco.com) is a leading supplier of additives and accessories to the aquarium industry. The company was founded in 2006 and is headquartered in Utah. For media inquiries, contact Cindy Goldstone, 801-555-5555, cindy@reefco.com

Figure 17.2 *An online press release, formatted for online consumption.*

Writing for Search Engines

So the core audience for your online press releases is your customer base, not the press. But that's not the only audience; you also have to target your press releases at Google and the other major search engines.

For the search engines to display your press releases in their search results, which is something you want, they have to be able to *find* your press releases. Yes, that means implementing basic search engine optimization (SEO) techniques for each and every press release you write.

SEO for press releases involves carefully choosing the keywords you want to use, and then incorporating those keywords into the copy you write. The most important keywords should go into the press release's headline or title; all the keywords should be written into the main text.

✉ *Note*

Google and the other search engines treat online press releases no differently from how they treat legitimate news articles—which is why SEO is so important when you're writing a press release.

You want to make sure that whatever terms your customers are searching for are found within the body of your press release. If you sell small kitchen appliances, and potential customers are searching for things like "toasters" and "blenders" and "mixers," those are the words you should include in your press release. It doesn't matter that your company has just introduced a "premiere line of kitchen electrics," as your product people might refer to them (and an old-school press release might announce); you still want to say **ApplianceCo releases innovative new toasters, blenders, and mixers**. Write the words that people are searching for.

That's not to say, however, that you should sacrifice style and substance for keyword placement. The primary audience for your press release is your human customers, not Google, so make sure that it speaks to them. Get the message right, and then you can optimize the release for search.

18

Writing Online Help Files and FAQs

If your company or organization offers products or services to the public, chances are the consumers of your products or services will have some questions. They might even have problems. Somebody has to answer those questions and solve those problems.

Guess what? That somebody is you.

Don't worry; you're not being reassigned to the customer support department. Nope, your job is to write online help files that will provide support to your users. That might involve answering questions about services offered at your local community center, showing customers how to install industrial-strength widgets in their construction equipment, or walking users through a complicated computer hardware setup. Everybody needs a little help, and you can provide it.

Understanding the Goals of Online Help

Writing an online help file is a challenging assignment. You have to figure out what questions or problems are likely to arise, and then address them—in a manner that is easy to understand and follow. If you do your job right, you get happy customers (and reduced customer support costs); if you fail, your customers will have even more questions than they did before.

There are multiple reasons why a company or organization might want to provide online help to its customer base. Yes, it's about helping customers, but there's more than that. Consider that online help does the following:

- Answers user questions—both pre- and post-purchase.
- Shows users how to install, set up, and use the products/services they purchase.
- Decreases the costs of traditional customer and technical support; if they can find solutions online, they don't have to call your support line and talk to someone on your payroll.
- Provides prepurchase information to potential customers who might be wondering how something works.
- Improves your company's image by showing how helpful you are.

Your goal, then, is to answer enough questions and provide enough solutions to help a significant number of current and future customers, while keeping those people from using your human support resources. You can help people get quick and easy answers and reduce your company's costs, all at the same time.

Getting to Know the Target Audience (and Their Problems)

The first step in writing effective online documentation is to determine who it is you're writing for. You need to know who's using your products or services, or rather, who's most likely asking questions. You then need to determine what questions they're asking or what problems they're having. That will then dictate what you write in the help files.

How do you know who's asking the questions? The first step is to talk to your current customer support staff. Find out who's calling them now; get some sort of caller profile in terms of age, gender, education level, and the like. You should also find out the following:

- Are existing support clients current or potential customers?
- How long have they been using your product or service?

- What products/services are they using?
- How are they using your product or service—that is, to perform what specific tasks?
- What questions are they asking? What problems are they encountering? (That is, find out the current most-asked questions.)
- How detailed are the current responses? How much help—and what type of help—do customers currently need?

If your customer support staff can provide this information, great. If not, you have to go out into the real world and get your hands dirty. Talk to some customers and ask them what kinds of questions they have and what kinds of problems they've run into. Find out what they understand and what they don't. Determine what they find confusing and what they find helpful.

This is market research 101, but from a customer usage perspective. You can do this formally, by hiring a research firm to ask the questions, or you can go out and start talking to people yourself. However you do it, you need to get a firm feel for who will be reading your help files and why. If you don't know this, you won't know what to write. It's that simple.

Planning and Presenting Your Content

With the needs of your audience in hand, it's time to start planning. Not writing—not yet, anyway—but planning.

What you need is a detailed table of contents (TOC). This TOC will detail the topics you'll cover and in what depth. Think of it as a master outline.

Your TOC should be structured in a logical fashion. It should easily flow from one topic to the next and be easy for users to navigate. Remember, people accessing your help file will want to quickly find a solution to a specific problem; they just want to know one thing and don't want to read the entire file. Make it easy for them to find that specific answer or solution they're looking for.

And how should that information be presented? The most effective help systems are those that present their information as a series of short articles. That is, each section in the TOC—each problem or question addressed—takes the form of a single-page article. The problem or question becomes the page heading, and the solution is the body text. Naturally, you should include any visuals that help explain or demonstrate things. (Figure 18.1 shows a fairly decent support page from Apple; note the screenshot in the middle of the numbered steps.)

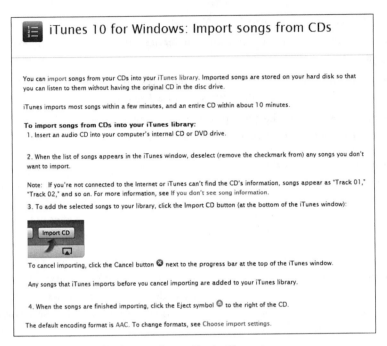

Figure 18.1   *A typical help page for an Apple iTunes issue.*

When writing help text, be as concise as possible. As with most online writing, use short paragraphs, short sentences, and short words. Don't confuse the already confused reader with unnecessary buzzwords and technical terms; explain things in plain English. You should also use the active voice and be as direct as possible in the explanations and instructions offered.

Your goal is to help customers, not further confuse them. Remember that.

Thinking Like the Customer

Your help documents need to include answers to the most common customer questions. You probably can't anticipate all customer problems, but you should know what problems crop up most often.

Those solutions need to be front and center in the help file—that is, they need to be near a top level in the TOC and be easily found by searching. This means you need to think in terms of search keywords for your content.

📩 *Note*

Most users will search rather than browse online help files. They're searching for a solution, not reading for pleasure.

What's important here is to consider a given problem or question the same way that users do—not the way people inside the company do. This means using the same terminology customers use, not the buzzwords you employ inside company walls. Nobody will ask you a question about a product's AccuTint Color Temperature Adjustment; instead, they'll ask how to adjust the color. Drop the formal, trademarked names, and go with informal, generic descriptions.

For that matter, don't assume that customers know everything there is to know about a product or service. Heck, don't assume they know everything they *should* know or that you want them to know. Assume the opposite—that, like Sergeant Shultz, they know nothing. See your products and services from the eyes of a newbie; start from the very beginning, or even before, and be prepared to do a lot of teaching along the way.

Showing Readers How to Do Something

Speaking of teaching, a lot of online help involves step-by-step instructions. If someone is having trouble doing a given task, you have to show the person how to do it.

This means employing a series of numbered steps, sometimes in painful detail. Again, you can't assume that customers know the proper procedures that you and everyone else in the company take for granted. You have to walk customers hand-in-hand from point A to point B, preferably with accompanying illustrations.

Even better, you might want to automate some of this process in the help file. Instead of showing someone how to do something, do it for them. Microsoft does a lot of this, employing web-based troubleshooters that actually open the proper dialog boxes and such to fix specific customer problems. This might not be practical for your particular business, but the easier you can make things for customers, the more helpful your help really is.

Remember, the primary goal of your online help is not to teach your customer all about a given product or procedure, but to get them up and running, as quickly and painlessly as possible. They don't have to become product experts: they just have to start using the darned thing.

Answering Frequently Asked Questions

Now we come to a specific subset of online help: the list of frequently asked questions, or FAQs. Many perplexed customers go directly to the FAQs on a company's website when they have problems; the expectation is that someone else has had the same problem or question, and thus the solution is known and easy to find within the FAQs list.

A FAQ is literally a list of those questions that your customers most frequently ask. They presumably address the most common issues regarding your product or service, and thus can help a large number of users who might be experiencing those same issues.

 Tip

How do you assemble a list of frequently asked questions? By asking your customer support staff. You can also examine web statistics for the most-visited pages on your help site.

Categorize and Prioritize

A primary benefit for customers using a FAQ page is being able to quickly find answers to common questions. For this to happen, you have to make those questions easy to find.

One approach is to put the most asked questions first—that is, to prioritize the list based on popularity or need, as it were. Answer the most common question first, then the second, then the third, and so on. With this approach you'll knock off the majority of issues pretty easily.

But what about those questions that aren't most common? An alternative approach is to categorize the questions (and answers, of course) on the FAQ page. Group all the questions relating to similar topics together, and make it easy for customers to browse the topics and the questions within each topic.

Figure 18.2 shows a particularly effective FAQ page from Southwest Airlines. Note how they don't even call these FAQs; instead, this is a page of "Questions We Hear the Most." Of course it is; the answers are short and sweet, and if additional information is required, there's a link for customers to click. It doesn't get more direct than this.

 Tip

This is kind of a page design thing, but if you have a lot of questions in a FAQ, you can condense them so that readers see only the questions, not the answers. To read an answer, a customer needs only to click the question to expand that section.

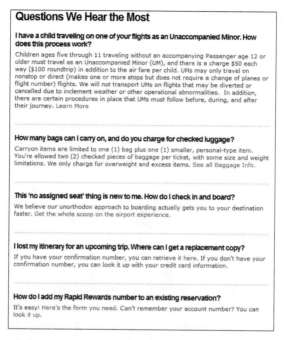

Questions We Hear the Most

I have a child traveling on one of your flights as an Unaccompanied Minor. How does this process work?

Children ages five through 11 traveling without an accompanying Passenger age 12 or older must travel as an Unaccompanied Minor (UM), and there is a charge $50 each way ($100 roundtrip) in addition to the air fare per child. UMs may only travel on nonstop or direct (makes one or more stops but does not require a change of planes or flight number) flights. We will not transport UMs on flights that may be diverted or cancelled due to inclement weather or other operational abnormalities. In addition, there are certain procedures in place that UMs must follow before, during, and after their journey. Learn More

How many bags can I carry on, and do you charge for checked luggage?

Carryon items are limited to one (1) bag plus one (1) smaller, personal-type item. You're allowed two (2) checked pieces of baggage per ticket, with some size and weight limitations. We only charge for overweight and excess items. See all Baggage Info.

This 'no assigned seat' thing is new to me. How do I check in and board?

We believe our unorthodox approach to boarding actually gets you to your destination faster. Get the whole scoop on the airport experience.

I lost my itinerary for an upcoming trip. Where can I get a replacement copy?

If you have your confirmation number, you can retrieve it here. If you don't have your confirmation number, you can look it up with your credit card information.

How do I add my Rapid Rewards number to an existing reservation?

It's easy! Here's the form you need. Can't remember your account number? You can look it up.

Figure 18.2   *Southwest Airlines' FAQs page—it's literally the questions they hear the most.*

Not Every Question Belongs in a FAQ

One of the nice things about a FAQ list is that it contains only the most *frequently* asked questions—not every possible question that could be asked. You go to a FAQ page to find answers to common questions, and to find those answers fast.

This nature of a FAQ list is defeated if you include too many questions. Throw a plethora of questions onto a FAQ page, and all of a sudden it's not so easy to find the answers you need.

How many questions is enough? Well, if a question isn't frequently asked, it shouldn't be included. You don't have to—and shouldn't—list every possible question in a FAQ list. Include only those questions that pop up with annoying regularity. Cut those questions you encounter only occasionally.

Whether you end up with a half-dozen questions, a dozen, or a hundred depends on the nature of your business, products, and services. Just make sure the FAQ list is easily scannable and that readers don't have to scroll too much to find the answers they need. It's not the number of questions in a FAQ list that matter, it's the number of queries that can be answered.

Keep the Answers Short

Conciseness is important in all support materials, but especially so in FAQs. You want the questions to be short, and the answers to be equally so. If you can answer a question in a few words, do it. You're not providing in-depth solutions here, just quick answers to common questions. Brevity counts.

 Tip

Your FAQ and help file aren't static documents. You need to update both based on the ongoing questions you receive and new products or services being offered. It's unlikely that you'll predict every single question your customers will ask, or issue they'll encounter. You need to keep adding to your support resources based on your company's real-world experience.

ONLY PART OF THE SOLUTION

Online help and FAQs should be only part of your organization's customer support resources. No matter how well you do your job, there will also be one more question asked, one more problem encountered than you anticipated when you started writing. You can't solve every conceivable problem; customers are going to ask other questions beyond what you cover in your help files.

Because of this, your company or organization needs to maintain live support staff. That might be a bank of customer support representatives available 24/7, or it might be one person answering the phone during business hours. Whatever is most appropriate for your organization, you need to give people a real human being to talk to, if they need it.

You also need to make it easy to find this contact information. It's a good idea to post your customer support phone number and email address on your main help page and provide links to any additional support resources. Naturally, you want to answer as many questions as you can online (it's both more convenient for your users and costs less for your company), but realize that at times, nothing less than a human voice will do.

19

Writing Web Interfaces

Copywriters are often called in to supply the words that accompany the navigational elements on websites. Sounds like an easy gig; just supply a "Home" and a "Back" and you're done, right?

Well, not necessarily. A good web interface is deceptively simple, and creating something simple requires a lot of hard work. It's also a lot more important than you might think; your interface work might consist of only a few words sprinkled about the page, but they're very important words. Choose the right words and site visitors quickly find what they want; choose the wrong words and people will get lost or—even worse—give up and abandon your site.

How best should you approach copywriting for your site's user interface? Read on to find out.

Planning Your Navigation

The first step in writing the copy for your website's navigational elements is planning your website navigation. After all, you can't write the text if you don't know where things are going.

The key to effective navigation is to make it as easy as possible to find all the content on your site. That means coming up with some sort of navigational scheme that makes sense to your site's various constituencies. You can't just put it all out there in a list and expect people to find what they need.

For example, if you have a business site, potential customers need to be able to easily click to specific product information. Current customers need a quick link to owner's manuals and support resources. The press must easily find the photos and press releases they need to write about your products. And everyone—on every site—needs immediate access to contact information, whether in the form of a web contact form, clickable email addresses, or honest-to-goodness real-world telephone numbers. Sounds obvious, but it's not always easy to achieve.

 Note

As a lowly copywriter, you might not be directly involved in designing your site's navigational structure. So be it, but you should still have some input based on your understanding of your company's customers. Learn more about how to work with your other team members in Chapter 23, "Working with Technical and Design Staff."

Devise a Hierarchy

The best place to start is to come up with some sort of easy-to-understand hierarchy, using the model of directories and subdirectories (and even sub-subdirectories). For example, consider a company that manufacturers yard machinery—lawn mowers, snow blowers, and the like. This company uses its website to present its products, offer customer documentation and support, provide service options, and steer visitors to local dealers. It also offers a press section for media support, a section for investors, and a general "contact us" page.

The first level of organization should probably be by these general areas. As such, the site's main menu system should include the following options:

- Products
- Documentation and Support
- Service
- Find a Local Dealer

The nonconsumer sections (press, investors, and contact us) probably don't belong on the main menu. Instead, they can be accessed via links at the bottom of the home page.

So far, so good. But this company offers a variety of products. So clicking the Products menu might display a Products page, with additional links to the various types of products—lawn mowers, snow blowers, weed whackers, and so forth. But that's two clicks to get to a more specific product line page, and then at least another click to view a specific model of product. Customers don't like to click so much; it's better if there are direct links or submenus to get to the product line pages faster.

The best way to do this is via submenus off the main menu items, like the ones shown in Figure 19.1. In this example, from Best Buy's website, clicking the Products item on the main menu displays a series of submenu items—TV & Home Theater, Audio & MP3, Mobile Phones, and such. Clicking a submenu item then takes the visitor directly to that product line page, without any intermediate pages (and clicks) necessary.

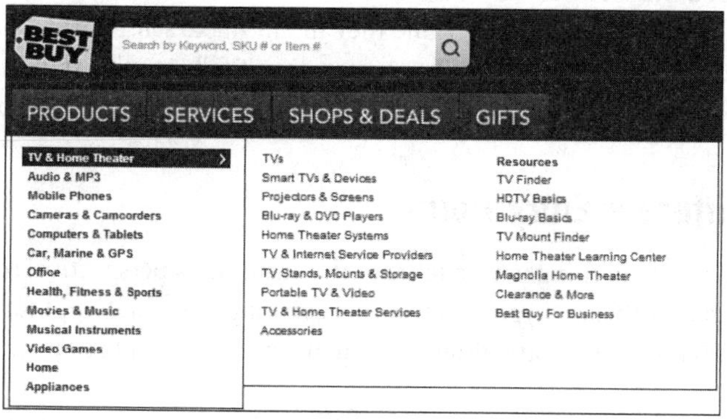

Figure 19.1 *Menus and submenus on Best Buy's website.*

The key is to figure out what visitors are looking for on your site, and then make it easy to get there. Minimize the number of clicks visitors have to make; it's always better to get there in one click than in two or three.

Be Intuitive

Your navigational system must be easy to find and easy to figure out. That probably means a set of pull-down menus or links across the top of the page or along the left side; that's where most people look for navigation.

Your menus don't have to be fancy, either. In fact, they probably shouldn't be fancy; it's better to use easy-to-understand text instead of impossible-to-comprehend graphics. Don't make it difficult on your visitors. Just point them to where they want to go.

You have to make the navigation as intuitive as possible; don't be cute about it. Be clear about what leads where and use wording that mimics how customers describe things, rather than how you might describe them internally.

Think Like the Customer

That last point is important. I was recently visiting a major consumer electronics manufacturer's site, looking for information about flat-panel TVs. I found the products section easy enough and quickly navigated to the section for LCD TVs. What I encountered next, however, totally confused me. Instead of letting me look at sets by screen size or price or features, I saw options for "G25 Series," "G20 Series," "S2 Series," "U2 Series," "X2 Series," and the like. (The names have not been changed to protect the innocent.) I don't know about you, but I have no idea what any of these series are. I just want to find an appropriate TV set; I don't know whether what I want is a U2 or S2 or X2 or whatever model.

So this particular website lost me, and I didn't buy any of their products. The folks who designed this site were not thinking like the customer; they were following internal product guidelines that, while they might make sense inside the company, don't mean a thing to the average consumer. Don't fall into this trap. Present your content the way your customers think of it, not the way you and your bosses do.

Employ Different Entry Points

When you're approaching your site from the customer's perspective, recognize that you might have different types of customers visiting your site—and for different purposes. That might dictate different concurrent entry points to your site's content.

If you're in the business of selling a specific type of product, for example, some visitors will be interested in buying those products. That's one navigational gateway. Other visitors will need support in using the products they previously purchased. That's another navigational gateway. Still other visitors might be interested in your company in general, perhaps in securing employment or investing in your company's stock. Still more navigational gateways.

Or consider this: an automobile company sells lots of different types of vehicles. Some people might know the model they want and want to navigate directly to that. Others might know the type of vehicle they want (minivan, SUV, and so forth) and want to navigate by that vehicle type. Still others might want to look for vehicles based on price, or passenger capacity, or gas mileage. You need to provide navigation based on all these various approaches to the available content.

Be Consistent

When you're working on your site's navigation and the necessary navigational elements, you need to be consistent. If you call something one thing on one part of your site, don't refer to it differently elsewhere. For example, your Help page shouldn't be labeled Support elsewhere on your site; your Shopping Cart shouldn't also be called a Shopping Basket. Consistency in nomenclature matters.

You should also be consistent in the navigational elements you show on each page. Visitors should have a consistent page-to-page experience, no matter where they are on your site. That means repeating basic page navigation, whether that's in the form of menus or buttons or links or whatever. Make sure the navigational elements are in the same position on every page, so visitors will know where to find them.

Let Them Know Where They Are

Speaking of knowing where to find things, visitors also want to know where they are in your site hierarchy. Show the current hierarchical position in directories and subdirectories; this often takes the form of a "breadcrumb trail," along the lines of **Products > Men's Clothing > Shirts > Long Sleeved**. This sort of trail can also be live-linked to make it easier for visitors to move back through the levels or directly to a specific level. It's all about making things readily apparent to and easily navigable by the user.

YES, IT'S YOUR JOB

I'm assuming that you, the copywriter, are asked to write the text for the static elements on your site's web pages. You might not be; some tech person or designer might assume the task is not germane or important enough to involve a trained copywriter and decide to do it himself. That would be a mistake.

You've seen sites where the navigation copy was written by the tech guys. These are the sites where there really isn't much useful navigation; maybe you get a Home button, but past that there isn't much there. I guess the techies think that people ought to be able to figure it out themselves, so why waste the time pointing out the obvious? (And, the thinking goes, if someone can't figure it out, they don't deserve to use the site, anyway.)

You've also seen sites where the designers handled all the navigation copy. These are sites that include navigational elements (lots of them, in many cases), but you can't figure out what the hell they are. You know, instead of "Home" you see things like "Enter," "Return to Base," and "all" (in all lowercase, of course). Designers like to be hip and trendy and don't care much for the practical details of life; remind me never to ask directions from one.

This is the reason you, the trained copywriter, need to get involved with the basics of site navigation and naming. You might be the only person on the team who is thinking about how real people really use your site. You have to inject a customer focus into the process and lay things out in easy-to-understand language for visitors who are neither uber-technical nor designer-cool. Plain English navigation for regular people—that's your assignment.

This is what you need to provide when asked to write the text for your site's navigational elements. And if you're not asked, insert yourself into the process anyway. You spent a lot of time writing all the other copy on the site; it would be a shame if poorly designed navigational elements kept people from finding and reading it.

Titling Your Pages

Let's pay a little special attention to what you call your web pages. I'm talking about page titles, the labels that are assigned to each page on your site.

✉ *Note*

A page's title is defined via the underlying HTML code, in the **<title>** tag. Most web design programs let you enter the page title as part of a form, without having to enter the HTML code directly.

Why Titles Matter

The page title is important because it's seen in so many places—and not just on your website. For example, you can see a page's title in all of the following:

- Title bar of the web browser
- Label on the tab of a web browser
- Favorites or Bookmarks menu in the web browser
- Back and Forward menus in the web browser
- History panel of the web browser
- Text of the browser button on the Windows taskbar
- App title when switching between programs with Alt+Tab in Windows
- Listing title in search results pages from Google and other search engines

Tip

> The page title is one of the first places that search crawlers look to deter-
> mine the content of your page. Crawlers figure that the title should accu-
> rately reflect what the page is about; for example, if you have a page titled
> "The Yellow School Bus Page," the page is about yellow school buses.
> Search crawlers will skim off keywords and phrases from the title to use in
> their search engine indexes.

When done correctly, a title tells visitors what they can expect to find on a page; it also helps search engines determine a page's content.

Determining Title Length

What's the ideal length for a page title? HTML rules dictate that a title can't exceed 64 characters or any additional text is truncated. So you have to keep the 64-character limit in mind, but aim to include from 3 to 10 words total. This makes the title both readable for users (short enough to scan) and useful for search engines (long enough to include a handful of keywords).

Determining the Best Title

What should you put in your title? Your page's official name, of course, if you have one. If a page doesn't have an existing title, you need to come up with a title that conveys the page content. You don't want to lie about these things. Tell current or potential visitors what the page is about, as concisely as possible.

▶ *Caution*

> What you don't want to do is give each page a default or generic name,
> such as Page01 or NewPage. Take the time to give each page on your site
> a unique and descriptive name.

Because search engines trawl page titles, you should also include one or more of the most important keywords for this page. It's best if the title includes the key-words organically, but you can always add the keywords after the formal title, following some sort of divider character—a colon (:) or semicolon (;) perhaps, or vertical line (|) or dash (-), or even a simple comma (,).

For example, if your page is named New Energy Sources, you could employ the following title:

New Energy Sources: Wind, Solar, Geothermal, Tidal, Biomass

That's 59 characters and 8 words, both of which fit within our guidelines. Visitors will see the name of the site in their title bar and in the search results, and search engines will link this page to queries regarding all types of new energy.

 Note

When counting characters, remember that a space counts as a character, the same as a letter or number or special character.

Captioning Buttons, Menus, and Links

How do visitors get from one page to another on your site? As previously noted, the main pages—Home, About Us, Help, and the like—need to be part of a consistent navigational scheme that appears on every page of your site. This might be at the top of each page, along a left sidebar, or at the bottom. (Or, perhaps, in multiple places; it's not uncommon for top-of-page navigational elements to be repeated at the bottom of each page.)

Now, there are a number of ways to present these navigational elements—clickable buttons, pull-down menus, text links, even clickable images. That's up to your designers to decide. Your job is to determine what text to use for each element.

Some text is easy to write. Your site's home page, for example, should always be labeled **Home**. That should be a no-brainer.

Other navigation requires more thought. For example, if you have multiple-page content, as with an online article, how do you title the button or link that goes to the next page? You could keep it simple, like this:

Next

Or even this:

Next page

You could tell the reader what to do by saying:

Click for next page

Although, to be honest, that's kind of insulting; you don't need to tell visitors to click *any* navigational element. They know that.

Even better, tell the reader what's on the next page, preferably by referencing that page's title. So if the content is about Abraham Lincoln and the next page consists of his biography, say that in the button or link:

Lincoln's biography

 Caution

> Don't use the word **More** as navigational text; it doesn't tell readers any-
> thing about what's coming next. Also avoid using the next page's URL in
> the link text. Again, it doesn't tell anybody anything.

When writing navigational text, keep the text active and to the point. Instead of saying **Creating a New Account,** say **Create a New Account** instead. And don't waste words; tell the visitor what the link is about and nothing more.

Make sure you use similar capitalization for all the navigational text on your site. You can choose title style (every word initial capped) or sentence style (only the first word capitalized) as it suits your overall site style, but be consistent about it. If the link text is a complete sentence, go ahead and put a period at the end of it—but if it's a one- or two-word caption, don't.

Tip

> Search engines look closely at link text when crawling your site. To opti-
> mize your search results, include one or more keywords in the navigational
> links to subsequent pages.

Writing Helpful Error Pages

There's one more element of your website for which you need to supply copy. It's not a place where visitors want to end up, although they sometimes do. I'm talking about error pages—those messages that pop up when someone encounters some sort of problem on your site.

The most common error page is the 404 error, which occurs when someone tries to access a page that for one reason or another doesn't exist. Maybe they typed in the wrong URL, or maybe you have a bad link on the site. In any case, this is the error type that pops up when there's nothing to display.

What a visitor sees, though, depends on the copy you supply for your site's 404 error page. You can opt to display a generic "page not found" message, but how is that helpful? It's better to give the visitor a little more information with a little more personality, along with some options on how to proceed. (Figure 19.2 shows a particularly inspired 404 error page; I like the links to other popular pages, a very useful touch.)

Figure 19.2   *A humorous and useful 404 error page from odopod (www.odopod. com).*

As to other types of errors, check with your tech staff to see what they're providing. Visitors might see an error message when a page is slow to load, when someone entered incorrect form information, or when the site is experiencing technical problems. Ask what error pages they've prepared, and then rewrite them as necessary. It's your job to interface with site visitors, and error pages are, unfortunately, one means of communication.

When writing an error page, you need to explain what's happening and tell the visitor how to recover from the problem—that is, what to do next. If it's a simple matter of reloading the previous page, say so. If the visitor needs to return to your site's home page, say that—or, even better, add a link or button to do it. Make sure your error messages are sufficiently informative and user friendly. Use a polite, positive tone and recognize that the reader is probably a little frustrated at the moment; be sympathetic and helpful.

20

Writing for Mobile Devices

The copy you write is dependent on what you're writing for. I'm talking about different online vehicles—websites, email campaigns, social media, and the like—but also different types of displays. Not so much the difference between a 15" laptop screen and a 21" desktop monitor; those two displays are close enough for jazz. (Or government work. Whatever.) The big difference comes when your content is displayed on smartphones and tablets, devices with much smaller screens.

The tough job of online copywriting gets more challenging when small-screen mobile devices are part of the mix. And part of the mix they are; more and more people are accessing the Internet from their iPads and iPhones. This means you need to consider mobile versions of all the online copy you write—and those mobile versions might be considerably different from what you wrote originally.

Why Mobile Matters

We'll get into how mobile content differs from traditional computer-based content in a moment. First, though, let's consider why you need to pay attention to mobile.

The reason mobile matters is because mobile web use is quickly gaining on traditional computer-based web use. If you've ever observed folks on a bus or plane, or waiting in line at a local movie theater or restaurant, you know this. It appears as if everybody and her brother reads Facebook feeds, checks email, and searches Google from their handy dandy cell phones. And, in this case, appearances are not deceiving.

Here's how it looks in numbers: at the end of 2011, there were more than 6 billion subscribers to cellular telephone services worldwide, with almost one billion of them in the Americas.[1] There were 1.7 billion new mobile phones sold worldwide in 2011, almost 500 million of them smartphones, which makes mobile a much bigger deal than the somewhat-anemic PC market (just 352 million PCs sold worldwide in 2011).[2]

It gets even more interesting when you drill down to look at mobile Internet usage. Research finds that 87% of smartphone owners sometimes use their phones to check their email or browse the Internet, with 25% of them using their smartphones as their primary source of web browsing.[3] That's a quarter of iPhone and Android users who prefer to browse the Web with their phones rather than with their computers.

This large and growing use of mobile devices to access the Internet makes it imperative for your company or organization to adapt its online activities for mobile use. You can't and don't want to dismiss hundreds of millions of potential customers; indeed, you want to reach Internet users no matter how they connect to your website or Facebook page. A mobile phone is another gateway to your web content.

 Note

The importance of the mobile web is more than just numbers. Unlike connecting to the web via computer, which can only be done while a customer is sitting in front of his PC, a customer can connect to the web via mobile phone anytime and anywhere. People always have their phones with them; this gives you non-stop connectivity to your customers.

---

1. The International Telecommunication Union, 2012

2. International Data Corporation, 2012

3. "Smartphone Adoption and Usage," Pew Internet Project, 2011

What's Different About Copywriting for Mobile

Writing copy for mobile vehicles (mobile web pages, mobile ads, and the like) is even more challenging than writing other forms of digital copy. It's all because of the size of the presentation—and the local nature of the message.

Working with a Smaller Screen

Let's talk about size first. When it comes to writing mobile copy, you have to adjust your text to fit the smaller screens of smartphones and other mobile devices.

Most online marketing has been done with traditional web browsers and the computer screen in mind. Web pages keep getting wider and wider to fill the space on widescreen monitors; we employ banner ads and full-screen graphics and fill every available inch of screen space. And online copy has expanded to fill that space.

That is not the tack to take with mobile devices. What works on the big computer screen doesn't work at all on the small screen of a typical mobile phone. You don't have much width; you don't even have much height if you want to avoid scrolling. Your onscreen message needs to be simplified and "smallerized," pure and simple.

You also have to make sure your content is visible on the small screen. Your content might look fine on a 22" diagonal monitor, but appear antlike on a 4" diagonal iPhone screen. Although this is a particular issue for images, it also affects your text.

Then, there's screen orientation. You're used to writing for computer displays that are wider than they're tall (landscape orientation). Most cell phone displays are in a portrait orientation, taller than they're wide.

It doesn't matter whether you're writing Twitter tweets or Facebook status updates, email promotions or blog posts, website home pages or online articles. The size and orientation of the mobile screen affects the way your copy is displayed.

This means you need to rethink your visual presentation—text included. You need to present less information on a smaller screen, and with fewer visuals. It's a challenge, and one that places a greater burden on the copywriter. (Yay!)

Target Marketing

It should go without saying that the information you present to the mobile market should be tailored to that market. It's not just how the content is displayed; I'm talking about revisiting the content itself with the needs of mobile users in mind.

How are mobile users different from PC users, in terms of Internet usage? Mobile users, although they have their phones with them all the time, aren't constantly connected as are computer users; they connect to the Internet on an as-needed basis. Your ability to communicate with them, then, depends more on them reaching out to you than the other way around.

This isn't necessarily a bad thing. When you think local marketing, think target marketing, not mass marketing. Instead of broadcasting a promotional message to thousands or hundreds of thousands of people, most of whom are wholly uninterested in what you have to say, you can send out a very targeted message to those few mobile customers who are interested in what you're promoting.

That's in part because of the local nature of mobile computing. People use their mobile devices to get the information they need while they're on the go. Quite often, this information is locality based—where's the nearest coffee shop, which store has the lowest prices, how do I get from here to there, that sort of thing. That makes mobile marketing synonymous with local marketing.

Therefore, your mobile message needs to be more locally targeted than the one you send to the general Internet population. It also should be more immediate; mobile users want their information now, because they're on their way to some place. Think short, local, and immediate—that's the key to successful mobile messaging.

Creating Mobile-Friendly Websites

Let's start by examining what you need to change about your website to make it accessible and friendly to mobile users. You can't assume that your current website will look good on a mobile phone; most websites aren't designed for small cellphone screens.

Take a test. Grab the nearest smartphone (you probably have one in your purse or pocket, right?), fire up the web browser, and browse to your normal website. How does it look? Not too good, probably; the home page is probably too wide and the elements too small to view comfortably. (Figure 20.1 shows a typical website not optimized for mobile use.) This no doubt includes that wonderful text you spent hours laboring over, which is now the size of the fine print you find in the instructions for a typical prescription drug. In other words, it's pretty much unreadable.

 Tip

It's not just about looks. Website functionality needs to be different—simplified, actually—for mobile users. That's because it's more difficult to navigate a website on a touchscreen phone than it is on a computer; you don't have a mouse to move around with. For that reason, a mobile website has to be navigable with fewer clicks (or taps) than a traditional site.

Figure 20.1 *The author's website viewed on an iPhone—the text is much too small for the mobile screen!*

If you want to play on the mobile web, then, you need a website that works with cellphones and other mobile devices. What exactly does that mean in terms of the content you create?

Reduce the Number of Elements

Designing a mobile website is all about simplifying. The first thing you need to simplify is the number of elements on a page. The typical cell phone screen is only so large; you can fit only a limited number of items on the screen and have them big enough to be visible.

To this end, you need to reduce the number of elements that appear on the screen at one time—including text elements. Instead of displaying a dozen different elements, opt for a half-dozen or fewer. It's a matter of what can fit in the limited space and choosing those elements that are most important.

🔍 *Tip*

When you're reducing the number of elements you present on your mobile site, prioritize those elements that remain. Browsing through pages on a mobile site can be quite time consuming; make sure users see the most important content at the top of the first page.

Orientation Matters

Pages on the traditional Web have a landscape orientation with horizontal menu bars because users typically have widescreen computer monitors. Cell phone screens, however, are more portrait or vertically oriented. This means you need to reorient your web pages to fit the format of the mobile screen.

Take, for example, the traditional home page of Minneapolis' Dakota Jazz Club, shown in Figure 20.2. It has a lot of elements, and the elements are organized to fit on a widescreen computer monitor; it's definitely a landscape orientation.

Compare that to the club's mobile page, shown in Figure 20.3. In addition to reducing the number of elements presented, those items are presented in a vertical list to match the vertical nature of the mobile phone screen. It's a much more pleasant experience for mobile users.

Figure 20.2   *The Dakota Jazz Club's traditional home page (www.dakotacooks.com) has horizontal content for widescreen viewing.*

Figure 20.3   *The Dakota Jazz Club's mobile home page: fewer elements, arranged vertically.*

Text Instead of Images

Here's something else about really good mobile websites: they don't use a lot of graphics. Space is at a premium, and you can't waste it with superfluous images. In most instances, you can present content more efficiently in text than in pictures—which puts more pressure on you, the copywriter.

Using text instead of images also affects the download time for your site's mobile pages. Mobile web access is typically slower than web access on a computer-based connection; it takes longer to download things, especially big images. And, since time is always at a premium, if your site takes too long to load on a mobile phone, users will simply click away before everything's loaded. That's less than ideal.

Keep this in mind and reduce the number of large elements that take a long time to download. Don't make visitors suffer through an interminable download just to look at a pretty picture.

▶ *Caution*

If you use tables on your main website, ditch them for your mobile site.
I know that tables are great for displaying complex sets of data, but they
simply don't display well on mobile devices. If a table is too wide (which it
probably is), it throws off the entire page.

Minimize Text Entry

If you require a lot of customer interaction on your site, rethink how you get visitor input. Put simply, it's difficult to enter text on a mobile phone; you have to
click here, press there, and then tap an onscreen keyboard multiple times just to
record a single letter. Consider accepting input via simple option buttons or lists
that visitors can select from. Require as few input keystrokes as possible.

Think Like the Customer

My final word of advice for designing an effective mobile website is one you've
heard throughout this book. When it comes to determining what you put on a
mobile page, you need to *think like the customer*. The goal is to know what your
customers are looking for on your mobile site, and then present that content in an
easy-to-find fashion.

This is important for any website, but more so for a mobile site, where you don't
have a lot of screen real estate to work with. You can't present multiple tunnels
into your content; you have to determine the one best way and present it front
and center. That means knowing, not guessing, what the mobile customer deems
important. If it's not there on that first small page, the customer won't stick around
to hunt for it.

In addition, know that mobile web surfers are more time constrained than users
sitting in front of a computer screen in their home or office. Mobile users are, most
often, *mobile*—that is, they're accessing the Web while they're on the go. They
need to get their information quickly, so they can get on with whatever else they're
doing (like driving their car or walking down the street). They're surfing in a very
directed fashion. Don't make them work for that information; give them what they
need as quickly as possible.

ONE SITE OR TWO?

Can a single website double for both mobile and traditional use? That's a fair question to ask.

In terms of overall design, probably not. Considering mobile's smaller portrait screen versus the larger landscape PC screen, it's tough to come up with a design that works on both. Whether you try to use your normal site for mobile users or your mobile site for PC users, there are just too many compromises. You and your site visitors are better off by designing specifically for each type of display.

In terms of website text, however, it might be possible to make one size fit all. That doesn't mean reusing your normal text for mobile use, however. It means honing your existing text for mobile displays, and then using that more concise copy for both versions of your site. If the constraints of mobile force you to create a more succinct version of your existing copy, all the better. Shorter copy is always more desirable—and more effective.

Writing Effective Mobile Copy

When it comes to writing effective mobile copy, the same advice holds no matter what type of copy you're writing—mobile web pages, blog posts, Facebook status updates, you name it. You need to keep it short, direct, and immediate.

I know, this is pretty much the same advice I gave for general online writing. But it's even more applicable for online copy, where screen space is smaller and the reader's attention span is even shorter. You have to give 'em what they want in one very small screen. That means being as succinct and direct as possible.

🔍 *Tip*

Keywords and search engine optimization (SEO) are as important on mobile sites as they are on traditional websites. It doesn't matter how your site is displayed, you still need to write for search engines and human readers.

Keep It Short(er)

Shorter is always better for online copy. On a small mobile screen, however, brevity is not just desirable, it's necessary. Let me demonstrate.

Figure 20.4 shows an email as displayed on an Apple iPhone. Note how the longer words squeeze out other words on the line, and how a single sentence takes up too many lines. It's difficult to read, and it requires a lot of scrolling to get through the thing.

It's even worse if you're writing text messages. (There's a lot of text-based marketing in the mobile space.) Figure 20.5 shows a similarly long-winded text message;

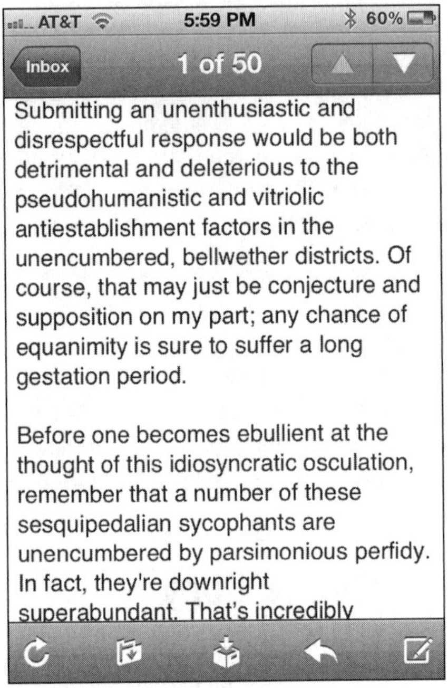

Figure 20.4   *Big words and long sentences are difficult to read on a mobile phone screen.*

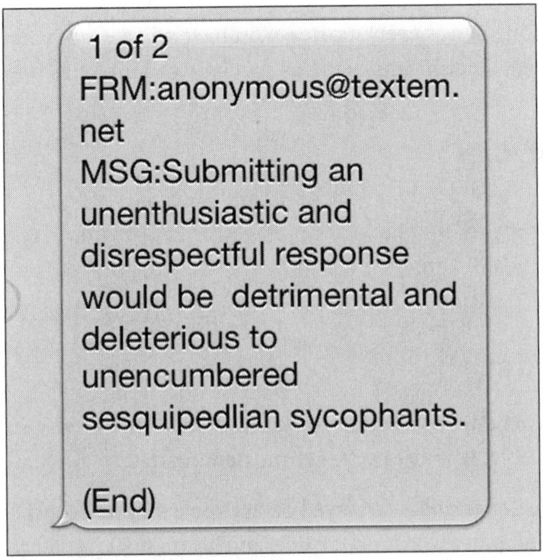

Figure 20.5   *An exceedingly difficult-to-read text message.*

it's even harder to read than the previous email. You're lucky to fit two long words onto the same line, which makes the line length inconsistent and rather jagged.

What does this mean for your writing? It's simple; you need to edit your text to use the following:

- Shorter words
- Shorter sentences
- Shorter paragraphs

Everything needs to be shorter—much shorter, in fact, than with standard website and online copy. Use words with fewer syllables, sentences with fewer words, and paragraphs with fewer sentences. Make every word count and watch your word count.

The goal of creating scannable content still holds. In the case of mobile devices, that means content that a reader can grasp with a single glance at the screen. Break it up into easily digestible chunks; it's better to have several easy-to-read chunks of information than a single long and difficult-to-read block of text.

 Tip

If you're prone to writing longer sentences, go through and break each one in two.

To that end, make appropriate use of bulleted and numbered lists. Tables are probably out, as we've previously discussed, but there's nothing so easily scannable as a bulleted list.

Be Direct

Mobile users want specific information and they want it now. So give it to them.

That means being extremely direct and action-oriented in your writing. Don't pontificate, don't elaborate, don't elucidate. Provide just the facts, ma'am, and nothing more. We're talking very goal-oriented writing; answer the question at hand and get out of the way.

You also need to say your piece as directly as possible. Instead of writing **Check out this terrific offer**, say **Terrific offer!** or **Check this out**. Instead of writing **Consult the documentation that came with the product**, write **Read the instructions**. Instead of **Don't wait to take advantage of these low, low prices**, tell readers to **Get it now**. Don't beat around the bush; say it simply and directly.

Front Load Your Content

Because you'll be writing shorter content, make doubly sure to put the most important stuff first—first in each paragraph and first in each sentence. Don't make readers hunt for what's important; give it to them clearly and early.

If more detail is necessary, put it later in the text—or, even better, link to it. That way you don't clutter the screen space with information only some readers might want.

21

Determining the Right Delivery Formats

As we've discussed various types of online copywriting, the tacit assumption has been that whatever writing you're doing, it's either being delivered over the Web or by email in HTML format. That is, your content is formatted with HTML code and displayed as an HTML document—either a web page or formatted email.

There are exceptions to this (the text you enter for a tweet or Facebook update), but the resulting content is still displayed on a web page. That's not the only way you can deliver your content, however. Not everything online is an HTML web page; you can also serve up your content as PDF documents, Word documents, and the like.

What are the pros and cons of the different document formats available to you online? And when should you use each type of document? That's what I'll talk about next.

What Works Best as HTML

HTML is the most common type of document format online. It's great for displaying both text and images on a computer screen. All web pages are HTML documents; that includes blog pages, social networking pages, and just about anything displayed by default in a web browser.

✉ *Note*

Learn more about what HTML is and how it works in Chapter 22, "Dealing with Web Page Design."

What HTML Doesn't Do Well

A web page designer with the right skills can create great-looking, visually sophisticated HTML pages that rival what you might see in a desktop-published document. Rival but not duplicate, that is, because HTML does have its limitations; you just can't do some intricate visual designs with HTML.

So here we have the first reason *not* to display your content in an HTML document. If your content is overly visual or requires a sophisticated page design, HTML might not be the way to go. I'm talking about precise placement of various text and graphical elements; HTML can't always guarantee that what you place in a given spot will always appear in that same spot.

That's due in part to limitations of the HTML language, in terms of available positioning commands. There are only so many HTML tags, and sometimes you can't make them do what you want done. This sort of precise page layout is not a forte of HTML; an HTML page will never be as visually sophisticated as a fancy desktop-published document.

The design problem also occurs because different web browsers interpret HTML code differently. You can demonstrate this by opening a given web page in Internet Explorer, Google Chrome, Firefox, and Safari; chances are some things about the page will display differently in at least one of the browsers. In addition, individual users can affect the display of a page by changing the width of the browser window or even configuring the browser to use a larger or smaller font size. Bottom line, there's too much variability with HTML to guarantee the page you design will always look the same for all users.

So if your web designers can't entice their HTML editing programs to make a page look the way they want, or if precise placement of elements on the page is important, you'll want to use a different document format (probably PDF) for this particular content.

Not for Downloading

Beyond these strict formatting issues, HTML does a pretty good job of displaying most forms of content and making it look good. If all you want is your content displayed in a web browser, HTML is the way to go. However, if you want visitors to download and save your content for future viewing, HTML isn't the best choice. Yes, you can download HTML documents, and yes, you can view saved HTML documents in a web browser. But viewing saved documents isn't HTML's forte, nor is it something that most users know how to do.

 Note

Do you know how to use your web browser to open a saved HTML-format document from your hard disk? I didn't think so, and neither will most readers.

If you want a document to be saved and possibly passed around to other readers, you need to use a document format that works better for that—either the PDF or Word formats. HTML documents are best for online reading, not for offline use.

So What's HTML Good For?

Okay, now you know that HTML is not a good format for visually sophisticated layouts or for saving and sharing. That leaves a lot of uses for which HTML is quite well suited.

First and foremost, HTML is the best format to use for online viewing. Most HTML documents download and display quickly over even anemic Internet connections, and you can be reasonably assured of fairly consistent reproduction in different browsers and on different types of computers.

The reproduction consistency issue is important. All web browsers have their own little quirks of usage, but a reader using Internet Explorer and another using Google Chrome (or Firefox or Safari) will see pretty much the same page you designed. It doesn't matter whether the reader is running Windows or Mac OS, or viewing your page on an iPhone or other mobile device; HTML is HTML and displays the given elements in the same way no matter how you're viewing a given page.

HTML is also the preferred format when you want to embed or link to content elsewhere on the Web. Although other document formats can do the linking thing, to a limited extent, HTML is the only format that can both link to and embed live content. If you need to link to other web pages or embed images or videos from other sites, HTML is the only way to go.

You will probably create HTML-format documents when you want to distribute your content in the following ways:

- Web pages
- Blogs
- Social media
- Email

This means that most—but not all—of your copywriting will ultimately be displayed in HTML format. It also means that even if you don't do your own coding (and you probably won't), you'll still have to deal with both the useful features and design quirks of the HTML language.

 Note

HTML is also the format you'll likely use when distributing content to mobile devices, because mobile web pages work the same as traditional ones.

What Works Best as a PDF Document

I mentioned previously that HTML is somewhat lacking when it comes to creating complex page designs. When precise placement of the elements on a page is imperative, you need to choose another document format.

Designing for PDF Viewing

Most professional designers are used to working with desktop publishing (DTP) programs such as Adobe InDesign or QuarkXPress. These programs allow the creation of visually sophisticated pages and documents, such as brochures and newsletters. (I can assure you that the pages of this book were laid out using one of these programs.)

What you can do, then, if you have sophisticated page design needs, is have your designers use a DTP program to design and lay out your document. No matter whether it's a single-page document or something longer, any desktop publishing program can do a better job with page design than is possible with HTML.

When the document is finalized, it can then be output as a PDF-format file. PDF, which stands for *Portable Document Format,* is a file format designed by Adobe with the goal of accurately reproducing document pages on any type of display or device. A PDF-format document looks exactly the same whether you're viewing it on a 12" netbook, a 22" desktop monitor, or a 4" iPhone screen. It looks the same on a Windows PC or a Mac. It looks the same anywhere and everywhere—which has much appeal to the designer crowd.

So have your designers use their DTP program of choice to lay out your content and then save it as a PDF-format document. The PDF document can then be uploaded to your website, where it can be displayed online in most web browsers or downloaded for viewing in Adobe Acrobat or some similar PDF reader application.

> ✉ *Note*
>
> Most web browsers let users add-in PDF reader functionality, so they can view PDF-format documents from within the browser window. To cover all bases, you can also include a link to download the Adobe Reader software, in case your site visitors don't yet have it installed.

When to Distribute Content as a PDF File

Now that you know how to port your content to PDF format, you need to understand when this makes sense.

Naturally, any document that requires a sophisticated visual layout can benefit from DTP design and PDF viewing. PDF is also preferred for any document that must be viewed exactly as laid out; that is, if you don't want to deal with the modest differences in HTML interpretation that exist between different web browsers. (Not all things look identical from one browser to another—close, yes, but not identical.)

What kinds of content are we talking about? How about schematics and product instructions to start. These documents are heavily visual, need to be readable when zoomed in or zoomed out, and have no latitude for display error. PDF provides the exact reproduction you need.

In addition, many providers prefer to distribute newsletters and brochures in PDF format, especially if they want exact reproduction of the original document. Electronic books also work well in PDF format, especially four-color books or those with fancy page designs.

🔍 *Tip*

I prefer to distribute brochures online in PDF format. I've experienced too many instances of font and spacing irregularities when trying to do brochures in HTML format to return to that format. When I want readers to see exactly what was designed, PDF is the only way to go.

The common theme here is that if you want readers to see the same document as originally designed, PDF is your go-to document format. Most programs these days let you save documents in PDF format; you can even save Word documents as PDF documents, if you like. It's easy to do, nearly universal, and guarantees a precision of display not possible with other document formats.

When *Not* to Use PDF

That's not to say that PDF is always the ideal format for your documents. First, you might not need it; if precision of reproduction isn't that important, or if your document is mainly flowing text with a few images, then porting to PDF is probably a waste of effort. For most online documents, HTML works just as well and doesn't carry the same overhead as does the PDF format.

What overhead, you ask? PDF documents are essentially large image files with the text being treated as part of the image. (That's how a PDF document exactly reproduces the original document; it essentially takes a snapshot of it.) Because images take up more space than does simple text, a PDF file is going to be considerably larger than a comparable text or HTML document. That means more storage space is required to host the file and, more important, it's going to take longer—much longer, in many cases—for readers to download the file for viewing on their computers. When speed is important—and when isn't it?—PDF is not a good choice.

PDF is also a little cumbersome. In most instances, the entire PDF document has to download before it can be viewed (even in a web browser), so if the document is large, the reader has to sit and wait (and wait and wait) for the download to complete. That's a lot of wasted time in front of an empty browser window.

Then, there's the whole process of saving a PDF file to then open it in a different program. That's okay for more experienced or technical users, but a lot of casual users will find it confusing at best and difficult at worst. If you want a simple, unencumbered online reading experience, stick with HTML.

DOCUMENTS FOR DOWNLOADING

When you provide a document in something other than the HTML format, you're probably intending that document to be downloaded by users and then read or viewed offline, using the appropriate companion software program. All well and good, but what is the best way to offer a document for downloading?

The simplest approach is to introduce a short text link, along the lines of **Click to download this file** or something similar. (Sometimes I see just the name of the file as the link, which isn't a clear call to action.) Your tech guys will do the coding, but when the link is clicked, the user sees some sort of "save file" dialog box and is prompted to download and save the file.

Personally, I like a more visually obvious approach. Again, your tech guys will do the heavy lifting, but it's relatively easy to create a clickable button for the download process. Provide appropriate button text (or text around the button); when a user clicks the button, the download process begins.

In any case, you want to make the downloadable file obvious on the page, and make it easy for users to complete the download. If you want people to download it, don't hide it from them; position it where they'll visually stumble over it and do what you ask them to do.

What Works Best as a Word Document

Another popular format for online documents is Microsoft Word's DOC format. Most people have Microsoft Word installed on their computers, so providing your content in Word format shouldn't create a lot of hassles.

Sharing Documents

In fact, Word-format documents are so ubiquitous that they're easy to pass around. This is the primary benefit of offering your online content in Word format; users can download the Word document to their computers and easily share it with friends or co-workers. It's a great pass-around format.

Of course, to share a Word document, one must first download it. That's an extra step some folks might find bothersome, but it shouldn't be a problem for business users—and they're the primary targets for Word documents online. It's fairly common to see white papers, research reports, even forms and notices offered for downloading in Word format. After files are downloaded, users can email or otherwise transfer the Word file to colleagues, who can open (and edit, if necessary) the document in their own copies of Microsoft Word.

Easy-to-Create Documents

Word documents are also good for distributing content created by casual users—regular folks who might not have the skills or wherewithal to create fancy HTML documents. I'm talking about things like class schedules, team rosters, community bulletins, and the like. It's easy to create a short document in Microsoft Word, upload it to a website or blog, and let interested parties download it for their own use. If that's what you're doing, by all means use Microsoft Word. It's not as easy to access as an HTML web page, but you don't have to spend a lot of time or effort doing the HTML coding. That's a big plus.

Editing and Collaboration

Finally, if you're creating a document meant to be edited or collaborated on with other users, nothing beats the Word format. The people you work with should all have Word installed on their computers, and editing a Word document is a skill everybody learns at birth these days. PDF documents can't be edited by the average user, and HTML documents are not easily editable by regular users; Word documents, however, were designed with editing in mind. When editing is part of the plan, Word is the way to go.

Other Types of Documents

HTML, PDF, and DOC are the three most common types of documents on the Internet (with HTML far and away the most popular). But you might want to use other, less common, types of document formats in specific instances.

Ebook Formats

If you're distributing an ebook online, using the electronic publication (EPUB) format makes sense—especially if it's primarily a text-based book (that is, not a graphically intense coffee table book). EPUB is a format that lets readers change the text display to better fit the reading device and their own personal needs; it's easy to increase or decrease the size of the text on viewing.

The EPUB format is kind of the MP3 format of ebooks, in that it's nearly universal; Kindles and Nooks and iPads can all read EPUB-format books, as can any number of ebook reader applications for PCs and Macs. Amazon's competing MOBI format works pretty much the same as EPUB but is limited to Amazon devices and software and comes with digital rights management (DRM) complications. My recommendation is to stick to EPUB or, if you have a design-intense book, convert to PDF for a more exact representation.

> ✉ *Note*
>
> DRM is a form of digital copy protection, designed to prevent unauthorized copying or piracy of a copyrighted work.

Image Formats

If your content is graphics heavy, you can always save it as an image file, in either JPG, GIF, or PNG format. Because every web browser can display images, you won't have any compatibility issues.

If you go this route, JPG or PNG are better for full-color and higher-resolution photographic images, whereas GIF is fine for illustrations and line drawings. Note, however, that image files are pretty lousy for displaying text; if text is a big part of the image, consider going the PDF route, instead.

Other Microsoft Office File Formats

By all means, if you have an Excel spreadsheet to display or distribute online, upload it in the native XLS file format. Same thing with PowerPoint presentations; upload the original PPT-format file to distribute the entire presentation online.

Here's the thing: just about every computer user in the free world has Microsoft Office (and the Word, Excel, and PowerPoint applications) installed and ready to run. Providing an Office file for downloading shouldn't create any issues and in fact is a good idea if you intend for the file to be viewed or used offline.

> ▶ *Caution*
>
> The ubiquity of Microsoft Office does not extend into the mobile world, where few smartphone users have Office readers installed on their devices.

22

Dealing with Web Page Design

The copy you write is only part of the content of a typical web page. You also have to deal with images, photographic and otherwise, as well as videos, animations, text boxes, and the like.

All these elements get put on the web page via a coding language called HTML. As a copywriter, you might not ever be called on to enter a single HTML code (or you might; you never know), but it helps to know a little about how HTML works in order to maximize the effectiveness of your overall content—and know when and how you can supplement your text with additional elements.

Understanding HTML

Before we go much further, a quick explanation is in order, not because you need to be well versed in the inner workings of HTML code, but because it helps to know exactly what HTML is and how it works, at least in general terms.

What HTML Is

First, let's get a little background info on this whole HTML thing. If you don't know, HTML stands for *HyperText Markup Language,* and it's the lingua franca of the World Wide Web.

By that I mean that HTML is the programming language used to create web pages, which are HTML-format documents. An HTML document, like a word processing document, consists of lines of text, images, sounds, and links, all organized on the page in some fashion or another. Each element on the page is defined by a specific HTML code or tag. These codes work in the background to define what people see when they view a web page in their web browsers.

HTML is actually a fairly versatile language. It's simple enough that just about anyone can use it to create a basic web page, but it contains enough advanced codes that professional web page developers can create more complex and lively pages. And, rest assured, there are lots of software programs out there that enable WYSIWYG (What You See Is What You Get) editing and then generate the corresponding HTML code for you, so you don't necessarily have to know HTML coding to create a web page.

How HTML Works

HTML coding might sound difficult, but it's really fairly easy. First, know that HTML is nothing more than text surrounded by instructions, in the form of simple codes, called *tags.* These tags tell a user's web browser how to display any given element on the web page—including the page itself.

Tags are distinguished from normal text by the fact that they're enclosed within angle brackets. Each particular tag turns on or off a particular attribute, such as boldface or italic text. Most tags are in sets of "on/off" pairs; you turn "on" the code before the text you want to affect, and then turn "off" the code after that text.

For example, the tag **<h1>** is used to turn specified type into a level-one headline; the tag **</h1>** turns off the headline type. The tag **<i>** is used to italicize text; **</i>** turns off the italics. (As you can see, an "off" code is merely the "on" code with a slash before it, **</like this>**.)

So, for example, if you want to specify a line of text as a level-one heading, the full code looks like this:

```
<h1>This is the level-one heading</h1>
```

And if you want to italicize a word in the middle of a line, the code looks like this:

```
Here's a line of text with a single <i>italicized</i> word.
```

✉ *Note*

Any text *not* surrounded by HTML tags uses the document's default formatting—normal Times Roman text.

There are tags for bold, italic, and underlined text. Some tags specify the family, size, and color of text. Other tags affect paragraph alignment. And there are tags—lots of tags—that insert things, such as hyperlinks and images and lists and tables.

Obviously, things can get a lot more complex than that, especially when we start talking about Cascading Style Sheets (CSS), XHTML, and the new HTML5 standard. These newer forms of HTML enable more sophisticated page design, although they require a bit more skill to use. But the general concepts still apply; you use various HTML codes to tell web browsers how to display various elements on the page. It's all about the code.

HOW MUCH HTML DO YOU NEED TO KNOW?

So now you have a little idea of how HTML works. The question is, does it really matter? Or, put differently, how much HTML do you, a lowly copywriter, need to know?

The answer is: it depends. (Yeah, I know, you really hate that answer. Tough.)

Most larger organizations will employ dedicated staff to design a website. That means you'll have designers and/or technical staff doing the HTML coding, and you'll be responsible only for supplying the content. In fact, you might have to supply only text content; the designers will probably want to create or source all the graphics. In this situation, you don't have to know any HTML at all.

If you're working for a smaller organization, or if you're putting together your own personal website, you might not have the luxury of separate design and technical staff. You might find that the entire responsibility of creating the website falls solely on your shoulders. Before you panic, know that even in this situation, you probably have tools at your disposal that simplify the task of web page design—either form-based page creation or WYSIWYG editing with programs like Adobe InDesign. It wouldn't hurt to know a little HTML if you need to tweak things, but you'll mainly be placing elements on the page and letting the application generate the HTML code for you.

For most copywriters, the only times you need to know HTML is when you want to apply some special formatting to a page or blog post and don't have technical staff handy. This happens, more often than not, in blog posting, where the default post-editing tools might not offer the flexibility you need. Rather than fighting the tool, it's sometimes easier to get your hands dirty and manually enter a few HTML tags—especially because you probably don't want to involve your design staff for a simple blog post. If you know some basic HTML coding, you'll be able to take things into your own hands and do a little designing of your own.

What You Can—and *Can't*—Do with HTML

For a copywriter, the main reason to get familiar with HTML is to know what it can and can't do. This way you can avoid asking your designers for some impossible, fancy schmancy page design and having them laugh in your face.

HTML Can Do a Lot

So what can you do, designwise, with HTML? A lot, actually. You can

- Specify the formatting of single word, block of text, or all the text on the page. I'm talking about boldface, italic, and such, as well as font family, size, and color, and paragraph alignment. If you want one paragraph to be left-aligned green 24-point Verdana and the next to be centered red 12-point Times New Roman, HTML can handle that just fine.

▶ *Caution*

Although HTML allows underlining, you should avoid this type of formatting; underlined text looks like a clickable web link, which can be quite confusing. Save underlining for anchor text only. (And you don't have to specify the underlining of anchor text; when you make text a link, it automatically gets underlined.)

- Format lines of text as numbered or bulleted lists.

- Specify the background color or background image of a page.

- Create hyperlinks for a word or block of text. You can also link from images to other web pages.

- Insert images and align (left, right, or center) them relative to a specific paragraph on the page. You can also specify the display size of the image and put a border around it if you like.

- Insert images and text boxes into absolute positions on the page. That is, you specify an exact location on the page and the element stays there, no matter what else is happening around it.

- Insert images and text boxes that float on the page. That is, the element is positioned in a static position so that other elements on the page flow around it, even if the page is scrolled.

- Insert videos and Flash animations, the same as you insert images.

- Create multiple-column layouts, at least to some degree. This is done with the more advanced CSS coding, which has become somewhat standard on the Web.

- Insert tables, even complex ones, on the page. You can also insert images and other elements within individual cells of a table, change border width and color, and specify background color for individual table cells.

- Embed items from elsewhere on the Web. These can be images from other web pages, videos from YouTube, or even "gadgets" with data supplied from sites such as Google Maps.

What does this mean for you, the copywriter? Simple—you can utilize any or all of these techniques to display content on the page. That probably means asking the designers to do it, and then giving them the individual content elements to insert where necessary. But if you want a table or a text box or a certain-sized photograph to accompany your basic text, it can probably be done.

 Note

I've deliberately avoided talking about web page design in this chapter and throughout this book. Although content and design should go hand in hand, your responsibility as a copywriter is for the content; in most instances, the design will be handled by separate design or technical staff. Learn more about how this collaboration should work in Chapter 23, "Working with Technical and Design Staff."

HTML Doesn't Guarantee Display Integrity

However, there are some design tricks you just can't do with HTML. We discussed some of these in Chapter 21, "Determining the Right Delivery Formats," but they bear repeating here.

First and foremost, HTML cannot guarantee that a web page will look the same when displayed on different web browsers. There's a lot of variability in page display from browser to browser, which means that your intricate, well-thought-out web page design might look different when you view it on something other than Internet Explorer.

HTML Doesn't Display All Special Characters

In addition, certain special text characters are not included in the HTML standard. If you employ any of these characters in your copy, chances are they won't display properly—if at all—in most web browsers.

Which characters are they? Here are the ones to avoid:

- Smart quotes ("''). Use straight quotes (") instead.
- Fraction characters (¼, ½). Use written-out fractions (1/4, 1/2) instead.
- Accented letters (á, é, ç, ü).
- Em dash (—). Use two dashes (--) instead.

 Note

Smart quotes are often automatically inserted by Microsoft Word and other word processing programs. Because HTML has no problem displaying straight quotes ("), you should use these instead of the Word-generated smart quotes in your text.

This seems like simple stuff, but there you have it. Just make sure you follow the rules and avoid doing things that HTML doesn't do or doesn't always do well.

Working with Images

I want to spend a moment discussing one optional feature of HTML that concerns the display of images on the page. By default, an inserted image is just that—an image file inserted onto the page via HTML code. It's a picture and nothing more.

You can, however, add a description of any image via an HTML attribute in the **<img>** (image) tag. This *alt text*, as it's called, will display if for some reason the image itself doesn't display. More important, it's what the search engines read when they're trying to figure out the content of an image on the page. (Remember: search engines can't read images, only text.)

So if you want to do your readers a small service, and if you want the content of your images indexed by Google and the other search engines (which, of course, you do), you want to supply alt text for every image on every page on your website. Technically, this is done by using the following HTML code:

```
<img alt="This is the alt text for this image" src="image.jpg">
```

The alt text is enclosed in quotes following the **alt=** attribute.

Practically, you can probably enter the alt text from within a form in your HTML editing program. Just enter the alt text in the required box (or give it to your web designer to enter for you), and you're set.

 Note

.You can (and should) also add alt text for videos and animations on a web page.

23

Working with Technical and Design Staff

Creating a website is a team effort; it's seldom something attempted, let alone accomplished, by a single actor. As the copywriter, you'll be working with lots of other people on this product—other marketing staff, technical staff, and designers.

How can you best work with the other members of your website team—and achieve the results you want? Short of trying to do everything yourself, working together as a team is the only way you can turn your words into the complete content package for your website visitors.

Who's the Boss?

Building a website requires a mix of skills. The site needs to look good and have the content flow properly, which means you need a designer of some sort. The site also needs to be properly coded in HTML and should take advantage of all the latest technological tools, which means you need a web developer—a tech person of some sort. Finally, the site needs content, most of which is in the form of text on the page, which means you need a copywriter—which is you.

The big question is who puts together and leads this multitalented team? The answer could determine the success or failure of all your web marketing efforts.

The reality is ownership of a website is often claimed by multiple parties within an organization. The designer thinks she's in charge, the developer thinks he's in charge, and the copywriter isn't sure who to pay attention to. The result is either some form of power struggle or pure inertia if no one takes the lead.

Even worse is when the wrong party runs the thing. Imagine if your company's finance department ran your website; no doubt it would be extremely cost effective, but at the expense of meaningful content or attractive design. Although that's an extreme example, similarly inappropriate results will occur if you turn over site design and management to parties who don't have an overt customer focus.

Someone has to take charge, and it helps if it's the right someone. If there's no lead player, the site will likely suffer from a lack of focus. (It's also likely the project will run behind schedule with no one driving things—and no one responsible for it.) If the wrong person takes the lead, the site is likely to suffer from an imbalance leaning toward one of the three key disciplines: design, technology, or content.

There needs to be both a balance in approach and one person or department responsible for the site's vision and the completion of the project. Who should be the responsible party? As you might suspect, I have some thoughts on that.

Why Marketing Should Run the Show

In most organizations, website development is a joint effort between the marketing, design, and technology departments. All three parties have much to contribute, but only one of these departments is charged with thinking with the customer in mind. Designers want to make something pretty, and the developers want to employ all the latest technology; marketers are the only folks at the table representing the site's users.

For this reason, having either the design or developer folks take charge could be disastrous. Your site could end up being either design heavy or tech heavy, instead of incorporating the right blend of design and tech in service to the customers' needs.

What kind of sites would your designers like to create? Well, if left to the designers, your website would likely be as hip as all get out with a marked emphasis on cutting-edge design. A designer's site would be stylish, yes, full of cute little fleur-de-lis and other totally useless design elements—useless in terms of obvious customer value, that is. The site would pop and sizzle and crackle, and it wouldn't matter if any substance existed beyond the style. All eye candy, no real content.

Of course, it wouldn't be much better if the developers ran the project. These folks, God bless 'em, love to throw in all the latest technological doodads, in the form of animations and movies and things that peek out here and pop out there. In fact, a tech-designed website would be so technologically advanced that many, if not most visitors, wouldn't be able to view it; it would require the latest browsers and a super-fast broadband connection, and who knows what else. Oh, and maybe there'd be some room for real content in there somewhere, providing you could slip it in between the animations and such.

What both these approaches have in common is that they're not thinking about how and why visitors might actually use the site. Designers want to put pretty pictures in front of your visitors without a thought as to what the visitors actually want to see. Developers want to utilize all the latest technologies without a thought as to how those technologies are used—or whether they're actually usable.

It's up to the marketing department, then, to consider what your site's visitors want—to *think like the customer*. Most customers want something specific, something meaty, something useful; they want substance, not style, and they want to find what they want quickly and easily. It's about useful content presented in a user-friendly fashion. Design and development come into play only in the service of these needs.

This means that the marketing department—represented by you, the copywriter—truly needs to research and deliver on these customer needs. You can't just spew forth the latest corporate platitudes and branding guidelines; you have to get beyond what the corporation and its executives like and create a site that focuses exclusively on your current and potential customers.

So you, the lowly copywriter, somehow need to take charge of your website project. You need to work with the designers and developers, incorporating their suggestions without letting them run wild. And you have to manage the higher-ups who have their own ideas about how things should look, instead of driving the site in a customer-focused direction. That shouldn't be too difficult, should it?

WHEN DESIGNERS AND DEVELOPERS WRITE

Throughout this chapter I've been assuming that you, the copywriter, are part of the marketing department. You might not be.

It's common, especially in smaller organizations, for other members of the team to absorb the copywriting duties. Maybe the designers or the developers think that the actual text on a page isn't that important (or that it's subsidiary to the design or technology), or maybe they just don't have the resources or the budget for a separate copywriter. In any instance, it's possible that you might be a designer or a developer charged with filling in the blanks on the page with text, as it were.

If you're a not a full-time copywriter and you're reading this book, you've already received a ton of advice that will help you put the right words on the (web) page. But it's more than just writing style; it's also about guiding the project with your site visitors in mind. It's your responsibility—as the copywriter, not as a designer or developer—to steer the site's content and design in a way that delivers what site visitors need and expect. Your designer and developer pals probably won't be thinking this way, so you have to.

Every word you write has to be in service to the customer, as do how those words (and other content) display on the page. No one else is responsible for this but you, so you need to step up and make sure it gets done. Even if you're not a professional copywriter by reputation, you have to think like one when working on your website. It's part of your job.

Focus on Content—Not Design or Technology

As the representative of your site's target visitors, you need to stand firm in insisting that technology and design are subservient to the site's content. You can't let the designers or developers run roughshod through the process; design can't dictate content, nor can technology. Content is king and should at least influence your site's design and use of technology.

Besides, there are a lot of fancy technological and design elements that can get in the way of your site's content: Flash animations, videos, and those things that in general exist to "wow" site visitors.

In other words, all the things that visitors love to hate.

That's right; all those fancy elements your design and technology people love are roundly despised by many web users. People just want to do what they want to do; they don't want to be interrupted in their quest. And trust me, animations and movies and things that go "pop" are interruptions—unwanted and unnecessary interruptions. They get in the way of getting to where people want to go.

As a user, I'm sure you've experienced this. You go to a site, and before you get to see the home page, you're greeted with some sort of animation or video. You're forced to sit through this thing, which takes several seconds (or more) to load and then just as long to play, before you can start looking for the information you want. It's a huge roadblock, one which many visitors simply click away from without ever visiting the site beyond.

Think of this pre-home page interruption as the online equivalent of making customers at a bricks and mortar store wait outside while you put on a little puppet show; you don't let them in the front door until the production is finished. If you did this in the real world, most of your customers would just walk away. So why would you do this online?

It's the same thing with other technological and design gimmicks. Yeah, they're fun, and I'm sure your designer and developer staffs really like them. But do they truly serve your site visitors or merely annoy them? That's the question to ask—and most of the time, the right answer will be to avoid these doodads completely and focus instead on the core content.

So when it comes to websites today, forget what your designers and developers might think and remember that content is always king. It's nice to have a pretty design, and there's nothing wrong with including the most up-to-date technology, but content is really the only thing that matters to your site's visitors. You could have the worst-looking website in the world, but if your content is useful and unique (and well written, of course), you'd still grab the visitors. Not that design and technology should be totally ignored, but your primary focus should be in providing the content that your customers want. And, as your site's copywriter, that's your job.

✉ *Note*

Want an example of strong content triumphing over weak design? Look no further than Wikipedia, one of the top 10 sites on the Web, and hardly an example of cutting-edge design; it's quite ugly, really. But the content is first rate, which is why it attracts millions of visitors each day. Wikipedia proves that content matters; design, less so.

How to Lead the Team

So you have a team of people assembled to create your website. As the representative from the marketing department, you've been assigned (or taken it upon yourself) to lead the team. How exactly does that work?

Assess Your Skills

The first thing you need to do is assess the skills possessed by your team members and match them with the skills you need to complete the project. I tend to view the core skills sets needed as follows:

- Strategy and planning
- Project management
- Content (that's you!)
- Information architecture and user interface design
- Graphic web design
- Web technology
- Site production

Any single member of your team might possess more than one of these skills, and that's great. But if you come up short—that is, if you need a skill that no one possesses—you'll need to augment your team either with other players from inside your organization or with freelancers from the outside.

Assign Responsibilities

For larger projects, you'll want to assign specific roles to each member of the team. Figure 23.1 shows a typical web design project organization chart with the following lead roles:

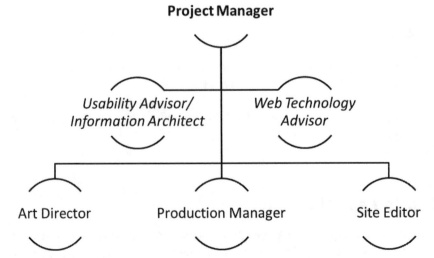

Figure 23.1 *A typical web design project organization chart.*

- **Project manager:** This individual coordinates the day-to-day implantation of the project. The manager works within the budget and schedule set by the stakeholder and communicates progress to the stakeholder. This person is responsible for keeping other team members focused and on track—that is, on budget and on schedule—and manages all communications between team members. Call this individual "the boss," at least on a daily level.

- **Usability advisor/information architect:** This individual's role is to shape the overall user experience and organize the website content and structure. This person is the primary user advocate on the team and is most active early in the process as the site is first taking shape. This is not a line responsibility; think of this position more as a consultant than a manager or hands-on worker.

✉ *Note*

Smaller projects might not have a usability lead or information architect. In these instances, another team member (such as the site editor) will take on these user-focused duties.

- **Web technology advisor:** This optional position (common on larger sites, less so on smaller ones) is responsible for choosing which technologies will be used for the website. Like the usability advisor, this is another consulting position. For larger sites, this individual is charged with designing the database integration, assigning or outsourcing custom web programming, addressing security concerns, and the like.

- **Art director:** This team member's primary responsibility is the look and feel of the website. This person (and the team) makes the big decisions regarding visual interface, typography, color palette, page layout, and graphics. Call this person "the designer."

- **Production manager:** This individual, along with the production team, is responsible for converting all the page mockups and designs into functioning HTML pages. This is an ongoing position, in that the production manager keeps the site up and running on an day-to-day basis.

- **Site editor:** This is you, the copywriter and the person responsible for assembling all content (text and images) for use on the site. You and your team are also responsible for keeping all content up-to-date, so this is an ongoing position even after the site is up and running.

> ✉ *Note*
>
> A website is never completely finished. Websites must change and evolve
> as the underlying business evolves; new products and services require new
> pages, employee movement requires updated contact information, and
> evolving web design standards require rethinking your site's design. As
> such, consider your website a work in progress, one that you must return to
> over time to rethink and rework.

As noted, the usability advisor and web technology advisor are more consulting
positions that function outside the day-to-day operations. The other positions exist
in no defined hierarchy, other than they all report to the project manager. The art
director is no more or less important than the production manager or site editor;
everyone has a role and must function together as a team to build the site and keep
it up and running. Naturally, it's the project manager's job to make sure this happens and to keep all the team members happy and working well together.

Functioning as Site Editor

If your role is strictly that of site editor, you need to focus on providing the appropriate content, on a timely basis, for the art director and production manager to
use in their designs. You should also be proactive about what content should be
included on each page; that's as much your responsibility as anyone's.

The best way to do this is to be actively involved in all upfront planning. You want
to tell (excuse me—suggest to) the other members of the team what content needs
to be on the page. It's tough to do this after a page has been designed or produced.
You need to be there with your proposed content as early and as proactively as
possible. Make your case, show 'em what you've got, and let them build their pages
around the content your customers need.

Managing the Project

If you have the good fortune to also function as project manager, good luck to you.
Managing such disparate personalities and skill sets is bound to be challenging;
everyone likes to think that his role is the most important and that everyone else
is just a flunky to the cause. You might let him think that, but in reality, you have
to manage all of them in a way that brings together all their skills in service to the
final project—and to your target customers.

It's easy to lose sight of your ultimate goals when you're in the trenches managing
a daily workload; that's understandable. But someone—presumably the project

manager—must keep the big picture in mind and manage everyone else to the big-picture goals.

Bottom line: you always have to keep the site's users in mind. The users—or, more precisely, the needs of the users—should drive every decision you make, from the technologies employed to the design applied to the content included. Do what's right for your users and you'll develop a winning site. Ignore your users, or get caught up in internal power struggles, and you'll end up with a site that no one wants to visit. I think you'll agree that the former is more desirable.

24

The Final Word:
Think Like the Reader

And now we come to the end—of this book, anyway. Your journey as an online copywriter will continue, and I hope what you've learned from this book will prove useful.

Before we part ways, however, I'd like to offer a few more words about what I believe is the most important component of copywriting, online or otherwise. I'm talking about the need to get inside the heads of your readers and deliver the content they need, in the manner most appropriate. It's what I like to call "thinking like the reader," and it's the key to successful copywriting.

Everything's Important, But Some Things More So

Throughout this book we've discussed various aspects of online copywriting, from basic structure to writing for specific vehicles and devices. All that information is useful, especially if you're new to or not entirely familiar with the business of writing. After all, it helps to know what words work best and how to place them on the page.

As important as the mechanics are, however, knowing how to employ the serial comma, use the active voice, and not dangle your participles gets you only so far. After all, anyone can learn how to write, but it takes a particular talent to write well.

That's not to say that punctuation and grammar and word choice aren't important; they are. But what you write is more important than how you write it. Putting the best, most useful content on the virtual page is the essential first step in writing copy of any sort for any medium. After you have that content in hand (or in your head), you can employ the appropriate rules and workarounds to make that content as easy to read, absorb, and retain as possible.

Give Readers What They Want

Knowing what to write, as well as how to write it, comes down to one central concept. It's all about thinking like the reader (or the customer or the site visitor or the social network friend—take your pick). When you know what the reader needs, it's relatively easy to deliver the most appropriate content.

I say it's easy; that might be hubristic. It's easy if you have a means for getting inside your readers' heads. You have to know what they know (and don't know), learn what they want and need to learn, think like they think. Then, you can deliver the information they want and need, in the fashion they'd like to read it.

This concept of "thinking like the reader" is important because it's very much reader focused—*not* writer focused. One of the biggest mistakes writers make is assuming their readers are just like them—that all readers know what the writer knows, are interested in what the writer is interested in, and like to receive that information in the same ways the writer does. That is seldom the case; writers who believe that nonsense end up writing for themselves, not for their readers. That's narcissistic, of course, but more important, it does not serve the reader well. You, the writer, are seldom your own target audience.

A similar mistake, when you're writing for a company or other organization, is to assume that your readers are like your company's employees or management, or like other industry insiders. That's a fatal mistake; visitors to a company's website seldom know as much as do your colleagues inside the company, nor are they interested in the same things. When you skew your writing to company insiders, you typically end up writing over the heads of potential customers. Just because your boss or the company's president likes it doesn't mean that it's well targeted to the desired reader base.

▶ *Caution*

It's a challenge to please both your targeted readers and your boss or company management. It's often difficult to get management on track with the whole "think like the customer" thing and move past their own personal likes and dislikes.

You have to deliver content that your readers want and need, not necessarily what the company wants to provide. Only by keeping a single-minded focus on the customer/reader will you be able to create effective and engaging content. If you take the eye off the reader, you're writing only for yourself.

Your goal, then, is to create and present content that is interesting and useful to the target reader. You can do this only if you know what the reader finds interesting and useful—which is where the whole "think like the reader" think comes in. If you know who they are and how they think, you can more easily write for them. If you don't have a clue about your readers—well, good luck, pal. You'll need it.

Presentation Matters

This knowledge of what your readers know and need dictates the content of your writing. It's also essential to know how and where your readers want this information; this dictates how you present your content.

When we're talking about online writing, this means becoming familiar with both the delivery vehicles (web pages, emails, social media, and the like) and the reading devices (computer monitors, laptop and smartphone displays, and such). When you know how these vehicles and devices work and how readers interact with them, you will come up with much of the online-specific advice I've presented throughout this book. Internet-based presentation is what leads us to write shorter and chunkier content and to think in terms of screens rather than printed pages.

Put another way, your presentation of the same information to the same readers will be different on a web page than it is in a book. It will be different in a blog post or tweet than it is on web page, too. It'll even be different if you think that post or tweet or web page is being read on a mobile phone.

The more you know about your readers and how and where they're reading, the more on-point your writing can be. When I say you need to think like the reader, it's not just a meaningless platitude; it's an essential approach for delivering the right content in the right format for the readers you're writing for.

Writing Web Words That Work

And that, dear reader, is what this book has been about—helping you to better target your writing for your target audience. Whether you take my specific advice to heart or not, you can always refocus your efforts by asking the simple question: **What do my readers want?** Answer that and you'll know what to write and how to present it.

That's what online writing is all about. Let your readers lead the way, and you'll soon be writing web words that work—and work exceptionally well.

FURTHER READING

This book is not intended to be the final word on effective online writing. I hope it's a useful guide, but a lot more can be said about the mechanics of writing.

To that end, consider the following supplemental texts that should be of value to any online copywriter:

- *The Complete Idiot's Guide to Search Engine Optimization*, Michael Miller, Alpha Books, 2009. I hate to toot my own horn, but search engine optimization (SEO) is an important component of most online writing, and this book is a pretty good guide to everything you need to know about SEO.

- *The Elements of Style*, William Strunk and E. B. White, Longman, 1918 (4th edition published in 1999). I've talked about Strunk and White elsewhere in this book and for good reason; this book is the essential reference for grammar, punctuation, and writing style. Every editor has a copy on her desk, and you should, too. (And don't let the initial publication date scare you; this book is as vital today as it was almost a century ago when it was written.)

- *On Writing Well: The Classic Guide to Writing Nonfiction*, William Zinsser, Harper Perennial, 1976 (30th anniversary edition published in 2006). Pretty much the bible for three generations of nonfiction writers, essayists, editors, and the like. Good, solid writing advice and inspiration.

- *The Ultimate Web Marketing Guide*, Michael Miller, Que, 2010. Another of my books, for anyone interested in the marketing strategy behind the various vehicles for your online writing.

- *The Yahoo! Style Guide: The Ultimate Sourcebook for Writing, Editing, and Creating Content for the Digital World*, Chris Barr (editor), St. Martin's Griffin, 2010. There was a time when Yahoo! ruled the online world, and this book builds on that experience and expertise to offer detailed guidance for what works and what doesn't when writing online content.

Any and all of these books are welcome additions to any online copywriter's reference shelf. The more help you can get, the better.

Appendix

200 Web Words That Work

Want to know some "action" words that will make your online copy more effective? Here are 200 of them, powerful words that will spice up any piece of online copy. Remember, with great power comes great responsibility, so don't overuse them; a few of these power words sprinkled throughout a piece of text can generate surprising results.

accomplish	big	control
achieve	bonus	convince
act	boost	cooperate
amazing	build	correct
answer	buy	create
apply	capture	custom
approve	cheap	customize
arrange	colorful	decide
attract	colossal	decrease
attractive	combine	defend
authentic	comfort	deliver
authorized	compare	demonstrate
award	complete	describe
bargain	confirm	detail
beautiful	contact	direct
begin	contribute	discount

discover

discuss

display

distinguished

earn

easily

eliminate

emphasize

employ

enable

encourage

enforce

enhance

enlarge

enlighten

enlist

enrich

enter

entertain

establish

evaluate

examine

excellent

exciting

exclusive

expand

explain

explore

express

extend

famous

fashionable

final

fix

focus

forecast

free

fund

generate

genuine

great

greater

greatest

guaranteed

help

highest

highlight

hurry

immediately

improve

increase

inform

innovative

inspire

instruct

introduce

invent

investigate

join

largest

latest

launch

leader

learn

manage

master

maximize

minimize

mobilize

model

modern

notify

order

outstanding

perfect

persuade

plan

popular

powerful

prepare

present

preserve

prevent

promotion

proven

purchase

qualify

quickly	secure	unlimited
rare	select	unveil
recommend	sensational	update
recruit	service	upgrade
reduce	show	valuable
reduced	simplify	value
register	sold	win
release	solve	
reliable	speak	
remarkable	special	
renew	specialize	
repair	start	
replace	startling	
report	strengthen	
respond	strong	
restore	success	
restrict	successful	
retain	superior	
retrieve	support	
revamp	surpass	
reveal	take	
revealing	terrific	
revise	tips	
revitalize	transform	
revolutionary	transmit	
sale	transport	
sample	tremendous	
save	uncover	
secret	unique	

Index

fair use doctrine, 111
with linked content, 110

length of writing. *See
short writing*

limiting detail, 41-43

line charts, 98

line drawings, 92-94

LinkedIn, 164-165

links, 103
adding, 104-105
captions, 216-217
in email newsletters, 172
in Facebook posts, 160
inbound links, 115
to landing pages, 178,
188
legal issues, 110
linking for scannability,
132
SEO (search engine
optimization), 118-119
what to link to, 105-106
when to link, 106-107

linkworthy content, 120

lists
bulleted lists, 67-68
numbered lists, 68-69

M

making promises, 74

managing projects,
256-257

marketing, role of, 250-
251

matching
style to audience, 82-83
style to content, 82
style with image, 81-82

menu captions, 216-217

<META> tag, 135

MOBI format, 238-239

mobile devices
effective mobile copy,
227-230
importance of mobile-
friendly copy, 220
mobile-friendly
websites, 222-226
overview, 219
screen limitations, 221
target marketing, 221

multiple pages, breaking
copy into, 64-65

MySpace, 153

N

navigation in web
interfaces
navigational captions/
text, 216-217
planning, 210-214

newsletters
headlines, 173-174
links, 172
overview, 167

reader expectations,
172-173
stories, 172
subject lines, 168-171
timely content, 172

numbered lists, 68-69

O

observing readers, 72

On Writing (King), 17

*On Writing Well: The
Classic Guide to Writing
Nonfiction* (Zinsser), 17,
263

online ads. *See* ads

online articles. *See* articles

online help files. *See* help
files

online press releases. *See*
press releases

opinions in blog posts,
145

optimizing copy for
web searches. *See*
SEO (search engine
optimization)

organizing
articles, 140
content
bulleted lists, 67-68
*chunks of
information, 53-54*

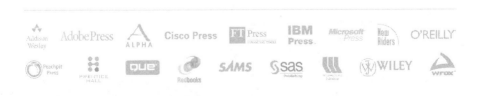